W9-ANE-884

# SLOW
# COOKING

# KNACK®

# SLOW COOKING

### Hearty & Delicious Meals You Can Prepare Ahead

**Linda Johnson Larsen**

**Photographs by Christopher Brown**

**KNACK**®
MAKE IT EASY

*Guilford, Connecticut*
An imprint of Globe Pequot Press

To buy books in quantity for corporate use
or incentives, call **(800) 962-0973**
or e-mail **premiums@GlobePequot.com**.

Copyright © 2009 by Morris Book Publishing, LLC

ALL RIGHTS RESERVED. No part of this book may be reproduced or transmitted in any form by any means, electronic or mechanical, including photocopying and recording, or by any information storage and retrieval system, except as may be expressly permitted in writing from the publisher. Requests for permission should be addressed to Globe Pequot Press, Attn: Rights and Permissions Department, P.O. Box 480, Guilford, CT 06437.

Knack is a registered trademark of Morris Publishing Group, LLC, and is used with express permission.

Editor in Chief: Maureen Graney
Editor: Imee Curiel
Cover Design: Paul Beatrice, Bret Kerr
Text Design: Paul Beatrice
Layout: Joanna Beyer
Cover photos by Christopher Brown
All interior photos by Christopher Brown with the exception of p. 9 (right) and p. 17 courtesy Crock-Pot; p. 13 © Monkey Business Images/Shutterstock; p. 16 (adjustable roasting rack) courtesy NorPro; p. 22 (left) by Viktor Budnik © Morris Book Publishing, LLC; p. 22 (right) courtesy ThermoWorks.com; p. 23 (right) courtesy Brookstone; p. 121 (left) © Dobri/Dreamstime.com

Library of Congress Cataloging-in-Publication Data
Larsen, Linda Johnson.
  Knack slow cooking : hearty & delicious meals you can prepare ahead /
Linda Johnson Larsen ; photographs by Christopher Brown.
     p. cm.
  Includes index.
  ISBN 978-1-59921-619-5
  1. Electric cookery, Slow. I. Title. II. Title: Slow cooking.
  TX827.L37 2009
  641.5'884—dc22
                                                2009022653

The information in this book is true and complete to the best of our knowledge. All recommendations are made without guarantee on the part of the author or Globe Pequot Press. The author and Globe Pequot Press disclaim any liability in connection with the use of this information.

Printed in China

10 9 8 7 6 5 4 3 2 1

*To my parents, Duane and Marlene, for teaching me that perseverance is a goal in itself.*

## Acknowledgments

Thanks, as always, to my agent Barb Doyen for her support and encouragement. I'd also like to thank Maureen Graney, my editor, for her good ideas and sense of direction. My husband, Doug, is always a great support and my best friend, too. And thanks to Christopher Brown for doing such a beautiful job on the photography and bringing the recipes to life.

# CONTENTS

# INTRODUCTION

Most Americans own a slow cooker, even if it's just languishing in a kitchen cupboard or basement storage room. But there are many reasons to pull out that neglected slow cooker and put it to work, including better tasting, healthier food; time, energy, and money savings; and ease of cleanup.

This book, featuring easy, delicious recipes, straightforward instruction and commonsense safety information, will help you become a slow cooker pro and feed your family excellent food for less money. When the slow cooker is used correctly, with staggered cooking times for different foods and judicious seasoning, you can produce excellent quality meals with very little work.

It's estimated that more than 80 percent of American households own a slow cooker. While this appliance was quite popular in the 1970s, it faded during the last few years of the twentieth century, and is now making a comeback. The ease of use, excellent results, and time and money saved make it a valued appliance in the kitchen.

This book will focus on familiar slow-cooked foods and introduce you to more exotic, delicious recipes. A simple, clear layout, with photos of not only the completed dish but also steps along the way, makes learning easy. Once you have discovered the many ways to use the slow cooker, you will be able to adapt recipes to your taste and create your own meals to satisfy your family.

Each spread is self-contained, with tips and instructions on how to perfectly and safely prepare and cook each recipe. Simple variations that transform the recipe into something completely new are highlighted, showing you that mastering several basic techniques will exponentially increase your repertoire. Ethnic flavors, like Pork Carnitas, Greek Chicken Stew, Shepherd's Pie, and Corned Beef, along with trendy new tastes and food combinations, are introduced via the variations.

Topics covered include how to cook multiple foods at the same time, how to use the slow cooker to make unexpected recipes like cheesecakes and salads, why slow-cooked food is healthier for your family, and how to make entire meals from the slow cooker. Slow cooker safety is stressed, with safe cooking ranges and final temperatures listed for each recipe. You'll also learn how to test the accuracy of your slow cooker.

You should own more than one slow cooker. Not only do the different sizes cook different types of food better, but you can make an entire meal in a collection of slow cookers. The main dish will cook in the largest appliance, while potatoes stay warm in another. A chocolate bread pudding cooks without any attention while you're eating.

There is more to slow cooking than just filling up the pot and turning it on. Once you learn the special preparation methods some slow cooker recipes demand, all of your attempts will turn out better.

There have been many advances in slow cooker technology over just the last five to six years. Electronic controls let you program a cooking sequence into the appliance. For instance, you can set it to cook for 1 hour on high to get the temperature up quickly, then set it to low for the rest of the cooking time.

The delayed-start and keep-warm features are also great advances. They let you safely stretch the cooking time by 2 hours on each side. This lets you be away from the house longer and still return to safe, perfectly cooked food.

## Food Safety

Food safety is one of the most important facets of cooking. If someone gets sick from food you cooked, not only is all your work, time, and money lost, but there can be serious consequences.

Some have questioned the safety of the slow cooker because it cooks at low temperatures. There's no need to be

doesn't reach the interior of whole birds fast enough to bring them quickly through the danger zone.

- Don't cool food in the slow cooker. The thick ceramic insert is designed to hold heat for a long time. If food in the insert is placed into the refrigerator, it will take too long to cool below 40 degrees F. Just transfer the food to a food storage container and refrigerate promptly.

- Finally, watch the time that the food is not cooking. Perishable foods, which include meat, dairy products, eggs, and cheese, cannot be left out at room temperature longer than 2 hours, cooked or uncooked. If the ambient temperature is above 80 degrees, that safe time shrinks to 1 hour. Promptly refrigerate foods after cooking.

concerned. The low setting cooks at 200 degrees F, and the high setting at 300 degrees F, well above the "danger zone" of 40 to 140 degrees F.

There are some food safety rules you need to follow:

- Don't cook frozen meats in the slow cooker. The cold temperature of the meats can keep the entire temperature of the dish in the danger zone too long.

- Don't cook a whole chicken or whole turkey in this appliance; the slow cooker just can't heat these birds fast enough to prevent bacterial growth. And the slow cooker's heat

It's important to understand preparation techniques and steps that improve the quality of food that comes from your slow cooker. Browned meats add color and remarkable flavor to the dishes, while precooking some foods like beans and grains makes the end result very delicious and appealing.

Some vegetables should be cooked before adding to the slow cooker. Onions and garlic are the most common ingredients that need precooking. These foods add great flavor and texture to recipes, but they can be harsh and overpowering when uncooked. Sauté them in oil or butter before adding to the recipe so they become sweet and mellow in the slow cooker.

Making a whole meal in the slow cooker is easy. Pick a main dish, a vegetable dish, and a dessert from this book. Choose the time when you want to serve dinner, and then write down a timetable.

Start the longest-cooking recipe first, then stagger the cooking times of the remaining dishes so everything will be done at the same time. You may want to delay dessert to finish cooking an hour after the other foods so you can leisurely enjoy your meal.

Dessert can sometimes be made ahead of time, so if that's the case, make it in the morning or the night before. Main dishes usually cook longer than side dishes, so plan those in advance as well. Work backwards from your chosen serving time to figure out when to start the slow cookers.

Start the longest-cooking recipe first, then stagger the cooking times of the remaining dishes so everything will be done at the same time. You may want to delay dessert to finish cooking an hour after the other foods so you can leisurely enjoy your meal.

## Care and Use

Caring for your slow cooker is easy. The inserts are usually dishwasher safe (read the instructions!) but it's a good idea, after you remove the food, to fill the insert with hot, soapy water and let it stand until you're ready to clean.

If you use a plastic slow cooker liner, cleanup is a breeze; just throw away the liner after you've removed the food. *Note:* Only use commercial liners that are specifically made for use in the slow cooker. Ordinary plastic bags, even cooking bags, may melt and ruin your food and the slow cooker. Spraying the insert with nonstick cooking spray will also help reduce cleanup to a wipe with a soapy sponge.

Never add cold water to a hot insert; the ceramic could crack. And speaking of cracks, if your insert develops cracks, even tiny hairline cracks, you shouldn't use it. Those cracks can harbor bacteria that may contaminate your food. And tiny cracks can develop into larger cracks, or the insert could break apart while it is holding hot food. Many companies offer insert replacements: Check their Web sites.

When you've learned how to make a basic recipe, start incorporating your own favorite flavors and ingredients. Almost all food can be cooked in a slow cooker (with the probable exception of lettuce!), and the appliance blends and accents flavors beautifully.

Enjoy these recipes. As you get more experienced in slow cooking, you'll be able to branch out and invent your own recipes. Be sure to write them down. It's hard to re-create a masterpiece from memory.

# HOW IT WORKS

## A slow cooker is a simple appliance that works wonders with inexpensive food

Your slow cooker is ready to go right out of the box. This versatile appliance stands alone, ready to transform tough cuts of meat and vegetables into flavorful feasts.

The true slow cooker consists of a round or oval metal housing that holds the heating element. It literally surrounds the food with heat as it cooks. This part of the slow cooker should never be immersed in water; wipe clean with a damp cloth or sponge.

Most slow cookers have inserts that actually hold the food. Stoneware inserts are very thick and heavy, and are meant to retain heat. Handle them carefully, because they can chip or break easily. A crack in the insert means it must be discarded.

### Slow Cooker Components

- Metal exterior
- Digital or manual controls
- Stoneware or metal insert
- Power cord
- Lid
- Instruction book

*Slow Cooker Housing*

- Slow cookers cook at two temperatures. Low setting reaches 200 degrees F, while the high setting reaches 300 degrees F. These settings are safe for food.

- Meats are the focus for food safety in a slow cooker. Meats need to be cooked to 155 to 180 degrees F, depending on the type, so these temperatures are sufficient.

- Try to keep the housing unit clean. Wipe up spills right away so they don't cook onto the housing.

The lid is an integral part of the slow cooker. It traps heat and moisture and helps heat circulate around the food. You must use the lid designed for your slow cooker so the food cooks properly.

The power cord is deliberately short to avoid accidents. Place the slow cooker on a heatproof surface, like the top of an oven or a large tile, to protect your countertop. And never use an extension cord with the slow cooker; a long cord invites accidents, especially if it hangs over the edge of a counter.

## YELLOW ● LIGHT

Because the stone inserts are so thick, and retain heat so well, do not keep the food in the insert after it is cooked. The insert will slow down cooling, and will keep food in the danger zone of 40 to 140 degrees F too long, even in the refrigerator. Always remove cooked food from the insert and store in food-safe, well-sealed containers.

## Inserts

- Most new slow cookers now come with a removable stoneware or metal insert.

- This insert makes it easy to clean the slow cooker and to serve food. If your older slow cooker is all one piece, use cooking bags to make cleaning easier.

- Be careful with the stoneware inserts. If they crack or chip, you'll have to discard them. These blemishes can harbor bacteria.

- Most inserts are dishwasher-safe. Be sure to read the instruction booklet and follow information about cleaning and storage.

## Sealed Lid

- Even though it's a loose fit, the lid on a slow cooker actually forms a seal with the insert.

- This seal is created by moisture and a little bit of pressure from the heat of the food.

- The low heat and the moisture circulate in the slow cooker. Condensation from evaporated liquid is kept in the appliance.

- There is little or no loss of moisture with this appliance; the food stays juicy and tender. Don't lift the lid more than you have to.

# HOW TO FILL IT
## Filling the slow cooker properly is key to best results

Because all the food cooks at the same time, variable cooking times come into play when filling the appliance. Follow these rules to the letter for best results.

The foods that cook most slowly in the slow cooker aren't meats, as you'd expect, but hard root vegetables like potatoes, carrots, and squash. These foods must be placed in the hottest part of the cooker, as close to the heat source as possible.

Always place root vegetables on the bottom of the slow cooker. They will become tender and sweet, and all of the juices from meats and broths, and flavors from herbs and spices, will infuse them.

Also place rice and grains on the bottom of the slow cooker. They have to be completely covered with liquid as they cook or they will never become tender.

### Place Root Vegetables

- Make sure that root vegetables are prepared as directed in the recipe. Most need to be peeled and cubed or diced.

- These vegetables should all be cut to about the same size, as they take the same amount of time to cook.

- Place vegetables evenly in the bottom of the slow cooker, and either layer them as the recipe suggests, or mix together.

- Even if you're making roasted vegetables, you need to add a small amount of liquid so the vegetables don't burn.

### Faster Cooking Foods

- Meats and more tender vegetables, along with dried fruits, are placed on top of root vegetables, beans, or grains.

- You can cook very tender produce in the slow cooker. Add peas, green onions, and fresh herbs at the very end of cooking time.

- Dairy products, like milk, cream, and cheese, are also added at the very end of the cooking time.

- Often, stabilizers like flour, cornstarch, or arrowroot are stirred in with dairy products to help prevent curdling and keep the sauce smooth.

Fill a slow cooker between one-half and three-quarters full. If you use less food, you run the risk of burning. And if you use more, the food may not cook through or the slow cooker could overflow as foods release juices.

As you get more accustomed to the slow cooker, filling it will become second nature and you'll learn how to eyeball quantities instead of precisely measuring foods.

········· GREEN ● LIGHT ·········

For recipes like soups and stews, you can alter the recipes "on the fly." Add ingredients until the slow cooker is properly filled, then add enough liquid to just cover the food. For less flexible dishes you have to keep the proportions of food to liquid the same, so follow the recipe carefully.

## Correctly Filled

- No matter the recipe, slow cookers should be filled between ½ and ¾ full.

- To decide which size slow cooker you need, add up all of the non-liquid ingredients in cups, then divide by 4 to calculate the number of quarts.

- Multiply the number of quarts by 3 and divide by 2 to get the size of slow cooker you need.

- Example: If recipe calls for 14 cups of food, you would need a 5-quart slow cooker. $14 \div 4 \times 3 \div 2 \approx 5$

## Stirring the Food

- Whenever you lift the slow cooker lid (even for stirring), it releases heat and extends the cooking time. Add another 20 minutes for each time the lid is lifted.

- When recipes specifically call for stirring, additional cooking time has already been factored in. Follow directions carefully and stir only as required.

- If you need to see the food, just spin the lid in place to remove condensation rather than lift the lid.

# SLOW COOKER SIZES
## Large or small: These are the slow cookers you need

Since filling slow cookers accurately is so crucial to recipe success, owning a variety of sizes and shapes of slow cookers is key.

Slow cookers are among the most inexpensive appliances on the market. They can, especially with liners made of metal, literally substitute for a stove and oven. You can bake, roast, boil, and simmer in a slow cooker; all for less than a hundred dollars.

Slow cookers range in size from diminutive 2-cup babies made for serving appetizers or condiments, to large 7-quart oval monsters that can serve a crowd.

The standard 4-quart slow cooker will handle most of your cooking needs. In it you can prepare a 12-cup pasta sauce or feed a family of four a meal of chicken and vegetables.

The next addition to your slow cooker family should be a

### Basic 4-Quart Round

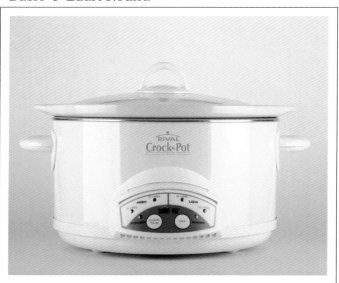

- The basic 4-quart slow cooker should be in every kitchen. It's the perfect size for making spaghetti sauce or soup.

- This size slow cooker is also ideal for keeping food, like mashed potatoes or other side dishes, warm during holiday meals.

- Most of these slow cookers come with a stoneware insert that fits snugly into the housing. Use cooking spray to grease the insert before use for easy cleanup.

- As with all appliances, follow directions for care in your instruction booklet.

### 1-Quart Slow Cooker

- Small slow cookers range from 2 cups to 2 quarts. The very small sizes are used for melting chocolate or making appetizers.

- 1½ and 2-quart models are ideal for small families, whether you're making soup or spicy chicken.

- Hot dips, snack mixes, and tiny sauces cook perfectly in the small slow cooker, and you can use it for serving.

- If there are 1-2 people in your family, a smaller slow cooker can prepare 2 chicken breasts or pork chops.

small slow cooker of 1 ½ to 2 quarts. With it, you can make a hot dip for a party and keep the dip hot and fresh while serving.

Then, a 5- to 7-quart oval slow cooker is a great addition. These slow cookers hold larger cuts of meat, like hams, roasts, and large pieces of chicken with ease. With slow cookers this size, you can feed 8 to 10 people a complete meal.

Keep your slow cooker family in good condition and it will serve you well for years.

## GREEN ● LIGHT

When choosing the slow cooker to use for a recipe, especially if you're creating your own, just add up the volume of the ingredients and choose a slow cooker based on filling it ½ to ¾ full.

Think about appearance as well. An attractive slow cooker can be used to serve as well as cook.

## 6-Quart Slow Cooker

- The 6-quart slow cooker is the one to purchase if you have a family larger than 4 people.

- It will cook 16 cups of soup or spaghetti sauce, enough to feed a family and freeze leftovers.

- A slow cooker of this size is also good for baking desserts and making breakfast cereals.

- A 7- or 8-inch springform pan or cake pan will fit into this slow cooker with room for heat to circulate.

## 7-Quart Oval

- These large slow cookers make preparing a holiday meal for a crowd a breeze.

- You should be able to fit a large roast or half a ham in this appliance, with room to spare.

- You can make whole meals for 6–8 people by adding vegetables or fruits to the large cuts of meat.

- If you routinely cook for more than 6 people, you may want to purchase multiple large slow cookers.

# SAUCES AND THICKENERS
## Many slow cooker recipes need these additions for stabilizing

One of the critical parts of slow cooker success is creating sauces. Since foods release liquid when they are cooked in the slow cooker, and that liquid doesn't evaporate, it's essential that the sauces have a little extra help so they don't break or separate.

This is why many slow cooker recipes call for canned condensed creamed soups. The soups have stabilizers, emulsifiers,

and other additives that keep the liquid stable over the long, slow, wet cooking time. Since condensed soups aren't very healthy, you can substitute a white sauce.

White sauces aren't difficult to make; they just take a little practice. Once you've learned how to make a white sauce, you can whip one up in about 10 minutes. And you control the sodium and ingredients that your family eats.

### Ingredients

2 tablespoons butter

2 tablespoons flour

$\frac{1}{4}$ teaspoon salt

$\frac{1}{8}$ teaspoon white pepper

1 cup milk or light cream

1 teaspoon cornstarch

*White Sauce*

- In small saucepan, melt butter over medium heat. You can add minced garlic, shallots, or onion at this point.

- Add the flour, salt, and pepper. Cook and stir with a wire whisk to incorporate the flour into the butter. Let simmer for 2–3 minutes.

- Slowly add the milk or light cream, whisking constantly.

- Cook and stir over low heat until the sauce thickens. Stir in cornstarch and remove from heat; use as directed in recipe.

KNACK SLOW COOKING

You can vary the white sauce with the type of liquid you use. You can add herbs, spices, condiments like mustard or flavored vinegars, and almost any kind of shredded or grated cheese.

If someone in your family is allergic to wheat or milk, you can still make a white sauce using a thickener other than flour, or a liquid other than milk or cream: variations are included.

**Yield: 1 cup**

## MAKE IT EASY

If you don't want to make a white sauce, you can substitute bottled Alfredo sauces. These products are higher quality than canned soups, and often have additional ingredients like roasted garlic, herbs, and cheeses. A 16-ounce jar of Alfredo sauce is equal to 2 cups of a homemade white sauce.

### *Sauces for Allergies*

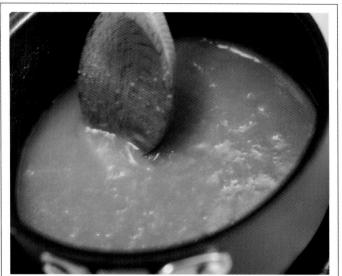

- For a milk allergy, simply substitute soy milk or rice milk for cow's milk. You can use dairy-free margarine in place of the butter.

- Or use chicken broth, beef broth, or vegetable broth in place of the milk. The result is called a *veloute sauce*.

- For wheat allergies, combine 1 tablespoon cornstarch or arrowroot with 1 cup milk. Add this to the melted butter and cook for 3–4 minutes.

### *Oil-Based White Sauce*

- An oil-based white sauce is based on the classic Cajun roux.

- Combine 2 tablespoons vegetable oil with 2 tablespoons flour in a small saucepan.

- Cook and stir over low heat just until the mixture takes on a tiny bit of gold. Then add 1 cup milk; cook and stir until thickened.

- Shredded cheese can be added to any of these sauces; use ⅓ cup of cheese for 1 cup of sauce.

# ENTERTAIN WITH SLOW COOKERS

## Slow cookers function as a personal chef, making entertaining a breeze

KNACK SLOW COOKING

Slow cookers are ideal for entertaining because the food cooks without any attention from you, it frees up your stovetop and oven, and you can serve directly from the appliance.

You can remove the insert and place it on a trivet or hot pad on the table, or keep the slow cooker fully assembled and plug it in for a buffet.

You have to keep an eye on the time, however. A keep-warm feature will keep the food at a safe serving temperature for 2 hours. If you only have low and high settings, place the slow cooker on low and stir it occasionally. After 2 hours, refrigerate the food.

It's possible to make an entire meal in a series of slow cookers.

### Multiple Slow Cookers

- The main problem if you are going to use multiple slow cookers is finding a heatproof surface.

- Slow cookers can damage laminate countertops, so look for large ceramic tiles at outlet stores to place under them.

- It's also helpful to place a sticky note near (not on) each slow cooker with a note about cooking time and any stirring instructions.

- Then relax, because everything is covered. All you need is a crisp salad, and dinner is served.

### Make a Complete Meal

- For cooking an entire meal in slow cookers, you'll need different sizes and shapes.

- A roast uses a larger, oval slow cooker, especially if you put vegetables around it, while mashed potatoes cook best in a 3- or 4-quart cooker.

- The smallest slow cookers are perfect for dips, while side dishes cook in the small to medium sizes.

- You can also easily stagger the starting times if the foods cook for different times.

Serve a flavorful mulled beverage along with a hot dip before dinner. Then offer a main dish like beef stroganoff or chicken verde; serve it over rice pilaf made in a small slow cooker, with some glazed carrots on the side. And for dessert, a chocolate cheesecake cooks to perfection in the slow cooker.

Even making one or two dishes in the slow cooker is like having your own personal kitchen assistant. And with the delayed-start and keep-warm features, entertaining has never been easier.

. . . . . . . . . . . . . . *GREEN* ● *LIGHT* . . . . . . . . . . . .

The slow cooker is the perfect choice when entertaining during the hot summer months. It doesn't heat up your kitchen, and you can prepare the food ahead of time and just add to the slow cooker, stir, and turn it on. Bean and vegetable dishes are a great complement to grilled meats.

## *Beverages*

- Any hot beverage can be made or kept warm in a slow cooker during a party.

- The keep-warm or low setting is perfect. But when the amount of liquid in the slow cooker drops to less than ⅓, turn it off.

- If you're serving a large party or are holding a long open house, have more than one beverage cooking.

- Just stagger times so you can remove the old beverage and put out the new when it's ready.

## *Buffet Sets*

- For a buffet, there's nothing better than a slow cooker set. You still have the flexibility of three separate slow cookers.

- Each has its own timer and heat regulation, so you can easily cook more than one dish.

- Set the buffet cooker on the table you'll use during the party; it will be too heavy to lift or move when full.

- Again, make sure to keep track of the time the food is sitting out—after 2 hours, remove it.

# HOW TO ADAPT RECIPES
## Adapt oven and stovetop recipes to the slow cooker

Many recipes that you cook in the oven and on the stovetop can be adapted to the slow cooker. There are just a few rules to follow.

First, choose a recipe. If it's a soup or stew, reduce the liquid by about half and you're ready to go. Add a browning step if the recipe calls for beef or pork, and ground meats must be cooked and drained before adding to the slow cooker.

Any recipes that call for long cooking times like braising or roasting are adaptable. Just remember to place root vegetables in the bottom of the slow cooker and top with meats and tender produce.

When cooking meat, first trim off any visible fat, since that will affect the taste and texture of the dish. Reduce liquids by ⅔ because of the slow cooker's moist environment.

### Reducing Liquid

- For a soup, the liquid should just barely cover the solid ingredients when cooking starts.

- If there is excess liquid in the slow cooker when the soup is done, there are a few ways to reduce it.

- Spoon out some of the liquid, or turn the heat to high and cook with the lid off for 20–30 minutes.

- Or transfer the liquid to a pan and simmer on the stovetop until reduced, then return to the slow cooker.

### Large Cuts of Meat

- Large cuts of meat cook well in the slow cooker; in fact, the cheaper the cut, the better the result.

- Coat the meat with seasoned flour and brown it first; this adds flavor and thickens liquid for gravy.

- Season the food well: dried herbs will stand up to the long cooking time, but their potency may be reduced.

- You can add some fresh herb of the same type at the end of cooking time to punch up the flavor.

For timing, multiply the time of your recipe by 6 for low heat cooking, or by 3½ for cooking on high. In general, to cook a 3-pound chunk of meat will take 4 hours on high or 7 hours on low, while chicken breasts take 5 hours and dark meat 6 to 7 hours on low.

Then always check the recipe at the shortest cooking time so foods don't overcook or burn.

## ZOOM

The slow cooker is a very healthy way to cook foods. The long, slow cooking time reduces unhealthy compounds that form in high heat, called advanced glycation end products, or AGEs. So using your slow cooker can help lower the risk of developing diabetes, heart disease, and cancer.

## Adjust Ingredients

- When adapting recipes, add milk, cream, sour cream, and cheeses at the end of cooking time just to heat through.

- Some recipes are exceptions: cheesy dips cook for only a short period and you can add cheeses at the beginning.

- Add tender vegetables like peas at the end of cooking time.

- Dried beans should be soaked before adding to a slow cooker recipe; avoid adding salt or acid ingredients until the beans soften.

## Layer Foods Properly

- Layering foods is crucial to success; hard vegetables go in the bottom, while tender vegetables go on top.

- Rice and pasta can be difficult to cook in the slow cooker. They should be placed on the bottom so they are covered with liquid.

- Usually, brown and wild rice work well. And smaller pasta like orzo or shells can be added during the last 15–20 minutes.

- Larger pastas should be cooked separately and added to the finished dish.

# LADLES, SPOONS, AND SIEVES

## These tools will help you rearrange and remove food with ease

You don't need a lot of extra equipment to cook in your slow cooker. Regular tools like knives, a swivel-bladed vegetable peeler, and a skillet to brown meats and cook onions and ground meat are standard in any kitchen.

Ladles and spoons are important tools for the slow cooker. You'll also need a strainer, especially if you make broths and stocks in your slow cooker. Have a selection of ladles on hand.

Ladles have a more rounded bowl, usually set at a right angle to the handle so it's easy to lift liquids. You should have a couple made of heat-resistant plastic, some made of steel or other metal, and some pretty serving ladles. Ladles are perfect for serving and for adding more liquid to the slow cooker.

Regular and slotted spoons should be on hand too. Slotted spoons are great for removing meats to shred or chop,

### Silicone Ladle

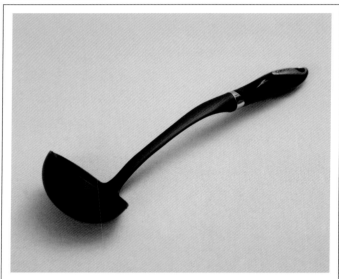

- You may want to have a variety of sizes of ladles on hand. They are also available in different colors.

- Silicone ladles easily release food, and are good for serving sticky items like sauce for chicken or cheesy appetizers.

- High-quality ladles, from Henckels or Kitchenaid, run around $15 to $20.

- For serving, you may want ladles of different materials, like sterling silver or china, to match your dinnerware or utensils.

### Slotted Spoon

- Slotted spoons have holes, slots, or decorative openings punched into the bowl. They are the same size as large serving spoons.

- They work like a sieve, but let slightly larger items like chopped onions or garlic pass through.

- Spoons should be sturdy, with long handles so your fingers stay away from the heat and steam.

- These spoons can be made from metal, silicone, heat-proof rubber, china, or ceramic.

and removing food from excess liquid. Stainless steel and wooden spoons are both good choices.

And sieves will help you strain broths as well as skim foam from the surface of simmering broths and stocks.

Be sure to buy the best quality, sturdiest items you can afford. Keep them in good working condition and on hand to help with your slow cooking chores.

········· GREEN ● LIGHT ·········

When you find a ladle, spoon, or sieve that you really like and that feels good in your hand, buy more than one. Utensils come and go on the market, and your favorite spoon may become unavailable. These tools are inexpensive and store easily.

## Ladles and Spoons

- 1 metal ladle
- 1 silicone ladle
- 1 stainless spoon
- 2 wooden spoons
- 1 heatproof rubber scraper
- 1 stand-alone sieve
- Graduated nesting sieves
- 1 large shallow strainer
- 1 pair spring-loaded tongs

*Bamboo Brass Skimmer*

- This type of skimmer or sieve usually has a bamboo handle and a brass mesh spoon.

- The handle stays cool when the spoon is immersed in boiling or simmering liquids.

- Strainers and sieves come in two forms: stand-alone models and those with a long single handle.

- A strainer with a handle usually has a hook on the opposite end so it can sit on top of a pot to receive broth or stock.

13

# COOKING BAGS AND FOIL
## Cooking bags and foil assist in preparation and cooking

A removable insert took the slow cooker to the next generation back in the 1980s. This advance made the appliance much easier to clean.

But making sure your slow cooker insert is sparkling clean is still a challenge. You can spray the insert with nonstick cooking spray before adding the food, but there is an easier way.

Heat resistant cooking bags, also called plastic liners, let you use your slow cooker with absolutely no cleanup at all. Just place the liner in the slow cooker, fill it with food, turn it on, and cook.

Then all you have to do is remove and serve (or store) the food, then lift out the liner and throw it away.

Foil is another essential slow cooker tool. Foil balls, made by crumpling the material in your fist, will help hold meat out of

### Heat Resistant Bags and Liners

- Be sure that the cooking bags you use are specifically made for use in the slow cooker.

- As the name suggests, heat resistant bags are specially designed to stand up to the heat of the slow cooker.

- Regular plastic bags should not be used in the slow cooker. They can melt and ruin your food.

- Products not designed for the slow cooker can emit chemicals into your food that can be harmful. So read labels.

### Foil Balls

- Heavy duty or regular foil can be used to make these balls. Keep the balls the same size so the meat sits solidly on them.

- This allows the meat to steam rather than braise sitting in liquid.

- The fat drains off the meat as it cooks, so the finished dish has much less fat.

- If you're concerned about aluminum, don't use the juices that accumulate around the foil balls. It won't affect the meat.

the liquid for roasting. And crossed foil strips fit neatly under a meatloaf so you can easily lift it out of the appliance when it's done.

Finally, paper towels also have a place in your slow cooker collection. When baking, place paper towels under the lid to catch moisture so it doesn't drip onto the baked goods.

With these inexpensive materials, using the slow cooker is even easier and less work for you.

············· RED●LIGHT ·············

Do not reuse heat-resistant cooking bags, foil, or paper towels. These materials are intended as one-use products, and can't be sufficiently cleaned to make them safe for reuse. These items are very inexpensive, so using new cooking bags, foil, and paper towels each time isn't prohibitive.

## Paper Towel under Lid

- Again, read labels to find out if the paper towel is approved for use with food.

- Microwave-safe paper towels are a good bet; they're approved for use with food, moisture, and heat.

- Place 3–4 layers of paper towel on top of the slow cooker; make sure the paper towel is large enough to sit on top.

- Then cover with the lid of the slow cooker. Because you're placing paper next to heat, don't leave the house when cooking with this method.

## Foil Strips

- To make the foil strips, tear off two 24-inch-long pieces of aluminum foil.

- Fold the foil in half lengthwise, then fold in half again to make two 24-inch-long x 3-inch-wide strips.

- Cross the strips over each other and place in the bottom of the slow cooker. Let the ends extend beyond the lid.

- Add the meatloaf or roast; cover and cook as directed. Use the foil to help remove the food from the slow cooker.

# RACKS AND HOLDERS

## Some recipes call for racks; and transporting the slow cooker is easy with travel cases

When you think of the slow cooker as an oven, the only thing that is different is the amount of liquid the recipe creates. For some recipes, the food needs to be lifted out of that liquid. That's where racks and holders come into play.

Some manufacturers sell racks that are made to fit perfectly into the slow cooker. But you can find inexpensive metal racks in any grocery store. Just make sure they fit in your slow cooker without tilting or tipping. And always use heatproof racks, never plastic.

Meat racks are another great gadget for your slow cooker. There are V-racks, which hold the meat out of the liquid, and racks to hold chicken or ham. Some of these racks have

### V-shaped Meat Rack

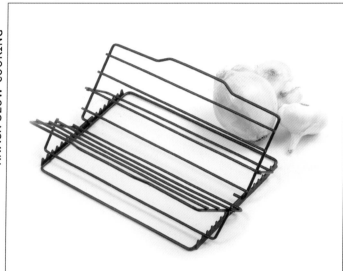

- Be sure that the rack fits into your slow cooker, and that the rack is short enough that the lid will fit snugly. There are even adjustable options.

- You can find racks made of aluminum, of metal coated with porcelain, and of stainless steel.

- The rack will hold the meat out of the liquid, while juices and fat drip down into the slow cooker.

- After skimming off the fat, the juices can be used in a saucepan to make delicious gravy.

### Rack with Lifting Handles

- When you're cooking a large roast or ham in the slow cooker, removing it becomes a challenge.

- Foil strips aren't sturdy enough to lift the food; and if the food drops, it can splash hot liquid over you.

- There are racks with handles and even lifter baskets that you put in the slow cooker before you add the meat.

- Just place the meat in the rack and make sure you can get to the handles. Use pot holders when lifting.

handles that make removing the food very easy.

And since slow-cooked recipes are the perfect choice for potlucks, you need a way to safely transport the food. Some slow cookers are made for transporting, with special locks; others have travel cases that hold in the heat.

Take some time to browse through a kitchenware store or even the baking supply aisle of your grocery store to see what's new in slow cooker gadgets and accessories. You may find something to make your life easier.

## YELLOW ● LIGHT

Even if you have an insulated carrier that will keep the food in the slow cooker warm, you still have to follow food safety rules. Don't let the food sit in the slow cooker without cooking for more than 2 hours. Make sure you get to your destination within that time frame.

### Round Rack

- When you're baking in the slow cooker, a rack is necessary to hold the pan.

- The heat has to circulate evenly around the pan for proper baking. A wire rack is ideal for this purpose.

- Be sure that the rack you use is heat-proof. You can use a slotted trivet; however, be sure it can be heated to 300 degrees F.

- The rack can also be used to hold meats above their cooking liquids.

### Travel Cases

- When you want to take your slow cooker along to a party, it's a good idea to have some kind of case.

- There are cases specifically made for round and oval slow cookers that are insulated to conserve heat.

- These cases usually have sturdy handles, and they help keep you safe from spills while traveling.

- If you don't have a case, you can wrap the slow cooker in newspaper tied together, then in blankets.

# TIMERS AND KEEP-WARM
## Timing is everything with a slow cooker; and many models have keep-warm features

Because the slow cooker cooks slowly and safely, just assemble dinner, turn it on, and leave the house. You can extend the cooking time to more than 10 hours, if you follow a few rules.

Many of the newer slow cookers have built-in timers and keep-warm features that can turn a 6-hour recipe into a 10-hour recipe, giving you more time away from the kitchen.

But you must follow the 2-hour rule. Never let perishable food (meat, eggs, dairy products) sit out at room temperature longer than 2 hours. And that time shortens to 1 hour when the ambient air temperature is 80 degrees F or higher. And, at the end of cooking, never let the food sit at room temperature longer than 2 hours, or 1 hour in the summer.

### Built-in Timer

HOT SURFACE

Hamilton Beach

- The newer slow cookers usually have built-in electronic timers for precise control of cooking times.

- Make sure that you read the manufacturer's instruction booklet completely so you understand how this feature works.

- Most of these slow cookers have three cooking temperatures: low, high, and keep-warm.

- Others have up to five settings, including a buffet setting to keep food safe during parties.

### Added Timer

- An added timer works by plugging into the slow cooker between the appliance and the electrical outlet. Set the timer, turn on the slow cooker, and walk away.

- For best results, use an added timer that has been developed specifically for the slow cooker.

- While lamp timers may work, for safety's sake use a timer made for this purpose.

- When cooking poultry, you should reduce the delayed start time to 1 hour for food safety reasons.

Only use these methods if they are built into your slow cooker. Attaching a timing device to the slow cooker can be risky. Some people have used devices made to automatically turn on lights to delay start of their slow cookers, but it's not wise to gamble with your food.

Follow these rules strictly and precisely and you'll give yourself more freedom in the kitchen than ever before. And you'll eat well too.

····· • GREEN●LIGHT ·············

If you'd like to prepare the food ahead of time and refrigerate it in the insert before putting it in the slow cooker, use delayed start. Putting a cold ceramic insert into the heating element can cause cracks. The 1- to 2-hour delayed start standing time will bring the insert to room temperature.

## Keep-Warm

- The keep-warm feature is built into many slow cookers. There really isn't a way to jerry-rig the appliance to create this feature.

- The timers made just for slow cookers often include this feature.

- Be sure that you count serving and eating time in that 2-hour window.

- If food stops cooking at 6:00 p.m., you have until 8:00 p.m. to serve and eat the food. Don't think you can serve it at 8:00 p.m. and be safe.

## Delayed Start

- All of the ingredients must be cold when added to the slow cooker if you're going to use a timer for a delayed start.

- Never use room temperature food or warm sauces if you use delayed start; this will keep the food in the danger zone of 40 to 140 degrees F too long.

- Don't use the slow cooker to reheat food, especially with a timer.

- Reheat slow-cooked food in the microwave or on the stovetop.

# OPTIONS

## The newest slow cookers come with some neat options

These aren't your grandmother's slow cookers! The new models come with all kinds of gadgets and options to make slow cooking even easier. Companies are constantly developing new products and updates to older products. In fact, it's worth your time to browse the Internet for cooking equipment sites to find out what's new.

Hinged lids, stainless steel liners that are safe to use on the stovetop or in the oven, and electronic controls are all huge advances in slow cooker technology.

When you place a hot lid with condensation on a countertop, a seal can form and the lid will stick tight to the countertop. Slide it to the edge of the countertop to lift off. A hinged lid automatically prevents this.

Electronic controls make the slow cooker even more

### Locking Lid

- A locking lid is another great feature that makes it easy to safely transport food in your slow cooker.

- Be sure that the locks really are fastened securely before you try to move the slow cooker.

- It's a good idea to place a hot slow cooker filled with food in an insulated case.

- These models often come with a spoon that attaches to the lid. Remember to wash off the spoon every time you stir, for food safety.

### Oven-Safe Insert

- Stainless steel inserts are a great new advance in slow cooker technology.

- In older models, if you want to brown meat or cook onions, you have to use another pan.

- If you have a stovetop-safe slow cooker (read the instruction booklet!) you can sauté right in the insert, saving you the hassle of cleaning another pan.

- These inserts may be used in the oven if indicated, and are also beautiful serving dishes.

versatile. Delayed start, keep-warm, and integrated meat probes keep your food safe for hours.

These improvements do make the appliance more complicated. You may want to read reviews of slow cookers at Amazon.com or Epinions.com before buying one. And don't be afraid to add your voice to the reviews.

·············· RED●LIGHT··············

If the power goes out while your food is cooking, and you don't know exactly how long it was out, you have to throw away the food. An outage of 2 hours or less is safe. Power outages are a concern for manually controlled slow cookers. If you're at home during the outage, monitor the time. It's better to be safe than sorry.

## Hinged Lid

- Lids drip hot water when lifted, and steam will rush up from the food. You can be burned by steam, and hot water can drip on your hands or arm.

- Hinged lids help prevent this from happening.

- If the lid is attached to the slow cooker and you have to unlock it before removal, it prevents sudden temperature changes.

- Glass lids can break or crack if they are put under cold water when they're hot.

## Electronic vs. Manual Controls

- Some of the new, more sophisticated slow cookers have complicated controls; read instruction booklets carefully.

- The newest even have built-in indicators that tell you if the power went off, and for how long.

- You can program these slow cookers for many different combinations of cooking times and temperatures.

- A meat probe is another great feature; it will let you know when meat is safely cooked.

# THERMOMETERS
## Final temperature of food is key to perfect results

If you don't have a food thermometer, go get one right now. They are that important to successful and safe cooking, not only with the slow cooker, but with every other method.

There are several types of thermometers, ranging from the simple probe with a dial reading, to electronic digital thermometers that keep track of food as it cooks, and instant-read thermometers that give you almost instant results.

Placement of the thermometer in the food is crucial. For accurate results, when checking the temperature of meat, the probe has to be in meat, not in fat, and not touching bone.

The least complicated thermometer, a dial thermometer, should be placed about 2 inches into the food for an accurate reading. Digital, instant-read, and fork thermometers can

KNACK SLOW COOKING

### Instant-Read Thermometer

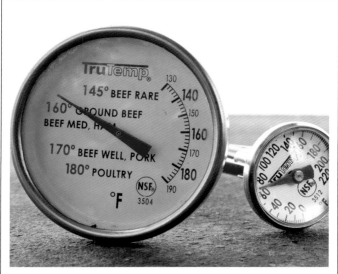

- There are several types of instant-read thermometers. Permanent models come with a dial or electronic reading.

- Single-use instant-read thermometers can be used only once and are made of temperature-sensitive material.

- These thermometers can't remain in the food as it is cooking because the controls aren't heatproof.

- You can find these thermometers in kitchenware stores and in most large supermarkets or department stores.

### Thermometer with Probe

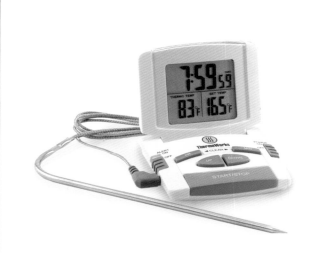

- This sophisticated thermometer does more than just check the temperature of food.

- You can program it to alert you with a beep at certain times in the cooking process, as when the meat reaches a certain temperature.

- This type of thermometer is more expensive, but worth it if you cook a lot of meat.

- The probe stays in the meat while it's cooking; a cord attaches the probe to the base unit.

take a reading with just a 1-inch insertion, making them useful for thin foods.

Before you use a new thermometer to check foods, make sure it's properly calibrated. Bring some water to a boil, and place the tip into the water. It should read 212 degrees F, or 100 degrees C. If it doesn't, you can return the thermometer to the store, or add or subtract the amount it's off to your readings in food.

GADGETS & ACCESSORIES

· · · · · · · · · · · YELLOW ● LIGHT · · · · · · · · · · ·
When you use a thermometer and find that the food isn't at the correct temperature, always wash the probe in hot soapy water and dry before using again. It's possible to transfer bacteria back into the food when you recheck the temperature.

## Built-in Thermometer

- Some of the newest slow cookers have built-in thermometers.

- These thermometers are inserted into the food through a small hole in the lid. Follow manufacturer's instructions for use.

- The hole is designed to hold the probe and not release much heat as the food is cooking.

- The probe stays in the meat during the cooking process, and an alarm will alert you to preset doneness.

## Thermometer on Fork

- A thermometer on a fork is typically used for grilling meats, but can also be used for other cooking methods.

- There is a sensor near the tip of the fork that has to be fully inserted in the food for an accurate reading.

- Be sure that the probe isn't touching fat or bone, which will skew the reading.

- Most food thermometers are reliable to within 2 degrees, plus or minus. Take this into account when determining doneness.

# MULLED BEVERAGES

## Hot beverages are a wonderful treat from your slow cooker

Mulling is the addition of spices to hot beverages, creating flavorful drinks. Mulling spices include cinnamon, cloves, nutmeg, allspice, star anise, and dried citrus peels. You can use whole, broken, or ground spices in your mulled beverages.

If you want to serve a clear liquid, wrap the spices in a cheesecloth bundle or use a tea ball; remove the spices just before serving. You can also grind the spices and add to the liquid. Or whole spices, like star anise and cloves, can be served with the liquid for a pretty appearance.

Serve the beverages directly from the slow cooker so they stay warm during your party.

**Yield: Serves 8**

### Ingredients

1 cinnamon stick

4 whole cloves

2 tablespoons grated orange zest

1 cup raisins

1 cup dried cherries

8 cups apple cider

2 cups orange juice

1/4 cup lemon juice

*Mulled Cider*

- Cut a 10-inch-square piece of cheesecloth and place on work surface.

- Place spices and orange zest on the cheesecloth. Pull ends to center and, using kitchen twine, tie into a bundle.

- Place cheesecloth bundle in 4-quart slow cooker. Top with dried fruit, then pour remaining ingredients into slow cooker.

- Cover and cook on low for 6–7 hours or on high for 3–4 hours until cider is hot. Remove cheesecloth bundle before serving.

**Mulled Wine**

In 4-quart slow cooker, combine 2 bottles dry red wine with ½ up honey and ½ up water. Place 1 broken cinnamon stick, 1 cracked nutmeg, 2 teaspoons orange peel, and 6 whole cloves in a tea ball and add. Cover and cook on high for 2–3 hours until hot.

**Glogg**

Pour 2 bottles dry red wine into a 3½ quart slow cooker. Add 2 cinnamon sticks, 1 cup raisins, 1 split vanilla pod, ½ teaspoon ground cardamom, and ½ cup sugar. Peel 1 orange in large peels and add to slow cooker. Add ½ cup aquavit. Cover and cook on high for 2 hours.

*Combine Spices*

*Add Liquids*

- Cheesecloth is used because it is so permeable. The flavors of the spices can easily escape through the porous cloth to flavor the liquid.

- You can usually find cheesecloth in the cleaning aisle or food storage aisle of the supermarket.

- Use 100 percent white cotton kitchen twine to tie the cheesecloth bundle closed.

- Remove the bundle before you serve the mulled cider. Fish it out with a spoon and squeeze liquid out, then discard.

- Apple cider and apple juice will both work in this recipe. Cider is unfiltered liquid with more body, while juice is more refined.

- Other fruit juices will be delicious in this recipe; try pineapple juice or mango juice.

- Encourage your guests to scoop up some of the plumped fruits along with the beverage as they enjoy this warming recipe.

- It's a good idea to offer small spoons so your guests can eat the flavored fruit.

DRINKS & APPETIZERS

# HOT PUNCH
## Serve a crowd easily with these simple and flavorful punch recipes

KNACK SLOW COOKING

Punch is traditionally served at large parties, but you can also serve it at a smaller gathering by cutting the recipe in half. The slow cooker is the perfect appliance for cooking and keeping the beverage warm.

A hot punch can be made with or without alcoholic beverages. Keep in mind that the low heat will not burn off all of the alcohol, even over long cooking times.

You can keep the punch warm for 2–4 hours after it finishes cooking. If you want to add more punch, it's better to make a new batch instead of just adding more ingredients to the original.

Serve your punch in handled mugs with cinnamon stick stirrers, a slice of orange or lemon, or grated spices.

**Yield: Serves 16**

### Ingredients

15-ounce can pineapple tidbits

1 cup whole macadamia nuts

6 cups pineapple juice

4 cups orange juice

4 cups guava juice

3 lemons, sliced

1 lime, sliced

2 cups citron vodka, if desired

*Hot Tropical Punch*

- Combine all ingredients except lemons, lime, and vodka in a 6-quart slow cooker.

- Cover and cook on low for 6–7 hours, or on high for 3–4 hours, until punch is steaming and blended.

- Add lemon slices, lime slices, and vodka to the slow cooker. Cover and cook on high for 30 minutes until punch is hot again.

- To serve, ladle punch, some of the pineapple tidbits, a few nuts, and a lemon or lime slice into each mug.

### Cranberry Punch

Place ½ cup dried sweetened cranberries in 3 ½-quart slow cooker along with ⅓ cup sugar. Add 8 cups cranberry juice, 1 cinnamon stick, and 1 cup orange juice. Cover and cook on low for 2–3 hours until steaming and blended.

### Wassail

In 4-quart slow cooker, combine ½ cup sugar, ½ cup honey, 2 cups water, and 1 cup orange juice and mix well. Add 6 cups apple cider, ¼ cup lemon juice, 1 inch peeled ginger-root, 2 cinnamon sticks, and 1 star anise. Cover and cook on low for 4–5 hours until steaming.

*Prepare Fruit*

*Stir Punch*

- Always wash fruits before slicing to avoid passing bacteria from the skin to the flesh.

- Use a food-grade soap or washing solution and rinse thoroughly before you slice or chop.

- Slice the fruit ⅛ to ¼ inch thick right through the rind. Carefully remove and discard any seeds.

- Other whole nuts you can use in hot punch are shelled cashews and walnuts; they keep their crispness even when cooked in liquid.

- Stir the punch gently so you don't break up the fruit. Use a wooden spoon or large ladle.

- Add the lemon and lime slices at the end of cooking time so the volatile oils in the skin don't become bitter.

- If you aren't going to use the citron vodka, add ⅓ cup of lemon juice just before serving.

- As they serve the punch, your guests automatically stir the punch so it stays blended.

DRINKS & APPETIZERS

# HOT CHOCOLATE
## Warm and creamy hot chocolate is a treat on cold days

The hot chocolate most of us have had is usually made from a mix. Real hot chocolate, made with cocoa powder and real chocolate, is another experience entirely.

The slow cooker melts the chocolate perfectly with less chance of burning. The long cooking time also brings out the complex flavor of real chocolate. Use all semisweet, all milk chocolate, or a variety for more depth of flavor.

For a nice froth, beat the hot chocolate with an eggbeater or immersion blender. The heavy cream will provide the foam.

Garnish your hot chocolate with anything from a candy cane to a cinnamon stick or tiny marshmallows. A sprinkle of freshly grated nutmeg or cardamom provides the perfect finishing touch.

**Yield: Serves 8–10**

### Ingredients

1 (13-ounce) can evaporated milk

1 1/2 cups heavy whipping cream

8 cups whole milk

2 tablespoons cocoa powder

1 (12-ounce) package semisweet chocolate chips

1 cup milk chocolate chips

1 cup white chocolate chips

1/8 teaspoon salt

2 teaspoons vanilla

*Classic Hot Chocolate*

- In 5-quart slow cooker, combine all ingredients except vanilla. Mix well.

- Cover and cook on low for 2–3 hours, stirring every 30 minutes, until chocolate is melted and mixture is smooth.

- Beat mixture with egg-beater or immersion blender until frothy. Turn off slow cooker while using immersion blender.

- Stir in vanilla and serve hot from the slow cooker, topped with marshmallows or whipped cream.

Because chocolate burns easily, don't use high heat to cook your hot chocolate. White chocolate burns more easily than darker varieties. As you stir the chocolate, scrape the sides so the chocolate isn't directly exposed to heat for long periods.

**Hot Chocolate Schnapps**
In 3 ½-quart slow cooker, combine 1 (14-ounce) can sweetened condensed milk, 8 cups whole milk, 8 ounces chopped semisweet chocolate, 1 cup milk chocolate chips. Cover and cook on low for 3–4 hours, stirring once. Add ½ cup peppermint schnapps, stir, and serve.

*Mix Chocolate and Milk*

- Combine all ingredients well, using a wire whisk or eggbeater.

- As the chocolate melts, incorporate it into the liquid. Use a heat-proof spatula to scrape the bottom of the slow cooker.

- If the chocolate sits at the bottom of the slow cooker too long, it can burn, so it's important to move it around.

- The little bit of salt may seem strange, but it brings out the flavor of the chocolate.

*Whipped Cream*

- Whipped cream melting slowly into the warm chocolate is decadent and delicious. And it's easy to make.

- Put ½ cup heavy whipping cream in a small chilled bowl. Add 1 tablespoon powdered sugar.

- Beat with an egg beater or an electric mixer until the cream forms stiff peaks. Beat in ½ teaspoon vanilla.

- The powdered sugar contains cornstarch to stabilize the cream, so you can make it ahead of time. Store it in the fridge.

# DIPS
## Dips cook to creamy perfection in your slow cooker

Most parties start with an appetizer dip. Warm dips are very welcome, especially during the cold fall and winter months. But keeping them hot is tricky.

You can place the serving bowl on a hot plate, but that can burn the bottom of the dip. A slow cooker is the perfect cooking and serving appliance for this type of food.

Hot dips are almost always creamy with cheese and dairy products. Those ingredients don't cook well in the slow cooker, so we need some buffering ingredients. A white sauce or Alfredo sauce is a good choice for this job.

The dip will brown a bit around the edges and on top as the cheese cooks; this is desirable. If you don't want this to happen, stir the dip twice during the cooking time.

**Yield: Serves 8**

### Ingredients

2 tablespoons butter

1 leek, chopped

4 cloves garlic, minced

16-ounce package frozen cut leaf spinach, thawed and drained

2 (14-ounce) cans artichoke hearts, drained and chopped

1 cup mayonnaise

16-ounce jar Alfredo sauce or 2 cups white sauce

1 1/2 cups shredded Havarti cheese

3/4 cup grated Parmesan cheese, divided

*Rich Artichoke Dip*

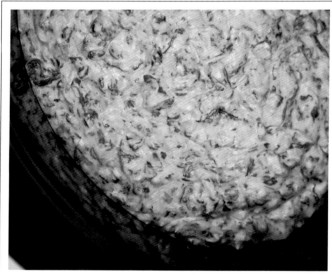

- Melt butter in medium skillet or stovetop-proof 3 1/2-quart slow cooker. Cook leek and garlic until tender.

- In slow cooker, combine leek mixture with remaining ingredients except 1/2 cup Parmesan cheese; mix well.

- Cover and cook on low for 6–7 hours, or on high for 3–4 hours, stirring once during cooking time, until mixture bubbles.

- Sprinkle with remaining 1/2 cup Parmesan cheese and serve with crudités and crackers.

### Cheese Fondue

Cook 2 cloves minced garlic in 1 tablespoon olive oil. Place in 3-quart slow cooker and add 1½ cups dry white wine and 1 cup apple juice. Toss 2 cups shredded Swiss and 2 cups shredded cheddar cheese with 2 tablespoons cornstarch and add. Cover and cook on low 1–2 hours, stirring occasionally, until cheese melts.

### Pizza Dip

Cook 1 chopped onion and 3 cloves minced garlic in 2 tablespoons butter. Add to 3-quart slow cooker along with 8 ounces cubed cream cheese, 1 (10-ounce) can pizza sauce, and 2 diced tomatoes. Add 1 cup shredded mozzarella cheese and ¼ cup grated Parmesan. Cover and cook on low 2–3 hours, stirring occasionally.

*Prepare Vegetables*

- Frozen spinach holds an incredible amount of water. For this recipe's success, the spinach has to be well drained.

- Squeeze the thawed spinach in your hands, then place in paper towels and press to remove more water.

- The chokes, or the prickly centers, of the artichokes should be removed; inspect them before chopping.

- If the choke remains, just scrape it off gently with a spoon. Be sure to use non-marinated artichoke hearts.

*Mix Ingredients*

- If your slow cooker has a metal insert, by all means use it to cook the leeks and garlic.

- Be careful with the insert; you may need to handle it with hot pads if it gets hot as the food cooks on the stovetop.

- You can use low-fat mayonnaise and Alfredo sauce in this recipe.

- Serve the dip with sturdy crackers and some crisp French bread, buttered and toasted.

**DRINKS & APPETIZERS**

# SNACK MIXES

## Snack mixes are well seasoned and crisp when cooked in the slow cooker

Crisp snack mixes don't have to be left to groups of men watching bowl games. They can be sophisticated and elegant, as well as flavorful and crunchy.

Once again, the slow cooker comes to the rescue with low, even heat that makes a crisp mix with no burned edges.

This is one of the few recipes where you cook the food uncovered. You want the low, consistent heat to glaze the cereal and crackers, but the moisture has to evaporate.

Stirring helps ensure that the crisp ingredients are evenly coated with the glaze and seasonings.

**Yield: 12 cups**

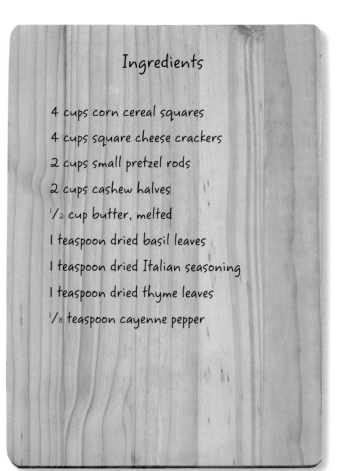

### Ingredients

4 cups corn cereal squares

4 cups square cheese crackers

2 cups small pretzel rods

2 cups cashew halves

1/2 cup butter, melted

1 teaspoon dried basil leaves

1 teaspoon dried Italian seasoning

1 teaspoon dried thyme leaves

1/8 teaspoon cayenne pepper

*Glazed Snack Mix*

- In 4-quart slow cooker, combine cereal, crackers, pretzels, and cashews.

- In small saucepan, melt butter over low heat. Remove from heat and add dried herbs and pepper.

- Drizzle herb mixture over cereal mixture in slow cooker; toss to coat. Cover and cook on low for 2 hours.

- Uncover; cook on low for 40–50 minutes longer, stirring once during cooking time, until mixture is glazed. Cool on paper towels; store in airtight container.

**Sweet and Salty Snack Mix**

Combine 4 cups corn cereal squares with 2 cups each pecan halves, pretzel rods, and round small pretzels in 3-quart slow cooker. Combine ½ cup butter with ¼ cup brown sugar in saucepan; cook until smooth. Drizzle over mixture; cook uncovered 2 hours. Cool and stir in 2 cups chocolate chips or candy bits.

**Caramel Corn**

Place 10 cups air-popped corn and 2 cups pecan halves in 4-quart slow cooker. Cook together ¾ cup butter, 1½ cups brown sugar, and ¼ cup honey in saucepan. Drizzle over corn and nuts; stir to coat. Cook, uncovered, on low 2 hours, stirring every 30 minutes, until crisp.

*Combine Ingredients*

- As long as you keep the total volume the same, you can use any kind and combination of crisp foods.

- Small crackers, whole or half nuts, straight or round pretzels, bagel chips, and plain cereals are good additions.

- Browse through the cereal and snack food aisles of the supermarket for more ideas.

- Store these mixes in airtight containers or heavy duty plastic bags at room temperature up to a week.

*Prepare Butter Mixture*

- Dried herbs are used because they stand up better to the heat of the slow cooker.

- You can use any combination of herbs and spices to create your own snack mix.

- Sprinkle on some finely grated Parmesan or Romano cheese at the end for more flavor.

- You can serve this mixture warm from the slow cooker; turn the appliance to low or keep-warm.

# MEATBALLS

## Meatballs, flavored with sauces and glazes, make perfect appetizers

Meatballs are always among the most popular appetizers at any party. And in the slow cooker, they are easy to make and serve.

With these types of recipes, make sure your slow cooker is attractive, because it should be used for serving. The slow cooker will keep the food warm and delicious up to 2 hours, if it lasts that long.

For best results, either choose fully cooked meatballs or sauces, or brown them thoroughly to make sure they are completely cooked before adding to the sauce in the slow cooker. You want to remove a good amount of the fat from the products before they cook in the sauce. And browning adds great flavor and eye appeal.

**Yield: Serves 8–10**

### Ingredients

2 tablespoons butter

1 onion, chopped

3 cloves garlic, minced

1 cup beef broth, divided

$\frac{1}{2}$ cup apple jelly

1 star anise

1 pinch ground cloves

$\frac{1}{3}$ cup brown mustard

$\frac{1}{4}$ cup brown sugar

$\frac{1}{4}$ cup apple cider vinegar

$\frac{1}{8}$ teaspoon cayenne pepper

$\frac{1}{2}$ teaspoon hot pepper sauce

50 small frozen fully cooked meatballs, thawed

1 tablespoon cornstarch

### Sweet and Hot Glazed Meatballs

- In small saucepan, heat butter and cook onion and garlic over medium heat for 5–6 minutes.

- Add ¾ cup broth and bring to a simmer; add apple jelly and stir to melt. Pour into 4- or 5-quart slow cooker.

- Add star anise, cloves, mustard, sugar, vinegar, pepper, and pepper sauce; stir; add meatballs. Cover; cook on low 7–9 hours.

- Remove star anise. In small bowl, mix cornstarch with rest of broth; add to slow cooker. Cover and cook on high until sauce thickens.

**Sweet and Sour Sausages**

Substitute 40–50 small fully cooked sausages for the meatballs in this recipe. Omit cloves and star anise, and use chicken broth instead of beef broth. Omit cayenne pepper and hot sauce; increase vinegar to ⅓ cup.

**Glazed Meatballs**

Bake 48 regular meatballs according to package directions. Place in 4- or 5-quart slow cooker. In skillet, cook 1 chopped onion in 2 tablespoons butter for 5 minutes. Add 1 (16-ounce) can whole berry cranberry sauce, 2 tablespoons mustard, 2 tablespoons brown sugar, and 1 cup barbecue sauce. Pour over meatballs; cover and cook on low 4–6 hours.

## *Chop Onions and Garlic*

- Onions and garlic should be chopped fairly fine so they melt into the sauce.

- Cut the onion in half, then peel off the papery skin. Place, cut side down, on work surface. Cut lengthwise through the onion 5–6 times, then cut crosswise to make cubes.

- Smash the garlic cloves with the side of the knife, then remove peel and mince.

- The onion and garlic flavor the butter so it permeates the sauce around the meatballs.

## *Stir Meatballs*

- Because the sauce has a lot of sugar from the apple jelly and brown sugar, you must stir fairly often to prevent burning.

- Use a wooden spoon, rubber spatula, or scraper and gently stir the mixture.

- Scrape the sides firmly so the sauce doesn't stick and burn. These recipes work better when cooked on low heat.

- Other varieties of jelly would work well. Try pineapple jelly, apricot preserves, or raspberry jelly for a new flavor.

DRINKS & APPETIZERS

# BREAKFAST CASSEROLES
These rich and savory egg casseroles cook while you're asleep

Breakfast casseroles are a great way to use your slow cooker. Put everything together the night before, let the food cook while you sleep and awaken to the wonderful aromas of breakfast cooking.

Eggs can be tricky in the slow cooker. So they don't curdle, you need to add a stabilizer: in this case, a white sauce (either a homemade white sauce or a bottled Alfredo sauce).

This sauce "cushions" the eggs so they don't curdle or separate while cooking. It also adds great flavor.

Vary the casseroles by choosing different herbs and cheeses. You can also use different breakfast meats and other vegetables.

**Yield: Serves 8**

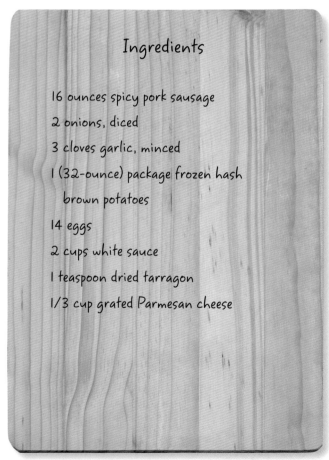

### Ingredients

16 ounces spicy pork sausage

2 onions, diced

3 cloves garlic, minced

1 (32-ounce) package frozen hash
   brown potatoes

14 eggs

2 cups white sauce

1 teaspoon dried tarragon

1/3 cup grated Parmesan cheese

*Sausage, Egg, and Potato Casserole*

- In large skillet, cook sausage, stirring to break up meat, until almost done. Drain and add onions and garlic; cook until sausage is done.

- In 5-quart slow cooker, layer ⅓ of potatoes and ⅓ of sausage mixture; repeat twice.

- In large bowl, beat eggs with white sauce and tarragon until smooth; pour into slow cooker.

- Cover and cook on low for 7–9 hours until browned around edges. Sprinkle with Parmesan cheese and serve.

## RED●LIGHT

If you choose the overnight cooking option, you must know your slow cooker and how it cooks. To check this, fill the cooker halfway with water. Cover and cook on low 8 hours. If the water temperature is higher than 185 degrees F, your slow cooker cooks "hot" and you may need to reduce cooking times.

## RECIPE VARIATION

Eggs Florentine: Cook ½ pound bacon until crisp; drain, crumble, and set aside. Drain pan; cook 1 chopped onion. Add 1 (10-ounce) package frozen spinach, thawed and drained, and 1 cup soft bread-crumbs. Beat 12 eggs with 1 (10-ounce) container Alfredo sauce and ½ cup Parmesan cheese; combine all in 4-quart slow cooker. Cover; cook on low 7–9 hours.

*Beat Eggs with Sauce*

- It's important that you combine the eggs with another ingredient just before adding to the slow cooker.

- Otherwise, ingredients like cheese, milk, salty bacon or ham, tomatoes, or salt will make the eggs separate before they are cooked.

- Beat with an eggbeater or wire whisk until smooth. You don't want to add too much air to the eggs.

- You can substitute a 16-ounce jar of any flavor Alfredo sauce for the white sauce.

*Pour Eggs into Slow Cooker*

- Pour the egg mixture slowly into the slow cooker so it diffuses throughout the food.

- You want the casserole to be evenly soaked with egg so it will spoon out easily. Let it stand 5 minutes before you turn the appliance on.

- If necessary, run a knife through the potato mixture before cooking to make sure the eggs have penetrated.

- When serving the casserole, use a large spoon to scoop through all the layers for each serving.

BREAKFAST

# VEGETABLE STRATA
## Savory vegetables add color and nutrition to a classic strata

A strata is a layered casserole that is held together with an egg custard mixture. Those eggs need to be stabilized, so a combination of evaporated milk and flour will substitute for the white sauce.

If the bread cubes float, you may want to spend a few minutes pushing them back into the custard. As the bread absorbs the custard it will sink. Then you can turn on the slow cooker.

Use your favorite combination of vegetables and cheeses in this easy recipe. Different types of bread can be used: try cubes of leftover waffles, croissants, or whole grain bread. Be sure to check the casserole at the shortest cooking time.

**Yield: Serves 6–8**

### Ingredients

1 onion, chopped

2 tablespoons butter

3 bell peppers, assorted colors, sliced

1/2 cup shredded carrots

1 (7-ounce) package basil pesto

14 slices sourdough bread

1 cup shredded Havarti cheese

8 eggs

1 (12-ounce) can evaporated milk

1 tablespoon flour

Salt and pepper to taste

*Three Pepper Pesto Strata*

- Cook onion in butter over medium heat for 4 minutes. Add bell peppers and carrots and remove from heat.

- Spread pesto on bread, then cut bread into cubes. Layer ⅓ each bread, vegetable mixture, and cheese in 5-quart slow cooker; repeat twice.

- Beat eggs with milk, salt, and pepper; pour into slow cooker.

- Cover and refrigerate for 6–8 hours. Then cook on low for 6–8 hours until strata is puffed and temp reads 165 degrees F.

**Loaded Hash Browns**
Start recipe as directed, except substitute 1 (32-ounce) package frozen hash brown potatoes, thawed, for the bread cubes. Omit pesto. Chop the bell peppers and add 1 cup shredded cheddar cheese. And add 6 slices cooked, crumbled bacon.

**Broccoli Strata**
Cook onion in butter; add 3 cloves minced garlic. Use 3 cups broccoli florets in place of the sliced bell peppers; omit carrots. Substitute 1 cup shredded Colby cheese for the Havarti. Sprinkle top with 2 tablespoons Parmesan cheese; cook as directed.

*Prepare Vegetables*

- To slice peppers, first cut them in half and pull out the stem, membranes, and seeds.

- Then place the peppers on the cutting board. Slice ⅓ inch thick and repeat.

- It's important to cook the onions before adding them to the slow cooker to mellow the flavor.

- As you cook onions and garlic, the flavor becomes mild and sweet, perfect for the first meal of the day.

*Layer Food*

- Make sure to layer the food evenly in the slow cooker, so every serving gets bread, cheese, vegetables, and egg.

- Other vegetables that would work well include chopped green onions or jarred, drained mushrooms.

- Vegetables high in water, like squash, zucchini, or fresh mushrooms, must be sautéed until dry or they will add too much water to the dish.

- You may want to sprinkle the top with more grated cheese before serving; let stand 5 minutes, then serve.

BREAKFAST

# FRUIT STRATA
## Sweet and tangy fruit makes this strata taste like sweet rolls

A sweet strata is comparable to a coffee cake or sweet roll, but it's healthier. Fruits will release liquid as they cook, flavoring the dish.

Cinnamon raisin bread is a good choice for this dish because it adds interest and flavor, but you can use other breads, like cracked wheat, croissants, multigrain, or oatmeal bread.

It's best to use firm fruits like apples or pears for this dish.

Soft fruits like strawberries or raspberries will become mushy and add too much water to the dish.

The fruit is tossed with lemon juice so it doesn't turn brown while it cooks. And for a topping that stays slightly crunchy, granola is a good choice; use your favorite variety.

**Yield: Serves 8**

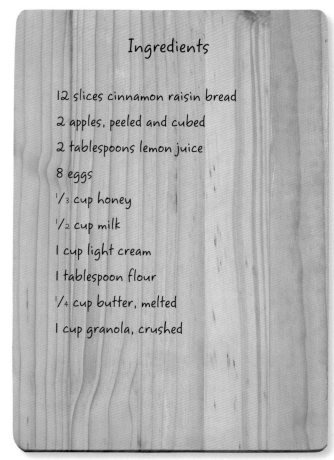

### Ingredients

12 slices cinnamon raisin bread

2 apples, peeled and cubed

2 tablespoons lemon juice

8 eggs

1/3 cup honey

1/2 cup milk

1 cup light cream

1 tablespoon flour

1/4 cup butter, melted

1 cup granola, crushed

*Apple Strata*

- Cut bread into cubes. Toss apples with lemon juice; layer in 4- or 5-quart slow cooker with bread.

- In large bowl, beat remaining ingredients except granola until smooth.

- Pour into slow cooker; cover and chill for 2–4 hours. Sprinkle with granola.

- Then cook mixture, covered, on low for 7–9 hours until strata is puffed and set. Serve with maple syrup.

## RED●LIGHT

Don't prepare this type of strata ahead of time, even if you keep it refrigerated. The fruit will start to break down and the recipe may be too watery. Savory stratas can be prepared ahead because the vegetables are cooked first. If the strata isn't thick enough, cook it for 20 minutes on high with the cover off.

## ●●●●● RECIPE VARIATION ●●●●●

**Chocolate Pear Fruit Strata**
Cube 8 1-inch slices of challah bread. Layer in 4-quart slow cooker along with 1 cup semisweet chocolate chips, ½ cup white chocolate chips, and 1 pear, peeled, cubed, and tossed with 1 tablespoon lemon juice. Beat 5 eggs with 1 cup light cream, 1 teaspoon vanilla, and ¼ cup brown sugar; pour over bread. Cover and cook on high for 2 hours until puffed.

*Prepare Apples*

*Layer Ingredients*

- Choose an apple that is good for baking for this recipe. Some apples break down too much when exposed to heat.

- Granny Smith, Golden Delicious, Rome Beauty, and Jonathan apples are good choices.

- Prepare the apples just before you are ready to turn on the slow cooker. Even when treated with lemon juice, they can turn brown.

- Peel the apples with a swivel-bladed peeler, then cut in half and remove centers with a melon baller; cube.

- Make sure that you evenly layer the ingredients in the slow cooker in the order described.

- Use more or less fruit and bread to fill the slow cooker ⅔ full.

- When you pour the egg mixture over, the bread

may float; just press it back down for a few minutes so it absorbs the liquid.

- You can cook the strata immediately without refrigerating as long as the bread has absorbed the egg mixture.

BREAKFAST

# OATMEAL

## Steel-cut oats cook to creamy perfection overnight

Oatmeal is the ultimate comfort food for breakfast. It's possible to cook it in the slow cooker, but there are some special ingredients and tricks to keep it creamy.

Oatmeal, especially when cooked overnight, is one of those foods that burn easily. We can solve this by placing the oatmeal in a heatproof bowl inside the slow cooker.

Steel-cut oats are really necessary for this type of cooking.

Even regular oatmeal, not the quick-cooking type, gets mushy when cooked this long.

Finally, toast the oats before cooking to create texture and bring out the flavor as the heat releases aromatic oils.

**Yield: Serves 4–6**

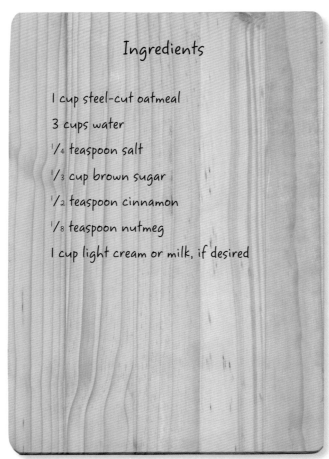

## Ingredients

1 cup steel-cut oatmeal

3 cups water

1/4 teaspoon salt

1/3 cup brown sugar

1/2 teaspoon cinnamon

1/8 teaspoon nutmeg

1 cup light cream or milk, if desired

*Brown Sugar Oatmeal*

- Spray a 2-quart Pyrex bowl with nonstick cooking spray containing flour. Place on a trivet in a 4-quart slow cooker; add 1 cup water to the slow cooker.

- In medium saucepan, toast oatmeal until fragrant. Place in bowl and stir in remaining ingredients except cream.

- Cover and cook for 7–9 hours or until oatmeal is creamy and tender. Stir in cream, if using.

- Serve with warmed maple syrup, brown sugar, or toasted nuts and granola.

### Apple Granola Oatmeal

Toast oatmeal as directed; place in sprayed bowl with water, salt, and ⅓ cup granulated sugar. Add 1 cup granola, ½ cup chopped peeled apple, ½ cup chopped walnuts, and 1 cup golden raisins. Cover and cook on low for 6–8 hours. Stir in ½ cup whole milk and serve immediately.

### Cranberry Oatmeal

Toast oatmeal as directed; place in sprayed bowl with 2 cups water, 1 cup cranberry juice, salt, and ⅓ cup brown sugar. Add 1 cup dried cranberries and 1 teaspoon vanilla. Cover and cook on low for 6–8 hours. Stir in 1 tablespoon butter and serve.

*Toast Oats*

*Combine Ingredients*

- Toast the oats in a dry saucepan over low heat. Stir occasionally so they toast evenly.

- You can toast the oats ahead of time and keep them in an airtight container up to 3 days.

- The oats are ready when they turn a slightly darker shade of brown and you can smell the toasted aroma.

- If you can't find steel-cut oats, toasting will help regular (not quick-cooking) oats keep their texture better in the slow cooker.

- A pinch of salt brings out the flavor in the oatmeal, but only add a small amount.

- You can use granulated sugar, honey, or maple syrup to flavor the oatmeal.

- If you choose maple syrup, reduce the water by ¼ cup.

If the oatmeal isn't sweet enough when it's done, just add more sugar to taste.

- You can substitute milk or cream for part of the water for a richer flavor and slightly thicker texture.

# FRUIT COBBLER
## Lots of healthy fruit cooks with a chewy topping in these fun recipes

Cobbler can be served as a delicious hot breakfast or as a dessert. Hard fruits like apples and pears work best in this type of recipe, but peaches and blueberries would be nice additions.

There are two kinds of cobblers: those with a chewy or crisp topping and those with a cake-like topping. The main recipe has a chewy topping. The Peach Cobbler variation has a cake-

like topping. Both are delicious and perfect for brunch.

For crunch, nuts, granola, and some brown sugar make a good combination that holds up to the wet environment.

Serve these cobblers with ice cream, ice milk, or any flavor of yogurt for a cooling contrast.

**Yield: Serves 6**

### Ingredients

3 Granny Smith apples, peeled

2 Bosc pears, peeled

2 tablespoons lemon juice

1/3 cup brown sugar

2 tablespoons flour

1/2 cup dried cherries

1 teaspoon cinnamon

3 cups granola cereal

1 cup chopped walnuts

1/4 cup brown sugar

1/4 cup butter

*Mixed Fruit Caramel Cobbler*

- Slice apples and pears into ½-inch slices; sprinkle with lemon juice as you work. Place in 3 ½-quart slow cooker with ⅓ cup brown sugar, flour, and cherries.

- In large bowl, combine cinnamon, cereal, walnuts, and remaining brown sugar.

- Drizzle melted butter over granola mixture and mix.

- Sprinkle granola mixture on top of fruit. Cover and cook on low for 7–8 hours or until fruit is tender. Serve with warmed caramel sauce, if desired.

**Peach Cobbler**

Sprinkle 4 peeled and sliced peaches with lemon juice. Place in 3-quart slow cooker with ⅓ cup sugar and ½ teaspoon cinnamon. Mix 1 cup flour, ⅓ cup sugar, and ½ teaspoon baking powder; add 3 tablespoons melted butter and ¾ cup evaporated milk; pour over peaches. Line cover with paper towels; cook on high 3–4 hours.

**Pear Cranberry Cobbler**

Increase pears to 4; peel and toss with lemon juice as directed. Substitute 1 cup dried cranberries for the dried cherries. Substitute 1 cup chopped pecans for the walnuts. Cook as directed.

*Prepare Fruits*

- The size you cut the fruits determines the texture of the final dish. The skin can stay on or be peeled off.

- Large slices will mean discrete pieces of fruit, while smaller slices or cubes will yield a sauce consistency.

- Choose fruits that are quite firm. In fact, underripe fruits work very well in this recipe.

- The heat and moisture will bring out their flavors and make them tender and juicy.

*Mix Topping*

- You can mix this topping ahead of time; keep it in an airtight container up to 1 day. Sprinkle over fruit just before cooking.

- Use your favorite granola; the crunchier and chunkier the better. Homemade or store-bought works just fine.

- This cobbler can be served warm or cool, but it doesn't keep well past 12 hours.

- Vary the dried fruits, spices, and nuts to create your own fruit cobbler.

BREAKFAST

# EGG CASSEROLES
## Ethnic flavors add great variety to delicious egg casseroles

Eggs are such a mild and versatile food; they combine with many different ethnic foods and flavors. The eggs need stabilization in the long slow cooking time; a white sauce, Alfredo sauce, or evaporated milk mixed with a bit of flour will all work.

A topping of cold chopped vegetables and herbs not only improves the appearance of these casseroles, but adds great flavor and temperature contrast as well.

Use your imagination to create other variations. For a Tex-Mex egg casserole, add chopped chorizo, Pepper Jack cheese, and drained salsa. For a Spanish casserole, add paprika, roasted red bell peppers, and oregano.

**Yield: Serves 6**

### Ingredients

2 tablespoons butter

1 onion, chopped

8 ounces sliced mushrooms

1 red bell pepper, chopped

4 cups cubed French bread

8 ounces Brie cheese, cubed

2 cups frozen hash brown potatoes, thawed

12 eggs

1 cup white sauce

½ teaspoon dried thyme leaves

½ teaspoon dried herbes de Provence

⅓ cup grated Parmesan cheese

*French Breakfast Casserole*

- Spray 4-quart slow cooker with nonstick cooking spray. In skillet, melt butter over medium heat. Cook onion and mushrooms until tender; drain.

- Combine with bell peppers. Layer with bread, Brie cheese, and potatoes in 4-quart casserole.

- In large bowl, beat eggs with white sauce, thyme, herbes de Provence, and Parmesan cheese. Pour into slow cooker.

- Cover and cook on high for 3–4 hours until casserole is set and puffed. Serve immediately.

### All-American Egg Casserole

Use cracked-wheat bread, cubed and toasted in the oven. Omit red bell pepper and Brie cheese. Use 1 pound breakfast sausage links, browned, chopped, and drained, in place of the potatoes, and 1 teaspoon dried basil in place of thyme and herbes de Provence.. Use Cheddar cheese; cook as directed.

### Southwestern Egg Casserole

Add 1 (4-ounce) can chopped green chiles, drained, to the egg mixture. Omit mushrooms and red bell pepper; add 1 green bell pepper and 3 cloves minced garlic. Add 1 tablespoon chili powder; omit thyme and herbes de Provence. Omit Brie; use Pepper Jack cheese. Cook as directed.

*Prepare Cheese*

- Cheese is a tricky ingredient in the slow cooker. It's usually added at the end of cooking time. But it can be included with lots of other ingredients to shield it from the heat.

- Brie cheese is easier to cube when it's very cold. Freeze it for 10–15 minutes before slicing.

- Don't prepare cheese ahead of time; it dries out very easily. Place in the freezer when cooking the onions.

*Assemble Casserole*

- Pour the egg mixture slowly into the slow cooker so the bread absorbs it. The potatoes will help hold the bread in place.

- Don't make the custard ahead of time; the egg mixture will separate and become runny.

- For a topping, combine 2 chopped tomatoes, ⅓ cup chopped green onion, and 1 tablespoon fresh thyme leaves.

- Serve the topping on the side, or spoon it directly onto the casserole when it's done.

# CHICKEN VEGGIE PITAS

## Chicken vegetable filling can be served hot or cold

Sandwiches are fun to make in the slow cooker. You can serve sandwich fillings hot or use the slow cooker to cook the ingredients, then combine with classic sandwich condiments like mayonnaise or mustard and chili.

Ethnic flavors are wonderful additions to the classic chicken sandwich. Just remember to place hard vegetables, like onion, potatoes, carrots, and garlic, on the bottom, and top with meats and tender vegetables. Cheeses and dairy products are stirred in at the end.

Serve these sandwich fillings in anything from croissants to hoagie buns to pita breads. Or you can assemble the sandwiches, butter the outsides of the bread, and grill them on a dual-contact grill or the stovetop.

**Yield: Serves 6–8**

### Ingredients

1 onion, chopped
1 leek, rinsed and chopped
3 cloves garlic, minced
6 boneless, skinless chicken breasts
1/2 teaspoon salt
1/8 teaspoon pepper
1 teaspoon dried oregano
1/2 cup chicken broth
1 cup crumbled feta cheese
4–5 whole wheat pita breads

### Topping

1 green bell pepper, chopped
1 cup thick Greek yogurt
1 tablespoon minced fresh mint
1/2 cup diced, seeded cucumber

*Greek Chicken Veggie Pitas*

- Place onion, leek, and garlic in bottom of 4-quart slow cooker. Sprinkle chicken with salt, pepper, and oregano and add.

- Pour chicken broth into slow cooker; cover and cook on low for 5–7 hours until chicken is thoroughly cooked.

- Meanwhile, combine all topping ingredients, cover, and refrigerate.

- When chicken is done, shred and stir into leek mixture with cheese. Make sandwiches with pita bread and yogurt topping.

## • • • • RECIPE VARIATION • • • •

**Tex–Mex Chicken Pita Sandwiches**
Increase onions to 2, and use 4 cloves garlic; omit leeks. Add 2 minced jalapeño peppers and use 10 boneless, skinless chicken thighs; omit oregano and feta. Pour 1 cup salsa over; cover and cook 7–9 hours. Shred chicken; serve in pitas with guacamole and shredded Monterey Jack cheese.

## YELLOW ● LIGHT

Use your judgment and adjust accordingly if the filling is too liquid or too dry. You can add more liquid and cook on high for 10-15 minutes to heat through or you can remove the cover and cook on high for 15-20 minutes to reduce liquid.

*Arrange Food*

- If you look at whole bone-in chicken breasts, you'll see there are actually 2 breasts.

- When a recipe calls for a chicken breast, it means 1 breast, or ½ of a whole breast.

- Place the chicken evenly over the onions and leeks, sprinkling each with seasoning as you do.

- You could substitute boneless, skinless chicken thighs; cook for 6–8 hours on low.

*Finishing Touches*

- Make the yogurt topping ahead of time and keep it in the fridge so it stays cold.

- The chicken will shred very easily using 2 forks. As you work, return the chicken to the slow cooker.

- The shredded chicken will begin to absorb some

- of the liquid in the slow cooker.

- At this point you can turn the slow cooker to keep-warm or low for another hour before adding the cheese.

# CHICKEN TACO WRAPS
## Tex-Mex flavors pair beautifully with tender chicken

Chicken thighs are one of the best meats to cook in the slow cooker. When tender, they shred with just a touch of a fork, and they pair beautifully with spicy Tex-Mex flavors.

This recipe is ideal for serving a crowd. Just make a buffet with the slow cooker, additional ingredients, and tortillas kept warm in some napkins; let everyone serve himself.

You can make this dish as mild or as spicy as you like. Use habañero peppers in place of the jalapeños, add more chiles or chili powder, or reduce them.

This recipe can easily be made ahead of time. Shred chicken, mix with remaining ingredients, and refrigerate. Then reheat on the stovetop or in the microwave just before you want to eat. Use the slow cooker to keep the filling warm.

**Yield: Serves 8**

### Ingredients

6 boneless, skinless chicken thighs

1 tablespoon chili powder

3 tablespoons flour

Salt and pepper to taste

1/2 teaspoon cumin

1 onion, chopped

3 cloves garlic, minced

2 jalapeño peppers, minced

1 (15-ounce) can black beans, drained

1 cup salsa

1 cup grape tomatoes, halved

8 flour tortillas

1 cup shredded Pepper Jack cheese

1 avocado, sliced

*Spicy Chicken Taco Wraps*

- Sprinkle chicken with chili powder, flour, salt, pepper, and cumin.

- Place onion, garlic, and jalapeño in 3 ½-quart slow cooker; top with chicken.

- Add beans and salsa. Cover and cook on low for 7–9 hours until chicken is cooked.

- Remove chicken and shred; return to slow cooker; cook on high for 30 minutes until blended.

- Stir in grape tomatoes. Make wraps with tortillas, cheese, and avocado.

**Chicken Enchiladas**
Prepare chicken recipe as directed, shred meat, and stir into remaining ingredients. Divide among 12 corn tortillas; sprinkle with 1 cup shredded Pepper Jack and 1 cup shredded cheddar cheese. Arrange in 9 x 13-inch baking pan; cover with 1 (10-ounce) can green salsa. Bake for 35–45 minutes.

**BLT Chicken Wraps**
Cook 5 slices bacon until crisp; drain, crumble, and set aside. Cook onion and garlic in drippings. Combine with chicken, salt and pepper, 1 (14½-ounce) can diced drain tomatoes, and 1 cup white sauce; cook as directed; shred chicken. Make wraps with bacon, lettuce, ½ cup sour cream, and flour tortillas.

*Shred Chicken*

*Spoon into Tortillas*

- The chicken will be very tender and will shred easily. Remove from the slow cooker with a slotted spoon.

- Using 2 forks, gently pull the chicken apart into long, thin pieces.

- Return the chicken and any accumulated juices to the slow cooker as you work.

- The mixture can be thickened at this point with a slurry of 2 tablespoons cornstarch and ¼ cup water.

- To warm tortillas, wrap in foil and warm in a 350 degree F oven for 10–15 minutes.

- You can also wrap in microwave-safe paper towels and microwave on high for 10 seconds per tortilla.

- Prepare the avocado at the last minute so it doesn't turn brown. You can sprinkle it with lemon juice, but prepare it only about 20 minutes before serving.

- You can use corn or flour tortillas. Flour tortillas are usually larger for larger sandwiches.

HOT SANDWICHES

# SLOPPY JOES

## This classic sandwich is easy to make in the slow cooker

Sloppy Joe sandwiches are the perfect slow cooker food. It's practically impossible to overcook or ruin this recipe.

The ground meat has to be browned before combining with the other ingredients. There's too much fat and water in that product; it would render the finished sandwich too wet and greasy. Brown the beef (and sausage, too) and drain very well.

This is another recipe that's perfect to make ahead of time; in fact, the flavors mellow in the refrigerator for several hours or overnight. Reheat in a saucepan on the stove, not in the slow cooker.

Season your Sloppy Joes any way you'd like. Add spicy ingredients like chili powder or jalapeños, or load up on cheese.

**Yield: Serves 8**

## Ingredients

1 pound ground beef

1 pound spicy pork sausage

2 onions, chopped

3 cloves garlic, minced

¼ cup tomato paste

1 cup barbecue sauce

½ cup ketchup

¼ cup mustard

2 tablespoons apple cider vinegar

Salt and pepper to taste

3 tablespoons butter

8 hamburger buns

*Classic Sloppy Joes*

- In large skillet, cook ground beef with sausage until almost done, stirring to break up meat. Drain well.

- Add onions and garlic; cook and stir for 2–3 minutes longer. Place in 3-quart slow cooker.

- Add tomato paste, barbecue sauce, ketchup, mustard, vinegar, salt, and pepper to skillet; bring to a boil and pour into slow cooker.

- Cover and cook on low for 6–7 hours until blended. Toast and butter hamburger buns; serve mixture on buns.

**Sloppy Janes**
Make the recipe just as directed, except substitute 1 pound ground turkey for the ground beef, and 1 pound turkey sausage for the pork sausage. Omit the ketchup and add 1 tablespoon Worcestershire sauce.

**Vegetarian Joes**
Make the recipe just as directed, except use 2 (12-ounce) packages vegetarian protein crumbles in place of the beef and sausage. You can find both beef substitute and sausage substitute. Add 1 teaspoon dried thyme and 1 teaspoon dried oregano.

*Brown Ground Beef*

*Mix Ingredients*

- Place the ground beef in a cold skillet; turn the heat to medium.

- As the beef browns, break it apart with a fork or spoon so it crumbles and cooks evenly. Turn the beef so the uncooked portion faces the heat.

- Choose a lean ground meat product. When the meat is cooked, spoon off and discard all of the fat.

- There will still be enough fat to cook the onions and garlic and add flavor.

- Because the meat is cooked, you don't need to layer ingredients in this recipe.

- Just combine everything and stir well. Cover and turn on the slow cooker. Stir again before serving.

- If the mixture needs to thicken, add a cornstarch slurry, or remove the cover and cook on high for 10 minutes.

- You can serve this mixture on buns, over split buttered baked potatoes, or over mashed potatoes or rice.

# MOROCCAN TURKEY WRAPS
## Travel to Africa with this exotic wrap sandwich

Moroccan food is rich and flavorful, full of spices. It is also characterized by the combination of meats and dried fruits, like apricots and raisins. Other common ingredients include gingerroot, nuts, onions, and garlic.

Turkey tenderloin is like chicken breast in that it's easily overcooked in the slow cooker. It's a very low-fat cut. Check on it after 5 hours of cooking.

If you want to cook this for a longer period of time, leave the tenderloin whole. Cook for 8–9 hours, then shred the turkey and return to the slow cooker.

Other dried fruits would be good additions to this recipe: golden raisins or chopped dates. Add cashews or chopped walnuts. Serve in tortillas or pita breads.

**Yield: Serves 8**

### Ingredients

1 onion, chopped

3 cloves garlic, minced

1 tablespoon grated gingerroot

1 (2-pound) turkey tenderloin

2 tablespoons flour

1/2 teaspoon salt

1/8 teaspoon cayenne pepper

1/2 teaspoon cinnamon

1 teaspoon ground cumin

1/2 cup dried currants

1/2 cup chopped dried apricots

1/2 cup chicken broth

1/2 cup plain yogurt

2 tablespoons cornstarch

8 flour tortillas

1/2 cup chopped pistachios

*Moroccan Turkey Wraps*

- In 3-quart slow cooker, combine onion, garlic, and gingerroot.

- Cut turkey into 2-inch cubes and toss with flour, salt, pepper, cinnamon, and cumin. Place over vegetables in slow cooker. Add currants and apricots.

- Pour chicken broth over all. Cover and cook on low for 5–7 hours until turkey is thoroughly cooked.

- In small bowl, combine yogurt and cornstarch; stir into slow cooker. Cover; cook on high for 20 minutes until thick. Serve mixture in tortillas with pistachios.

**Thai Turkey Wraps**

Use onion, garlic, gingerroot, turkey, flour, salt, and pepper. Omit cinnamon, cumin, currants, and apricots. Make sauce of ⅓ cup peanut butter, ½ cup barbecue sauce, and 1 tablespoon soy sauce; pour over turkey. Cook as directed; make sandwiches with tortillas and ½ cup goat cheese.

**Gyro Sandwiches**

Start with onions, garlic, and gingerroot. Add 2 pounds cubed trimmed lamb shoulder. Add remaining ingredients, but omit cinnamon, cumin, currants, and apricots. Add 2 peeled, seeded, chopped tomatoes. Shred lamb, then make sandwiches with ½ cup feta, olives, and pita breads.

## *Coat Turkey*

- Coat the turkey with flour and spices so the spices penetrate the meat, and the flour thickens the sauce.

- You can substitute cubed chicken breast (cook 5 hours on low) or chicken thighs (cook 7 hours on low) for the turkey.

- Prepare all of the ingredients ahead of time and refrigerate. Coat the turkey and layer the food when you're ready.

- Any leftover turkey mixture could be warmed and served on lettuce the next day as a salad.

## *Make Sandwiches*

- You don't have to add the yogurt mixture. If you'd like, you could just remove the ingredients from the slow cooker with a slotted spoon.

- Then make the wrap sandwiches with the drained turkey and fruits.

- You can make the filling mixture ahead of time; omit the yogurt mixture and serve it warm or cold.

- Think about using different types of bread in this and all of your sandwiches. Flatbread, pita breads, ciabatta, and French bread all work well.

# PULLED PORK SANDWICHES

## A barbecue classic can come out of your slow cooker, too

Pork shoulder roast is an inexpensive cut of meat that cooks to perfection in the slow cooker.

Classic pulled pork is cooked in a barbecue over low heat for a long time, then shredded and mixed with sauce. In the slow cooker, the pork is cooked with the sauce, which adds more flavor.

There are several ways to serve pulled pork. It can be served alone on a bun, or with coleslaw, which adds a great contrast in flavor, temperature, and texture.

It's hard to overcook the meat in this recipe; the longer it cooks the more tender it will get. But you do have to watch out for the sauce burning; stir occasionally.

**Yield: Serves 12**

### Ingredients

4-pound pork shoulder roast
1 1/2 teaspoons salt
1/2 teaspoon pepper
1 tablespoon Cajun seasoning
2 tablespoons apple cider vinegar
1 (16-ounce) bottle barbecue sauce
12 hoagie buns, split

### Coleslaw

6 cups shredded green cabbage
2 Granny Smith apples, chopped
1 cup golden raisins
1/2 cup mayonnaise
2 tablespoons sugar
1 cup chopped pecans

*Carolina Pulled Pork Sandwiches*

- Trim excess fat from pork. Sprinkle roast with salt, pepper, and Cajun seasoning. Place in 5- or 6-quart slow cooker.

- Pour vinegar and barbecue sauce over all. Cover and cook on low for 8–9 hours until pork is falling apart.

- Shred pork using 2 forks; return to slow cooker. Stir mixture and cook on low for another hour.

- Meanwhile, combine coleslaw ingredients and chill. Make sandwiches with hoagie buns, pork mixture, and coleslaw.

**Classic Pork Sandwiches**
Cook pork as directed, except add 1 (8-ounce) can tomato sauce to the sauce and omit the vinegar. Omit the coleslaw. Shred pork, stir into sauce, and serve on toasted and buttered onion buns.

**Homemade BBQ Sauce**
Cook 1 chopped onion and 4 minced garlic cloves in 1 tablespoon butter. Place in 2-quart slow cooker; add 1 cup ketchup, ⅓ cup vinegar, ¼ cup brown sugar, 1 teaspoon salt, and 2 minced jalapeño peppers; cook on low for 7–8 hours. Refrigerate up to 5 days.

*Cook Pork*

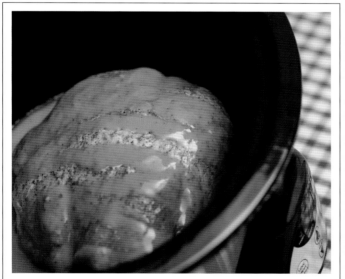

- Make sure that you trim any visible fat from the pork before adding it to the slow cooker.

- You can brown the roast on all sides in some olive oil or butter for 6–8 minutes for a deeper flavor.

- The pork will start to fall apart after about 8 hours. You'll know it's done when you insert a fork and twist; the meat should split easily.

- This type of meat cooks to temperatures well past 160 degrees F, so the fat and connective tissue melt.

*Shred Meat*

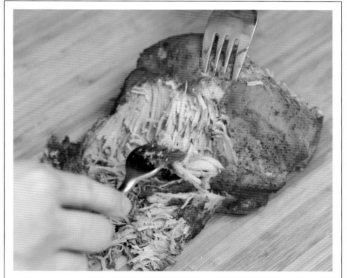

- Use tongs to remove meat from the slow cooker. A fork will just slip right through the tender meat.

- Place the meat on a large plate. You can pull the meat apart with 2 forks, or wear heatproof gloves and use your fingers.

- As you work, return the shredded meat to the juices in the slow cooker.

- The meat will absorb some of the juice, adding more flavor and thickening the sauce.

HOT SANDWICHES

# MU SHU PORK WRAPS

## This Asian stir-fry can be served as a sandwich

Mu Shu pork is usually made as a stir-fry. Thin strips of pork are quickly cooked and combined with vegetables and a sauce, then served over rice or rolled up in pancakes.

Traditional ingredients include lily buds, cloud ear mushrooms, and hard cooked or scrambled eggs. But these foods don't cook well in the slow cooker.

The pork roast will fall apart at the end, making it very easy

to shred. The pork mixture can be served hot or cold.

Onion, garlic, and gingerroot, along with hoisin sauce, add flavor and texture to the finished wraps. You can also serve these in Peking pancakes or crepes.

**Yield: Serves 8**

### Ingredients

2 carrots, sliced

1 onion, chopped

2-pound pork shoulder roast

2 tablespoons low-sodium soy sauce

1/2 cup chicken broth

1/4 cup hoisin sauce

2 tablespoons grated gingerroot

3 cloves garlic, minced

3 cups shredded Napa cabbage

1 tablespoon cornstarch

2 tablespoons oyster sauce

2 tablespoons water

2 teaspoons sesame oil

10 (10-inch) flour tortillas or Peking pancakes

*Mu Shu Pork Wraps*

- Place carrots and onion in bottom of 4-quart slow cooker. Place roast on top.

- Mix soy sauce, chicken broth, hoisin sauce, gingerroot, and garlic; pour over pork.

- Cover and cook on low for 7–8 hours or until pork is very tender. Shred pork; mix with sauce in slow cooker.

- Add cabbage; cover. Cook on high 30 minutes. Mix cornstarch, oyster sauce, and water; add and cook on high 15 minutes. Add sesame oil; make wraps with tortillas.

**Mu Shu Chicken Wraps**

Layer carrots and onion in slow cooker. Substitute 2 pounds boneless, skinless chicken thighs for the pork shoulder roast. Omit oyster sauce. Cover and cook on low for 6–8 hours until chicken is tender. Shred chicken, return to slow cooker. Make wraps with tortillas.

**Peking Pancakes**

In blender, combine 1 cup flour, ⅓ cup water, ⅓ cup milk, 2 eggs, and 1 tablespoon melted butter. Brush 6-inch non-stick pan with unsalted butter and heat over medium heat. Add 2 tablespoons batter; spread evenly; cook 2 minutes. Turn and cook 1–2 minutes longer. Do not stack together; separate with waxed paper. Can be frozen.

*Layer Ingredients*

*Shred Meat*

- You can brown the pork in some vegetable oil before placing in the slow cooker. Cook about 2 minutes per side on medium heat.

- Mu Shu Pork traditionally has some browner bits, and browning the meat would replicate this texture.

- Mushrooms could be added to this dish, but sauté them first on the stovetop until browned.

- Mushrooms release too much liquid to be added straight to the slow cooker in this recipe.

- Remove meat from slow cooker with tongs and shred using 2 forks. Return to sauce in slow cooker and mix.

- The sesame oil is added at the very end so its flavor is pronounced. Heating this oil reduces its flavor.

- You can add some sliced green onions to the sandwiches at the end, along with a small amount of hoisin sauce.

- This mixture is good hot or cold. It can be made ahead of time and reheated in a skillet.

HOT SANDWICHES

# BEEF STEW

## Chuck roast, cut into cubes, cooks tender in this stew

Beef stew is the quintessential slow cooker recipe. The meats usually used for stew are inexpensive cuts of round steak or chuck steak, which become very tender when cooked for a long time at low heat.

Traditionally, onions, carrots, and potatoes are added, but you can use any vegetable you'd like. Remember to add tender vegetables like peas and asparagus at the end of cooking time.

For a liquid, beef stock or broth makes a rich stew, but you can use water since the meat and vegetables add flavor.

It's easy to thicken this stew. Just add a mixture of 1 tablespoon cornstarch with ¼ cup dry red wine at the end of cooking time; cook on high for 15 minutes.

**Yield: Serves 6–8**

### Ingredients

2 russet potatoes, peeled and cubed

1½ pounds beef bottom round

¼ cup flour

1 teaspoon salt

⅛ teaspoon pepper

1 teaspoon dried marjoram leaves

½ teaspoon paprika

1 tablespoon olive oil

2 tablespoons butter

2 onions, chopped

4 cloves garlic, minced

4 carrots, cut into chunks

4 cups beef stock

¼ cup tomato paste

1 (14.5-ounce) can diced tomatoes, undrained

2 tablespoons Dijon mustard

*Beef and Potato Stew*

- Place potatoes in bottom of 4–5 quart slow cooker.

- Cut beef into 1 ½-inch cubes and toss with flour, salt, pepper, marjoram, and paprika.

- Cook coated beef in butter and oil in large skillet for 5 minutes; remove to slow cooker.

- Add onions, garlic, and carrot to pan; cook 4 minutes. Pour 1 cup broth into pan; bring to a boil.

- Pour into slow cooker along with remaining ingredients. Cover and cook on low for 7 hours, stirring once.

## RECIPE VARIATION

**French Beef Stew**
Prepare stew as directed, except add 1 (8-ounce) package cremini mushrooms, sliced. Omit marjoram and paprika; add 1 teaspoon dried thyme and ½ teaspoon dried herbes de Provence. Add ⅓ cup sliced black olives and 2 table-spoons orange juice.

**Belgian Stew**
Prepare as directed, except add 1 cup dark ale beer. Omit potatoes; add 2 bay leaves and 2 tablespoons brown sugar to stew. Reduce stock to 3 cups. When stew is done, remove bay leaves and serve.

*Prepare Ingredients*

- You don't have to brown the beef before adding to the slow cooker, but it does add good flavor and color.

- Cut the potatoes and carrots to about the same size so they cook through in the specified time.

- You can prepare the carrots, onions, and garlic ahead of time, but prepare potatoes just before cooking.

- Potatoes can become brown when cut due to enzymatic browning in the vegetables' cells.

*Place Ingredients in Slow Cooker*

- Because all of the ingredients are covered with liquid, it isn't necessary to layer the root vegetables in the bottom and place the beef on top.

- If you don't brown the beef, be sure to trim off any visible fat before cutting the meat into cubes.

- The flour should thicken the stew enough, but you can add more in a slurry during the last hour of cooking time for a thick stew.

- Add some fresh chopped marjoram leaves at the very end of cooking time for a punch of flavor.

# BEEF BRISKET
## The slow cooker makes all cuts of meat tender and juicy

Beef brisket is perfectly suited to the slow cooker. This cut can be tough, but the long, slow cooking and wet environment make it fork tender after 8 hours.

There are several types of brisket. Since the brisket itself is so large, it's cut into 2 pieces. First cut, also called flat cut, is the type usually found at the meat counter in your supermarket. It is fairly lean and thinner than the second cut.

The second cut is called deckle or point cut. This thicker cut has a lot more fat. It's not as commonly found in supermarkets. Either type can be used in this recipe

You can brown the meat before cooking, or place it in the slow cooker rubbed with spices and herbs.

**Yield: Serves 8–10**

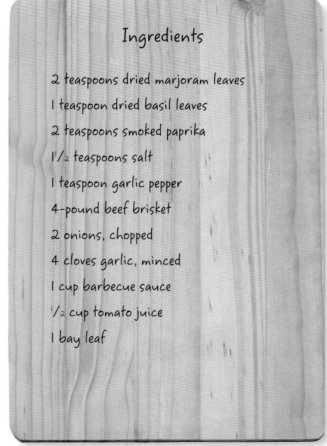

### Ingredients

2 teaspoons dried marjoram leaves

1 teaspoon dried basil leaves

2 teaspoons smoked paprika

1½ teaspoons salt

1 teaspoon garlic pepper

4-pound beef brisket

2 onions, chopped

4 cloves garlic, minced

1 cup barbecue sauce

½ cup tomato juice

1 bay leaf

*Barbecue Brisket*

- In small bowl, combine marjoram, basil, paprika, salt, and garlic pepper.

- Trim excess fat from brisket and sprinkle marjoram mixture over; rub in.

- Place onions and garlic in 5- or 6-quart slow cooker; top with beef. Pour barbecue sauce and tomato juice over beef; add bay leaf.

- Cover and cook on low for 8–10 hours until beef is tender. Remove bay leaf, slice beef, and serve with sauce from slow cooker.

· · · · · **RECIPE VARIATION** · · · ·

**Mom's Brisket**
Prepare as directed, except omit barbecue sauce and tomato juice. Place 4 cubed potatoes and 3 sliced carrots in slow cooker with onions and garlic. Top with beef; pour 1 cup beef stock over all. Cover and cook on low 8–10 hours until tender.

## YELLOW ● LIGHT

When you buy a large chunk of meat, you're spending a good amount of money. The beef should be firm and hold together well. There should be visible lines of fat running through it. The color doesn't matter as much, as exposure to air can change the color.

### Add Herb Rub

- Really use your fingers to rub the spice mixture into the meat so the flavors permeate as deeply as possible.

- When you create a spice or herb rub that you really like, make it in quantity.

- Store the rub in an airtight container for 3–4 months; be sure to label it.

- When you use it, pour out the amount you want rather than dipping your fingers back into the rub as you work to prevent contamination.

### Pour Sauce Over

- You can use a bottled barbecue sauce or make your own. Make the sauce as mild or as spicy as you like.

- The sauce is very important in this recipe, so buy the best you can find with ingredients you would use yourself.

- To make your own sauce, cook onion and garlic in oil; add chopped tomatoes, ketchup, mustard, and vinegar.

- Simmer for 1–2 hours or until the flavors blend. Store in refrigerator up to 4 days.

# POT ROAST

## This classic comfort food recipe cooks to perfection in the slow cooker

Nothing makes your home feel cozier than a simmering pot roast, and the slow cooker does such a good job with this cut of meat.

You can make any pot roast a one-dish meal by adding root vegetables: carrots, potatoes, parsnips, turnips, and onions all cook very well and impart their flavor to the tender meat.

Use vegetables like tomatoes and celery to make wonderful gravy to serve with your roast. Just remove the meat and root vegetables—if you've placed any under the roast—with tongs and a slotted spoon, then puree the remaining veggies. Thicken it with a cornstarch or flour slurry if you like.

**Yield: Serves 8–10**

### Ingredients

¹/₃ cup flour

2 teaspoons paprika

1 teaspoon salt

¹/₈ teaspoon pepper

4-pound beef chuck roast

1 teaspoon dried oregano leaves

1 tablespoon butter

2 tablespoons olive oil

2 onions, chopped

2 tomatoes, peeled and chopped

4 cloves garlic, minced

1¹/₂ cups beef stock

¹/₄ cup tomato paste

*Mom's Pot Roast*

- On plate, combine flour, paprika, salt, and pepper. Dredge roast in this mixture.

- Brown roast in butter and olive oil over medium heat on all sides, about 10 minutes. Remove roast to 6-quart slow cooker.

- Add onions, tomatoes, and garlic to pan; cook 4 minutes. Add beef stock and tomato paste; simmer and pour over roast.

- Cover; cook on low for 8–10 hours or until meat is falling apart. Remove meat from slow cooker; cover. Puree vegetables to make sauce.

## • • • • • • • • • • • • • • • RECIPE VARIATION • • • • • • • • • • • • • • •

**Pot Roast and Vegetables**
Make the recipe as directed, except use a 7-quart slow cooker. Place 4 potatoes and 4 carrots, scrubbed and cut into chunks, under and around the meat. Cook as directed. Remove meat and most of the vegetables to a serving platter when done; cover with foil to keep warm. Puree remaining mixture for gravy.

**Tex-Mex Pot Roast**
Cook recipe as directed, except add 2 minced jalapeños to the onion mixture. Peel and cube 2 sweet potatoes; place under roast. Instead of paprika, rub 1–2 tablespoons chili powder into the meat. And add 1 tablespoon chile paste to the liquid along with the tomato paste.

*Season Meat*

- It's important to season these large chunks of meat well. Enough salt is the secret to the best-tasting meat and gravy.

- Don't go overboard, but up to 2 teaspoons salt for a 4-pound piece of meat will work.

- For cuts of meat, you can use chuck, brisket, bottom round, or rump. Trim off excess fat before rubbing in the spices.

- Leftover pot roast makes wonderful sandwiches, or you can reheat it in the gravy to serve the next day.

*Prepare Tomatoes*

- To peel tomatoes, first bring a pot of water to a boil. Fill another bowl with ice water.

- Cut a small X in the blossom end of each tomato. This is the side of the tomato without the stem.

- Drop the tomatoes into the boiling water for 5–10 seconds. Remove with a Chinese skimmer and plunge into ice water.

- Let cool for 2–3 minutes, then remove and slip off the peel; it should come off easily.

# SAUERBRATEN

## A German specialty, this hearty main dish is special enough for company

This German specialty results in tender meat served with a very flavorful sweet and sour, thick gravy perfect served over mashed potatoes or little dumplings.

Traditionally, Sauerbraten is made by marinating meat in a vinegar mixture up to 4 days, then braising in the oven. The slow cooker method is much easier and just as delicious.

At the end, you'll need to taste the gravy several times, and add either gingersnaps or vinegar so it is to your liking. Have extra gingersnaps on hand for this purpose.

Serve this excellent dish with spaetzle or egg noodles, some glazed carrots, and a spinach salad with strawberries.

**Yield: Serves 8**

### Ingredients

3 pounds beef bottom round

1 teaspoon paprika

1/4 cup flour

1 teaspoon salt

1/8 teaspoon pepper

3 tablespoons butter

2 onions, chopped

4 cloves garlic, minced

4 carrots, sliced

1 1/2 cups beef stock

1/4 cup apple cider vinegar

1/4 cup red wine vinegar

1 tablespoon Worcestershire sauce

1 cup crushed gingersnap cookies

1/4 cup brown sugar

*Sauerbraten with Gingersnap Gravy*

- Dredge beef in mixture of paprika, flour, salt, and pepper. Brown in butter in large pan; remove to 5- or 6-quart slow cooker.

- Add onions and garlic to pan; cook and stir 4 minutes. Add carrots, stock, vinegars and Worcester-shire; boil.

- Pour over beef; cover and cook on low for 8–10 hours until tender.

- Add gingersnap crumbs and sugar to slow cooker and taste. Cover and cook on high for 20–30 minutes until gravy is smooth.

## • • • • RECIPE VARIATION • • • •

**Sauerbraten Stew**
Instead of using the whole chunk of meat, cut it into 1-inch cubes. Add 1 cup chopped celery. Cook as directed, but at the end, stir in ½ cup sour cream mixed with 2 tablespoons flour. Cover and cook on high for 15–20 minutes. Serve over egg noodles or hot cooked rice.

## • • • • • • GREEN ● LIGHT • • • • • •

Sauerbraten is the type of recipe that you can make ahead of time. Get everything ready, then coat the meat, brown it, and assemble the food in the slow cooker. Cook as directed. Remove the meat, vegetables, and gravy from the slow cooker, cover, then refrigerate. Reheat in a saucepan on the stovetop until the food is hot and the sauce bubbly.

## Brown Meat

- Browning meat means just that. You want to cook the meat in fat until the color is deep and rich.

- You'll know when the meat has been sufficiently browned: it will release easily from the pan.

- Cook the roast on all sides, lifting and turning when the meat moves easily.

- Do not brown the meat ahead of time. For food safety reasons, you can't partially cook meat and then refrigerate it.

## Add Gingersnaps

- Homemade or purchased gingersnaps work equally well. They can be crisp or soft.

- The cookies are used for their sweet taste, the spices, and how they thicken the gravy.

- If the gravy is too thick when the taste is right, thin it by adding more beef stock; cook on high 10–15 minutes to blend.

- Spaetzle are tiny dumplings that are usually served with Sauerbraten. Find them in the frozen foods aisle.

# BEEF STROGANOFF

## A smooth, rich sauce envelops tender beef cubes in this classic recipe

Beef stroganoff sounds rich, and it is. This is the perfect dish for entertaining. The food cooks all day while you're busy doing other things, and it's a very elegant meal.

Like Sauerbraten, beef stroganoff is usually made with marinated meat. Once again, the slow cooker comes to the rescue and omits the need for marinating.

The beef is cut into fairly large cubes because it will fall apart slightly as you stir in the sour cream mixture, and you want to see and taste discrete chunks of meat.

Sour cream and Worcestershire sauce are the usual seasonings for beef stroganoff. And it's served over hot cooked egg noodles. Add a green salad and some roasted asparagus and you have a meal fit for a king.

**Yield: Serves 8**

### Ingredients

2 pounds beef chuck roast

$1/4$ cup flour

1 teaspoon smoked paprika

1 teaspoon salt

$1/8$ teaspoon pepper

3 tablespoons butter

2 onions, chopped

4 cloves garlic, minced

2 cups beef stock

$1/2$ cup dry red wine

1 tablespoon Dijon mustard

1 teaspoon dried thyme leaves

2/3 cup sour cream

1 tablespoon flour

*Classic Beef Stroganoff*

- Cut beef into 2-inch cubes. Toss with flour, paprika, salt, and pepper. Brown in butter in saucepan; remove to 4- or 5-quart slow cooker.

- Add onion and garlic to pan; cook 4 minutes. Add stock, wine, mustard, and thyme; bring to a simmer.

- Pour mixture over beef in slow cooker. Cover and cook on low 8–9 hours.

- Mix sour cream and flour and stir into slow cooker; cover and cook on high for 20–30 minutes until thickened. Serve over hot cooked noodles.

## RECIPE VARIATION

**Rich Beef Stroganoff**
Prepare recipe as directed, except add 2 cups baby carrots. Omit the sour cream addition at the end, and omit the flour. Cube 2 (3-ounce) packages cream cheese and stir in at the end of cooking time; cook on high 15–20 minutes until thickened.

**Beef and Mushroom Stroganoff**
Prepare recipe as directed, except cook 1 (8-ounce) package mushrooms, sliced, in the drippings after the beef has browned. Add to slow cooker, then cook onions and garlic and proceed with the recipe. Serve over hot mashed potatoes made with sour cream.

*Prepare Beef*

- Trim off visible fat and cut beef into same-size cubes.

- Brown the beef cubes as you'd brown a large piece of meat. The meat will release from the pan when it's ready to be turned.

- Use tongs to turn the meat and place it in the slow cooker so you don't disturb the flavorful outer crust on the meat.

- You can use beef brisket, chuck steak, or top or bottom round for this recipe.

*Add Sour Cream*

- Make sure that the sour cream and flour are well combined before adding to the slow cooker.

- You can ladle a spoonful of the hot liquid into the sour cream mixture to temper it and bring it up to the temperature of the liquid.

- This will help prevent curdling, but as long as you stir thoroughly, it's not necessary.

- Don't make the sour cream mixture ahead of time. Stir it together just before you add it to the slow cooker.

# CORNED BEEF

## Corned beef can be tough, but not when cooked for hours in the slow cooker

Whether you are truly Irish or another nationality, corned beef is the dish to serve around St. Patrick's Day. This is the American version of a celebratory dish; it's an ordinary dish in Ireland and wouldn't be considered for a party.

Because corned beef can be tough, even when cooked correctly; the slow cooker is the perfect appliance for it. You must slice the meat very thinly, against the grain, for tender results. It usually comes with a seasoning packet made of pickling spices and other ingredients. If yours doesn't, you can make your own.

Serve with icy cold beer and a fruit salad.

**Yield: Serves 8**

### Ingredients

2 onions, chopped

4 cloves garlic, minced

4 carrots, sliced

3-pound corned beef brisket with seasoning packet or homemade corned beef seasoning

1 cup beef broth

1 cup beer

1 bay leaf

1/8 teaspoon cloves

1/4 cup Dijon mustard

2 tablespoons sugar

2 tablespoons cornstarch

1/4 cup water

*Corned Beef Dinner*

- Place onions, garlic, and carrots in 4- or 5-quart slow cooker. Top with brisket; sprinkle with seasoning packet.

- In bowl, combine broth, beer, bay leaf, cloves, mustard, and sugar; mix and pour into slow cooker.

- Cover and cook on low for 10–12 hours until beef is tender. Remove beef and bay leaf; cover beef.

- Add mixture of cornstarch and water; cover and cook on high for 30 minutes. Slice beef thinly against the grain and serve with vegetables and sauce.

## • • • • • • • • • • • • • • • RECIPE VARIATION • • • • • • • • • • • • • • • •

### Corned Beef Seasoning

Mix 2 tablespoons mixed pickling spices with 2 teaspoons paprika and 1 teaspoon garlic powder. Add 1 teaspoon salt, ¼ teaspoon pepper, ½ teaspoon mustard seeds, and 1 teaspoon dried onion bits. Store in an airtight container up to 3 months. Rub into corned beef before cooking.

### Corned Beef and Cabbage

Prepare recipe as directed, except omit carrots. When corned beef is cooked, remove from slow cooker and cover with foil to keep warm. Add 8 wedges red or green cabbage to slow cooker. Cover and cook on high for 25–35 minutes until cabbage is tender. Slice corned beef and serve with cabbage.

### *Place Food in Slow Cooker*

- You can vary the root vegetables you use in this recipe. Baby carrots are good, as are 1–2 peeled and cubed rutabagas.

- Try parsnips, turnips, or potatoes for a change of pace.

- Small red potatoes can be added whole; cut larger potatoes into chunks. Just make sure they're all under the beef.

- Any kind of beer will work well in this recipe; non-alcoholic, light beer, or a dark ale.

### *Slice Beef*

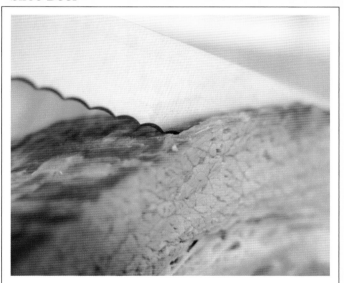

- To slice the beef, look carefully at the meat and you'll see the grain—thin lines running through the meat.

- Slice the meat against the grain; that is, perpendicular to the lines.

- Once the beef has been sliced, you can return it to the slow cooker and keep it warm for up to 1 hour on keep-warm.

- Serve this meal with some grainy brown mustard and the juices from the slow cooker.

# MEATBALLS

## Meatballs, whether homemade or purchased, can be slow cooked many ways

Meatballs are easy to make, fun to eat, and perfect to cook in the slow cooker. As with ground meat, they do better if browned first in butter, oil, or bacon fat.

The meatballs can also be baked in the oven or browned under the broiler before adding to the slow cooker. This forms a crust on the meatballs, for flavor and texture.

You can drop meatballs, unbrowned, directly into a sauce in the slow cooker, but you must use very lean meat so the dish doesn't become too fatty.

Serve these meatballs over mashed potatoes, hot cooked rice, or pasta, or on a Hoagie bun for a great sandwich.

**Yield: Serves 6**

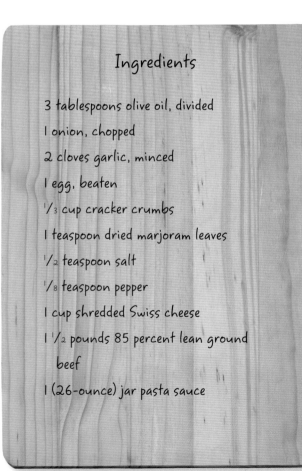

### Ingredients

3 tablespoons olive oil, divided

1 onion, chopped

2 cloves garlic, minced

1 egg, beaten

1/3 cup cracker crumbs

1 teaspoon dried marjoram leaves

1/2 teaspoon salt

1/8 teaspoon pepper

1 cup shredded Swiss cheese

1 1/2 pounds 85 percent lean ground beef

1 (26-ounce) jar pasta sauce

*Classic Meatballs*

- In large skillet, heat 1 tablespoon olive oil; cook onion and garlic for 5 minutes. Remove to large bowl.

- Add egg, crumbs, marjoram, salt, pepper, and cheese; mix well. Add beef and mix gently but thoroughly.

- Form into 1-inch meatballs.

Heat remaining 2 tablespoons oil in same skillet; brown meatballs; drain.

- Combine meatballs with sauce in a 4-quart slow cooker. Cover; cook on low 6–8 hours until done.

- Serve over pasta or cooked rice.

**Meatballs in Gravy**

Follow recipe as directed, except substitute 2 cups beef broth for the pasta sauce; cook as directed. Remove meatballs with slotted spoon; set aside. Mix 3 tablespoons cornstarch with ¼ cup water; add to slow cooker; cook on high 15–20 minutes until thickened. Return meatballs to gravy; cook 10 minutes longer.

**Southwest Meatballs**

Follow recipe as directed, except use ⅓ cup tortilla crumbs in place of the cracker crumbs. Omit marjoram; add 2 teaspoons chili powder. Add 2 minced jalapeño peppers with onions. Omit pasta sauce; add 2 (16-ounce) jars salsa. Cook as directed.

## *Mix Meatballs*

- You can make the meatball mixture ahead of time; refrigerate until you brown and add to the slow cooker.

- You can use breadcrumbs or crushed cereal instead of the cracker crumbs.

- When you're making meatballs, it's important to mix all ingredients except the meat first.

- Add the meat and work gently with your hands just until combined. Overhandling will result in tough meatballs.

## *Add Meatballs*

- Place about a cup of the pasta sauce in the slow cooker and add a layer of meatballs.

- Repeat until all sauce and meatballs are used. The meatballs are quite tender and have to be handled gently.

- You can make this entire recipe ahead of time; after cooking, refrigerate until ready to eat.

- Then place the sauce and meatballs in a saucepan and heat on low heat for 15–20 minutes until bubbly.

# BEEF CURRY

## Inexpensive ground beef is the base for this rich and elegant dish

Curry is an Indian dish, which was transplanted to England during its occupation of that country. Curry itself isn't a single spice, but a combination of spices. In India, every family has its own special curry blend.

You can make your own curry by combining different amounts of certain spices. The most common include cinnamon, paprika, cumin, dry mustard, turmeric, coriander, and cloves.

Curry is usually made with chicken. Beef is a nice alternative because the pungent flavors of curry powder stand up nicely to richly flavored meat.

The ground meat has to be fully cooked before combining with the rest of the ingredients so the finished dish has the proper amount of fat and liquid.

**Yield: Serves 6**

### Ingredients

1 parsnip, peeled and cubed

1½ pounds 85 percent lean ground beef

2 onions, chopped

4 cloves garlic, minced

1 tablespoon grated gingerroot

½ teaspoon salt

1 tablespoon curry powder

2 tablespoons flour

⅛ teaspoon cayenne pepper

¼ cup tomato paste

1 cup beef broth

1 cup crushed tomatoes

½ cup golden raisins

½ cup mango chutney

2 (8-ounce) packages couscous, cooked

½ cup toasted sliced almonds

*Beef Curry*

- Place parsnips in bottom of 4-quart slow cooker.

- In large saucepan, cook ground beef, onion, garlic, and gingerroot until meat is browned, stirring to break up meat; drain.

- Add salt, curry powder, flour, and pepper; cook 3 minutes. Add tomato paste and broth; simmer and pour into slow cooker with tomatoes and raisins.

- Cover and cook on low for 6–7 hours until sauce is blended. Stir in chutney. Serve over couscous, topped with almonds.

## • • • • RECIPE VARIATION • • • •

**Curry Powder**
For your own homemade curry powder you can vary the spices as you like. A basic recipe is 2 tablespoons ground cumin, 1 teaspoon cinnamon, 1 tablespoon turmeric, 2 teaspoons dry mustard, ½ teaspoon cayenne pepper, 1 teaspoon salt, 1 teaspoon paprika, and ½ teaspoon ground ginger.

## • • • • • • • GREEN ● LIGHT • • • • • • • • •

Make several different curry blends and use them interchangeably. The curry powder will keep, stored in the dark in an airtight container, for about 2–3 months. After that time the spices lose their potency. Be sure to label the bottles and store them away from heat.

### Brown Ground Beef

- Start by adding the ground beef to the skillet. As it begins to sizzle, break up the meat with a fork.

- Add onion, garlic, and gingerroot when some of the fat has rendered from the meat.

- Cook and stir until no pink remains. Drain by scooping out the fat and liquid with a spoon.

- There will still be enough fat and liquid in the meat mixture to cook the curry powder and flour.

### Add Chutney

- Curry powder tastes better after it's been heated. The heat brings out the aromatic oils in the spices.

- Chutney, however, tastes better when it hasn't been cooked for a long period of time.

- Add the chutney at the end of cooking time, then serve the curry immediately.

- If you want to make this ahead of time, don't add the chutney. Refrigerate the curry; reheat and add chutney just before serving.

# SHEPHERD'S PIE

## A pie without a crust, this casserole is great for a cold night

Shepherd's pie is made from a ground beef and vegetable mixture that is topped with mashed potatoes or cornbread. The pie doesn't have a bottom crust.

You can use mashed potatoes made from scratch, refrigerated, or made from dried potato buds. The ground beef mixture has to be hot so the potatoes start cooking immediately and don't turn brown.

You can make shepherd's pie with ground lamb, beef, pork, sausage, chicken, or turkey. And it can be flavored with foods from every cuisine in the world. Middle Eastern shepherd's pie would use ground lamb, with allspice and pine nuts, while a Cajun pie would use jalapeños, green bell peppers, and Tabasco sauce with chicken.

**Yield: Serves 8**

### Ingredients

3 cups refrigerated mashed potatoes

I cup canned sweet potato cubes, drained

1/2 cup shredded Asiago cheese

1 1/2 pounds 85 percent lean ground beef

2 onions, chopped

3 cloves garlic, minced

4 carrots, sliced

2 tablespoons flour

Salt and pepper to taste

I tablespoon Worcestershire sauce

I cup beef broth

1/2 cup ketchup

3 tablespoons mustard

1/3 cup grated Parmesan cheese

*Easy Shepherd's Pie*

- Heat refrigerated mashed potatoes as directed. Mash in sweet potatoes and stir in Asiago; set aside.

- In large saucepan, cook beef with onions, garlic, and carrots until beef is browned. Add flour, salt, and pepper; simmer.

- Add Worcestershire sauce, broth, ketchup, and mustard; simmer for 3 minutes, then pour into 4-quart slow cooker.

- Top with potato mixture and sprinkle with Parmesan. Cover and cook on low for 7–9 hours until hot.

**Tex-Mex Shepherd's Pie**
Make as directed, except add 2 minced jalapeños with onions. Omit carrots; add 2 cups frozen corn. Omit ketchup; use 1 cup salsa. For topping, combine 4 cups refrigerated mashed potatoes with 1 cup sour cream, 1 tablespoon chili powder, and ⅓ cup grated Parmesan. Pour over hot meat mixture; cook as directed.

**Greek Shepherd's Pie**
Prepare as directed, except add 1 chopped and peeled zucchini in place of the carrots. Omit sweet potatoes; add ½ cup crumbled feta cheese to the potato topping. Omit ketchup; use ½ cup yogurt plus 1 tablespoon cornstarch in its place.

### Simmer Mixture

- The ground beef mixture can be made ahead of time. Just refrigerate it, and when you're ready to cook, heat in a saucepan until bubbly.

- Because the beef is fully cooked, you can stop cooking and hold it for later.

- You can add other vegetables to the beef mixture if you'd like: mushrooms or bell peppers would be good.

- Spray the slow cooker with nonstick cooking spray before adding the food for easy cleanup.

### Add Potatoes

- Refrigerated mashed potatoes are a very high quality product and easy to use.

- They usually just involve reheating, in the microwave or in a saucepan. You can add other ingredients to them, like sour cream or cheese.

- Adding sweet potatoes not only changes the color, but provides great flavor and lots of vitamin A.

- You could also add ½ cup sour cream or softened cream cheese to the potatoes for a richer taste.

# MEATLOAF

## Meatloaf "bakes" to a moist and tender finish in the slow cooker

Meatloaf is an easy meal that's easy to make badly. Everyone has had a dry meatloaf full of dry pieces of bread, or bland meatloaf that's tough.

To make the best meatloaf, follow a few rules. First, always precook any additions to the meatloaf, like onions or shallots. Then, combine all of the filler ingredients—breadcrumbs, egg, ketchup, and seasonings—first. Then add the ground

meat and mix gently. Overmixing will make the meatloaf tough.

The slow cooker's moist environment will ensure the meatloaf is always juicy. Let it stand 10 minutes after you take it out of the slow cooker and enjoy your perfect meatloaf.

**Yield: Serves 6–8**

### Ingredients

1 onion, chopped

3 cloves garlic, minced

1 tablespoon olive oil

$1/3$ cup chopped kalamata olives

$1/2$ cup soft breadcrumbs

$1/2$ cup ground almonds

$1/2$ cup shredded Manchego cheese

1 egg, beaten

$1/2$ teaspoon salt

$1/8$ teaspoon pepper

1 teaspoon smoked paprika

$1 1/2$ pounds 85 percent lean ground beef

$1/4$ cup grated Asiago cheese

*Spanish Meatloaf*

- Cook onion and garlic in olive oil. Mix with olives, breadcrumbs, almonds, Manchego cheese, egg, salt, pepper, and paprika.

- Add beef; mix gently. Form into round loaf. Form 2 long foil strips, 3 x 24 inches, and crisscross in 4-quart slow cooker.

- Place meatloaf in slow cooker. Cover; cook on low for 6–8 hours or until meat thermometer registers 160 degrees F.

- Lift out of slow cooker using foil strips, sprinkle with Asiago, cover, and let rest for 10 minutes.

**Mom's Meatloaf**
Make recipe as directed, except increase breadcrumbs to 1 cup. Omit almonds, olives, and Manchego cheese; increase eggs to 2 and add ⅓ cup ketchup. Omit Asiago cheese; instead, mix ¼ cup ketchup and 2 tablespoons mustard; spread over meatloaf; cook as directed.

**Tex-Mex Meatloaf**
Make recipe as directed, except add 4-ounce can chopped green chiles, undrained, in place of the olives. Omit almonds; add ¼ cup yellow cornmeal and 1 tablespoon chili powder along with ¼ cup salsa to meatloaf mixture. Cook as directed; sprinkle with Parmesan cheese.

## Add Ground Beef

- It's important to mix all of the other ingredients before adding the ground beef.

- This ensures that the ingredients will be evenly mixed throughout the meatloaf, making it tender and flavorful.

- The more you handle ground beef, the tougher the final product will be. Handle gently.

- Form the meatloaf into a round if you have a round slow cooker; into an oval shape for an oval slow cooker.

## Place Meatloaf in Slow Cooker

- Make sure that the foil strips are crossed and placed evenly in the slow cooker.

- The ends of the foil strips should extend beyond the slow cooker edges so you can grab them to lift the meatloaf.

- After the meatloaf has been removed from the slow cooker, cover it with foil and let stand 10 minutes.

- This will give the juices time to redistribute so the meatloaf is tender and juicy.

# STUFFED CABBAGE
## Old-fashioned comfort food is easy to prepare in the slow cooker

Stuffed cabbage is a comforting, old-fashioned dish. It is delicious when well seasoned and cooked in the slow cooker.

Green cabbage is usually used because it's milder than red cabbage and the finished product has nice color. Choose a head of cabbage that is heavy and firm, with no soft spots or brown edges.

For food safety reasons, it's best to cook the ground beef completely before you fill and cook the cabbage rolls.

Traditionally, the beef is mixed with rice. Barley is a less common filling, but it has lots of nutrition and fiber and adds a wonderful nutty taste to the cabbage rolls.

Serve with gelatin salad and green beans for a retro meal.
**Yield: Serves 6**

### Ingredients

1 (8-ounce) can tomato sauce

1 (14.5-ounce) can diced tomatoes, undrained

3 tablespoons Dijon mustard

3 tablespoons brown sugar

2 tablespoons lemon juice

1 teaspoon dried thyme leaves

Salt and pepper to taste

1 head green cabbage

1 pound lean ground beef

1 onion, chopped

3 cloves garlic, minced

1 cup cooked barley

1 egg

*Old-Fashioned Stuffed Cabbage*

- Combine tomato sauce, tomatoes, mustard, sugar, lemon juice, thyme, salt, and pepper; set aside.

- Cut core out of cabbage. Remove 8 outer leaves; set aside. Chop rest of cabbage.

- Cook ground beef with onion and garlic; drain.

- Stir in barley, chopped cabbage, egg, and ½ cup tomato mixture.

- Fill cabbage leaves with beef mixture; roll up and place in 4-quart slow cooker.

- Pour remaining tomato sauce over all. Cover and cook on low for 8–9 hours.

**Rice Stuffed Cabbage**
Make recipe as directed, except omit barley. Add 1 cup cooked brown, basmati, white long-grain, or wild rice. For sauce, omit mustard; add 2 tablespoons cider vinegar and ⅓ cup ketchup. Cook rolls as directed.

**Mushroom Stuffed Cabbage**
Make recipe as directed, except add 2 cups chopped mushrooms to the ground beef mixture. Cook with onions and garlic until browned. Add 1 teaspoon marjoram in place of the thyme leaves. At the end of cooking time, stir in ½ cup sour cream mixed with 1 tablespoon cornstarch; cook 10 minutes on high.

## Add Filling

- For 1 cup cooked barley, cook ⅓ cup medium barley in ⅔ cup beef stock or water for 25–30 minutes until tender.

- Each cabbage leaf should take ⅓ to ½ cup of the filling.

- Don't pack the filling tightly in the leaves because it will expand when heated.

- To remove cabbage leaves, cut out the core. You can soak the cabbage in very hot water for 5–6 minutes to soften the leaves.

## Place in Slow Cooker

- Roll the leaves up gently, folding in the sides. Place them seam side down in the slow cooker.

- You don't need to use toothpicks to seal the rolls. The cabbage will cook around the filling and stay in place.

- If you'd like, you can substitute your favorite pasta sauce for the tomato mixture.

- To make ahead of time, make the filling, stuff the rolls, and refrigerate. Then put everything in the slow cooker and cook as directed.

# TAMALE PIE

## With a few extra steps, you can make this pot pie in the slow cooker

A tamale pie consists of a cornbread mixture that is baked on top of a well-seasoned combination of beef and vegetables.

Cornbread mix or corn muffin mix works well in this recipe. It's just a combination of flour, cornmeal, some seasonings, and baking powder. Adding corn kernels to the topping imparts a wonderful fresh flavor and texture.

This Southwest dish usually contains beans, for added texture and nutrition. You can use pinto beans, black beans, or kidney beans. They must be cooked before combining with the other ingredients.

You can make this dish as mild or as spicy as you like. Add more or less jalapeños; use a mild or spicy salsa. Serve with guacamole and sour cream for cooling contrast.

**Yield: Serves 8**

### Ingredients

1 ½ pounds ground beef

2 onions, chopped

3 cloves garlic, minced

1 jalapeño pepper, minced

2 (15-ounce) cans black beans, drained

1 cup red salsa

½ cup barbecue sauce

1 (6-ounce) package corn muffin mix

½ cup frozen corn

1 egg, beaten

½ cup heavy cream

½ cup green salsa

½ cup shredded Cotija or Parmesan cheese

1 cup sour cream

1 (4-ounce) can chopped green chiles, drained

*Tex-Mex Tamale Pie*

- Cook ground beef with onions, garlic, and jalapeño; drain. Add beans, red salsa, and barbecue sauce; simmer.

- While sauce simmers, combine muffin mix, corn, egg, cream, green salsa, and Cotija cheese; mix.

- Pour hot beef mixture into 4-quart slow cooker. Immediately top with corn muffin mixture.

- Top with folded paper towels; cover and cook on low for 6–8 hours until topping is done. Combine sour cream and chiles; serve with pie.

**Refried Bean Tamale Pie**

Make recipe as directed, except substitute 1 (16-ounce) can refried beans and 1 (16-ounce) can of kidney beans for the 2 cans of black beans. For topping, combine muffin mix with 1 egg; 1 (4-ounce) can chopped green chiles, undrained; and 3 tablespoons oil. Cook as directed.

**Homemade Cornbread Topping**

To substitute for the cornmeal muffin mixture, combine 1 cup cornmeal, ½ cup flour, 1 teaspoon baking powder, ½ teaspoon baking soda, ½ teaspoon salt in bowl. Add ¾ cup buttermilk and 1 beaten egg with 2 tablespoons heavy cream. Mix; pour over hot mixture in slow cooker.

## *Add Cornbread Topping*

- The meat filling has to be hot when the cornbread mixture is added so the bread starts to cook immediately.

- If the meat filling isn't hot, there will be an uncooked layer of cornbread mixture right on top of the filling.

- If you want to make the filling ahead of time, you must bring it back to a simmer on the stovetop. Then pour it into the slow cooker and add the cornbread topping.

## *Paper Towels*

- Do not make the cornbread mixture ahead of time; the leavening will rise before it should and the topping will collapse.

- After the mixture has cooked for 3–4 hours, you can remove the paper towels.

- At this point, the cornbread mixture will have risen to cover the beef mixture and there will be less condensation on the lid.

- This pie can be served with salsa, guacamole, or a mixture of sour cream and chili powder.

# CHICKEN CACCIATORE
## Shorter cooking time ensures chicken breast is tender and juicy

KNACK SLOW COOKING

Cacciatore literally means "hunter" in Italian. This doesn't mean food prepared with game, but made "hunter-style," using onions, mushrooms, tomatoes, and wine.

Chicken is probably the most common meat made with this cooking method and ingredients, because its mild taste blends well with these assertive flavors.

You can use chicken breasts or thighs. For thighs, use boneless, skinless meat and cook for 7–9 hours on low.

You can vary the type of mushrooms you use, and the vegetables to some extent, but to be true to the basic flavors of the dish, keep tomatoes, onions, and wine in the recipe.

Serve this hearty dish with a spinach salad and a rice pilaf to soak up the wonderful sauce.

**Yield: Serves 6**

*Chicken Cacciatore*

### Ingredients

1 onion, chopped

3 cloves garlic, minced

1 (8-ounce) package cremini mush-
    rooms, sliced

2 tablespoons olive oil

2 tablespoons flour

$\frac{1}{2}$ teaspoon salt

$\frac{1}{8}$ teaspoon pepper

1 teaspoon dried oregano

1 teaspoon dried thyme

1 (14.5-ounce) can diced tomatoes,
    undrained

1 (6 ounce) can tomato paste

$\frac{1}{2}$ cup red wine

6 boneless, skinless chicken breasts

Salt and pepper to taste

1 green bell pepper, chopped

- In saucepan, cook onion, garlic, and mushrooms in oil until tender. Add flour, salt, pepper, oregano, and thyme; cook 3 minutes.

- Add tomatoes, tomato paste, and wine; simmer 4 minutes.

- Sprinkle chicken with salt and pepper to taste and place chicken in 4- or 5-quart slow cooker. Top with green bell peppers; pour sauce over.

- Cover and cook on low for 5–7 hours until chicken registers 165 degrees F on a meat thermometer. Serve over hot cooked pasta.

**Chicken Cacciatore on the Bone**
To cook this meal using bone-in, skin-on chicken breasts, first brown the meat, skin side down, in 2 tablespoons olive oil, then cook as directed, except increase cooking time to 7–8 hours. For thighs, brown the meat and cook on low for 8–9 hours.

**Triple Mushroom Cacciatore**
Make recipe as directed, except add 1 cup sliced button mushrooms and 1 cup sliced shiitake mushrooms. Omit the green bell pepper at the end; instead, add 2 cups frozen green beans. Cook 15–20 minutes on high and serve over pasta.

*Sauté Onion Mixture*

*Mix Sauce*

- When you cook onions, they become sweet and tender. The sugars in the onion develop in the heat.

- The sulfur compounds that are harsh and make your eyes tear will evaporate as the onions cook.

- When cooking mushrooms in the slow cooker, you must sauté them first. The mushrooms can add a lot of water, which dilutes the dish.

- Cook the onion and garlic mixture until the liquid evaporates. This concentrates the flavor, too.

- You can make the sauce ahead of time. Cook the onion, garlic, and mushrooms, and add the flour and seasonings.

- Stir in the tomatoes and wine and simmer. Then refrigerate the sauce.

- When you're ready to cook, heat this mixture to a simmer again and assemble the recipe in the slow cooker, layering as directed.

- Serve this dish over hot cooked rice, a rice pilaf, mashed potatoes, or hot cooked pasta.

# EASY DRUMSTICKS
## The kids' favorite can be flavored many ways

Drumsticks are a child's favorite kind of chicken. They are easy to hold and eat and come with a built-in handle!

Drumsticks cook very well in the slow cooker. The meat tends to fall off the bone unless the drumsticks are browned first. Broiling them is an easy way to brown, adding flavor and color without adding fat.

You can remove the skin from the drumsticks before cooking if you'd like; in that case, don't brown them first. Just grasp the skin firmly with a paper towel and pull it off.

If you cook with the skin on, and then remove the skin at serving time, the chicken will be moist and juicy. Removing the skin after cooking also removes most of the fat.

**Yield: Serves 8–10**

Ingredients

3 cloves garlic

1/2 teaspoon salt

1/8 teaspoon pepper

1/2 teaspoon five-spice powder

3 pounds chicken drumsticks

1/4 cup honey

2 tablespoons soy sauce

2 tablespoons lemon juice

1/2 cup ketchup

2 tablespoons hoisin sauce

*Sticky Drumsticks*

- Mince garlic and work together with salt using the back of a spoon. Add pepper and five-spice powder; set aside.

- Place drumsticks under broiler; broil for 5–7 minutes, turning once, until browned. Rub with garlic mixture.

- Combine honey, soy sauce, lemon juice, ketchup, and hoisin sauce. Layer drumsticks and honey mixture in 4- or 5-quart slow cooker. Stir to coat.

- Cover and cook on low for 7–9 hours until chicken registers 170 degrees F on a meat thermometer.

**BBQ Drumsticks**

Make recipe as directed, except add ½ cup barbecue sauce and 1 teaspoon chili powder. Omit five-spice powder, soy sauce, and hoisin sauce. Broil the drumsticks, rub with the garlic mixture, then cook as directed.

**Sweet and Sour Drumsticks**

Make recipe as directed, except add ⅓ cup apple cider vinegar and ⅓ cup sugar to the honey mixture. Omit five-spice powder, soy sauce, and hoisin sauce. Broil, rub, and cook drumsticks as directed.

*Make Sauce*

- One of the nice things about slow cooking is that you can vary proportions in a recipe and it will still work beautifully.

- You can use more or less honey or ketchup, or substitute cocktail sauce or pasta sauce for the ketchup.

- Add your favorite herbs to this recipe, too. Some dried oregano and thyme would be nice.

- You can make the sauce ahead of time; just store it covered in the refrigerator. Layer with the chicken when you're ready.

*Layer Drumsticks*

- If you want to make part of this recipe ahead of time, you can't broil the drumsticks and set them aside.

- Whenever you partially cook meat, whether broiled or browned in a pan, you must fully cook it immediately.

- If you don't follow this rule, bacteria could grow on the meat. Be safe, not sorry.

- Because of the high sugar content of this sauce, it can burn easily. Check the food after 5 hours.

# STUFFED CHICKEN BREASTS
## Chicken breasts are easy to stuff and are delicious with any filling

Stuffed chicken breasts are such an elegant entree. They impress guests and the flavor combinations are really delicious. And they're easier to make than you might think.

There are a few ways to stuff chicken. One is to pound the boneless, skinless breasts so they are thin enough to wrap around the filling. For a second method, you can cut a pocket in the side of the breast and fill it. Or you can stuff the filling

mixture between the skin and the flesh.

Invent your own fillings by using these basic proportions, and then combine your favorite ingredients and flavors. When you create a masterpiece, write it down so you don't forget it.

**Yield: Serves 6**

### Ingredients

4 slices bacon

1 tablespoon butter

2 shallots, minced

2 cloves garlic, minced

1 cup chopped ham

1 1/2 cups shredded Swiss cheese

6 boneless, skinless chicken breasts, flattened

1/4 cup sour cream

1 cup white sauce

1/2 cup chicken broth

1/2 cup grated Parmesan cheese

*Chicken Cordon Bleu*

- Cook bacon until crisp; crumble and set aside. Drain skillet; add butter. Cook shallots and garlic.

- Remove to bowl; add ham and bacon; cool 10 minutes. Add Swiss cheese.

- Divide mixture among breasts; roll up, enclosing filling; use toothpicks to secure. Place chicken in 4- or 5-quart slow cooker.

- Mix sour cream, white sauce, and chicken broth; pour over chicken. Cover; cook on low for 7–8 hours until done.

- Sprinkle with Parmesan and remove toothpicks. Serve.

**Easier Chicken Cordon Bleu**

Make recipe as directed, except use boneless, skin-on chicken breasts. Make the filling and stuff it between the skin and the flesh. Dredge chicken in flour; brown in 2 tablespoons oil, skin side down. Place in slow cooker, add sauce, and cook on low 8–9 hours.

**Tex-Mex Cordon Chicken**

Make recipe as directed, except add 2 minced jalapeño peppers to the garlic mixture. Omit shallot; add 1 chopped onion. Omit ham; use 1 cup chopped cooked chorizo sausage. Use Pepper Jack cheese instead of Swiss. And use 1 cup salsa in place of the chicken broth for the sauce.

## *Pound Chicken*

- To pound chicken, place smooth side down on plastic wrap; top with more plastic wrap.

- Gently pound the chicken using the smooth side of a meat mallet or a rolling pin. Don't pound too hard or you'll tear the flesh.

- When the breasts are ¼ inch thick, remove the top sheet of plastic wrap and add filling.

- You can pound the chicken ahead of time; wrap well and store in the refrigerator.

## *Fill Chicken*

- You should use about ⅓ cup of the filling mixture for each chicken breast.

- If the breasts are large, you may be able to use more. Don't overstuff the chicken; you want the filling to stay enclosed.

- Use the plastic wrap to help you roll the chicken around the filling; don't wrap the plastic into the chicken!

- Use toothpicks to hold the seam together. You can also tie the chicken closed with kitchen twine.

# CHICKEN MEATBALLS

## Meatballs made with chicken are tender and delicate

Meatballs aren't usually made of chicken, but when properly seasoned and cooked, they can be meltingly tender.

These meatballs are naturally lower in fat than beef or pork meatballs. For best results, use mixed dark and white meat ground chicken. If you use all white-meat chicken, the meatballs can dry out easily. In meat dishes, the fat not only carries the flavor, but conserves moisture.

As with beef and pork meatballs, combine all of the filler ingredients before you add the chicken. Then when they are well mixed, add the chicken and work gently with your hands to incorporate everything.

Flavor your meatballs any way you'd like: with Asian ingredients, Tex-Mex flavors, or Mediterranean ingredients.

**Yield: Serves 6**

### Ingredients

½ cup minced onion

1 tablespoon minced gingerroot

2 cloves garlic, minced

1 tablespoon butter

1 teaspoon salt

⅛ teaspoon cayenne pepper

1 egg

¾ cup soft breadcrumbs

1 ¼ pounds ground chicken, dark and white meat

2 cups white sauce

½ cup chicken broth

1 cup shredded Havarti cheese

*Creamy Chicken Meatballs*

- In medium saucepan, cook onion, ginger, and garlic in butter; remove to large bowl.

- Add salt, pepper, egg, and breadcrumbs; mix. Add chicken and mix gently.

- Form into 1-inch meatballs. Gently brown in butter in skillet; remove to 3- or 4-quart slow cooker.

- To skillet, add white sauce, broth, and Havarti cheese; pour over meatballs. Cover and cook for 5–7 hours on low until chicken registers 165 degrees F.

**Greek Chicken Meatballs**
Cook onion and garlic in butter; omit gingerroot. Add salt, pepper, egg, and breadcrumbs. Add ½ teaspoon dried oregano, ¼ cup grated Parmesan cheese, and ½ teaspoon lemon zest. Add chicken; brown as directed. Add ½ cup lemon juice and ½ cup sliced olives to white sauce; omit cheese.

**Tex-Mex Chicken Meatballs**
Cook onion and garlic in butter; add 1 minced jalapeño. Omit gingerroot. Add ⅓ cup grated Cotija cheese and 2 teaspoons chili powder to breadcrumbs. Brown meatballs; place in slow cooker with white sauce and 1 cup salsa. Omit broth and Havarti.

*Form Meatballs*

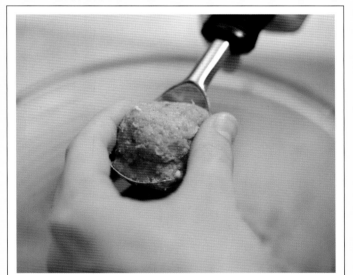

- For perfectly sized meatballs, use a small ice-cream scoop. This tool won't compact the mixture, so the meatballs stay tender.

- Spray the scoop with non-stick cooking spray so the meatballs release easily.

- You can roll them lightly between your hands so they are perfectly round. You can make them ahead of time and refrigerate until you're ready to cook.

- The meatballs are very delicate, so handle with care. Don't press down on them as they cook.

*Layer Meatballs and Sauce*

- The tender meatballs will hold together well if they are first browned, either in a pan or under the broiler.

- Still, be careful when you layer them in the slow cooker. If some break apart, that's okay. The dish will still taste wonderful.

- When testing the final temperature, be sure that the thermometer probe sits in the middle of a meatball.

- You can also break a meatball in half and test it with a thermometer.

# MOROCCAN CHICKEN SALAD
## A hearty and nutritious chicken salad

Chicken salads, made with ingredients cooked in the slow cooker, are a real treat, especially when the weather is hot. Use root vegetables along with the chicken; this is a fancy variation on potato salad.

The foods of Morocco include couscous, lemon, cumin, and cilantro. Fresh vegetables are used in quantity.

This salad uses the liquid in the slow cooker to cook the couscous. Not only is this easy, but it flavors the couscous with all of the ingredients that cooked into that liquid.

Regular plain yogurt works well, but if you can find thick Greek yogurt, use it. It has a fabulous tang and texture that will set the salad apart.

**Yield: Serves 6–8**

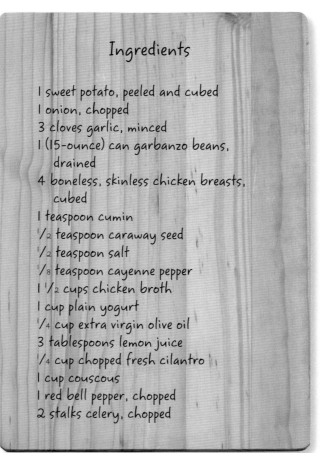

### Ingredients

1 sweet potato, peeled and cubed
1 onion, chopped
3 cloves garlic, minced
1 (15-ounce) can garbanzo beans, drained
4 boneless, skinless chicken breasts, cubed
1 teaspoon cumin
$1/2$ teaspoon caraway seed
$1/2$ teaspoon salt
$1/8$ teaspoon cayenne pepper
$1 1/2$ cups chicken broth
1 cup plain yogurt
$1/4$ cup extra virgin olive oil
3 tablespoons lemon juice
$1/4$ cup chopped fresh cilantro
1 cup couscous
1 red bell pepper, chopped
2 stalks celery, chopped

*Moroccan Chicken Salad*

- In 4-quart slow cooker, layer potato, onion, garlic, and garbanzo beans; top with chicken.

- Sprinkle with cumin, caraway, salt, and pepper; add chicken broth. Cover and cook on low 7–8 hours.

- Mix yogurt, olive oil, lemon juice, and fresh cilantro. Remove chicken mixture from slow cooker with slotted spoon; add to salad.

- Add couscous to liquid in slow cooker; let stand 5 minutes, then add to salad along with bell pepper and celery. Stir and chill for 3–4 hours before serving.

### All American Chicken Potato Salad

Use 4 peeled, cubed russet potatoes in place of the sweet potato. Omit garbanzo beans, cumin, and caraway. Add 1 teaspoon each dried basil and thyme leaves. For dressing, combine ½ cup each mayonnaise and yogurt, 3 tablespoons mustard, and ¼ cup milk. Add chicken, potatoes, celery, and bell peppers.

### Wild Rice Chicken Salad

Place 1 ½ cups wild rice in slow cooker. Add 2 cups chicken broth, onion, garlic, 1 teaspoon dried marjoram, and ½ teaspoon each salt and pepper. Omit sweet potatoes, beans, cumin, caraway. Add chicken; cook. Add chicken mixture to 1 cup yogurt, ½ cup mayonnaise, 3 tablespoons mustard, and 1 cup cubed Havarti cheese.

## *Layer Ingredients*

- It's important that the potatoes are in the liquid, so place them in the bottom of the slow cooker.

- You can substitute chicken thighs for the breasts; just increase cooking time to 8–9 hours.

- The combination of potato, garbanzo beans, and couscous is classically Middle Eastern.

- This salad should be made ahead of time. Add the chicken to the dressing while it's hot, so it will stay juicy.

## *Mix Salad*

- By adding the hot ingredients to the salad dressing, the food will absorb the flavors of the dressing.

- Make sure you use quick-cooking couscous that will absorb the liquid without additional cooking.

- It's a good idea to make extra dressing. After the salad has chilled in the refrigerator, you may want to add more.

- Or you can pass additional dressing at the table, letting your guests dress their own salads.

# CHICKEN THIGHS

## Dark meat combines beautifully with sweet cherries in this rich dish

Chicken thighs cook very well in the slow cooker. They have more fat, so they won't dry out or become tough, as can happen with white meat.

The only difference between preparing chicken thighs or chicken breasts in the slow cooker is the cooking time. The thighs do take a bit longer. Remember that boneless meat always cooks for a shorter time period than bone-in cuts.

Chicken thighs have a stronger flavor than breasts, so they can stand up to more intense flavors. Think about incorporating assertive ethnic flavors, like chiles, peppers, strong cheeses, and herbs such as oregano or rosemary.

Serve this dish or any sauced chicken dish with hot cooked rice or pasta.

**Yield: Serves 6**

### Ingredients

2 onions, chopped

8 boneless, skinless chicken thighs, cubed

1 teaspoon salt

1/8 teaspoon cayenne pepper

1 teaspoon dried tarragon leaves

1 cup chicken broth

1 (15-ounce) can dark cherries in water, drained

2 tablespoons cornstarch

1/3 cup cherry preserves

2 tablespoons lemon juice

1/3 cup sliced almonds, toasted

*Cherry Chicken Thighs*

- Place onion in bottom of 3 ½-quart slow cooker. Sprinkle chicken with salt, pepper, and tarragon; add to slow cooker.

- Pour chicken broth over all. Cover and cook on low for 6–8 hours until chicken is done.

- Add drained cherries to slow cooker. Combine cornstarch, preserves, and lemon juice; stir into slow cooker.

- Cover and cook on high for 20–30 minutes until sauce is thickened. Sprinkle with almonds and serve over rice.

**Italian Chicken Thighs**

Cook recipe as directed, omitting tarragon, cherries, preserves, lemon juice, and almonds. Add 1 (14.5-ounce) can diced tomatoes, undrained, ¼ cup tomato paste, 3 cloves minced garlic, and 1 teaspoon dried Italian seasoning. Thicken mixture with 1 tablespoon cornstarch in ¼ cup water.

**Lemon Chicken**

Place 2 chopped onions and 3 cloves garlic in slow cooker. Add chicken, sprinkle with salt, pepper, and tarragon. Add broth, ⅓ cup lemon juice, and ¼ cup honey. Cook as directed. Thicken mixture with 1 tablespoon cornstarch in ¼ cup water.

*Season Meat*

*Cherries and Cherry Preserves*

- Make sure that you trim off any visible fat, especially if the meat isn't browned before it is added to the slow cooker.

- It's important to season the meat well. This brings out the flavor of the meat.

- You can use purchased or homemade chicken broth or stock. Boxed stocks are usually higher quality than canned.

- For bone-in, skin-on thighs, brown first, then cook for 8–9 hours on low.

- Make sure that you use plain cherries, not pie filling. They are found in the canned fruit aisle of the supermarket.

- Check the cherries carefully before adding to the slow cooker to make sure there are no pits.

- Cherry preserves have pieces of whole fruit, while cherry jelly is made from juice.

- Serve this dish, which is intensely flavored, over plain white or brown hot cooked rice.

SLOW COOKED CHICKEN

# CHICKEN DUMPLING STEW
## Slow cookers were made for stews; the aroma is irresistible

Dumplings are a very old-fashioned food that is pure comfort. Dumplings and chicken are a classic combination.

Dumplings, which are basically soft drop biscuits, cook well in the slow cooker as long as you follow a few rules. Mix the batter very gently; overworking makes tough dumplings. Be sure the liquid is bubbling when you add the dumplings. Don't lift the lid while the dumplings are cooking.

You can use these dumplings in soup or stew, with beef or pork. Make the dumplings just before you want to cook them; the batter doesn't hold well.

This one-dish meal needs just a fruit or spinach salad for a perfect evening.

**Yield: Serves 6**

### Ingredients

1 onion, chopped
3 cloves garlic, minced
4 carrots, cut into chunks
2 stalks celery, chopped
8 boneless, skinless chicken thighs, cubed
4 cups chicken broth
1 cup apple juice
2 cups water
$1/2$ teaspoon salt
$1/8$ teaspoon pepper
1 teaspoon dried thyme leaves
2 tablespoons lemon juice
1 $1/2$ cups baking mix
$1/3$ cup sour cream
$1/4$ cup milk
$1/3$ cup grated Romano cheese
$1/3$ cup chopped flat-leaf parsley

*Grandma's Chicken Dumpling Stew*

- In 4- or 5-quart slow cooker, place onion, garlic, carrots, and celery. Top with chicken thighs.

- Pour over chicken broth, apple juice, water, salt, pepper, and thyme. Cover and cook on low for 8–9 hours.

- Stir in lemon juice. Place baking mix in a medium bowl. Add sour cream, milk, and cheese; stir just until mixed.

- Drop dumplings onto bubbling chicken mixture; cover; cook on high 20–30 minutes until dumplings are cooked. Sprinkle with parsley and serve.

## •••• RECIPE VARIATION ••••

**Bacon Chicken Dumpling Soup**
Cook 5 strips bacon until crisp; drain, crumble, and refrigerate. Drain all but 2 tablespoons drippings from pan; cook onion and garlic 5 minutes. Combine all stew ingredients in slow cooker as directed; omit apple juice. Mix dumplings as directed. Add bacon to soup, then dumplings; cook as directed.

## YELLOW LIGHT

Be sure that your baking mix is fresh. There should be an expiration date or "best if used by" date stamped onto the package. If it's too old, the baking powder won't react with the liquid and your dumplings will be hard and flat.

### Prepare Ingredients

- To mince garlic, first hit with the side of a knife to loosen the peel. Remove peel and discard.

- Slice garlic into strips, then cut across. Gather the pieces together and cut through again until pieces are fine and even.

- Cut carrots into 1 ½-inch chunks. Peel the carrots before cutting them.

- Remove visible fat from the chicken thighs and then cut into even pieces about 1 inch square.

### Add Dumplings

- Measure the baking mix by lightly spooning into a measuring cup; level off with back of knife.

- Stir dumpling mixture just until dry ingredients are moistened.

- Work quickly when dropping the dumplings into the stew. Use a tablespoon measure and drop batter from the side of a spoon.

- Don't lift the lid until 20 minutes have passed. Cut a dumpling in half to check doneness; the dumplings should not be doughy, but should be evenly cooked through.

POULTRY STEWS

# MULLIGATAWNY STEW

## Chicken, cooked with curry and vegetables, makes a classic English stew

Mulligatawny is an Indian word that means "pepper water." The soup is spicy with curry powder, also called garam masala. You can find curry powder in the grocery store. The more expensive blends have saffron for flavor and color. The inexpensive brands use turmeric, which provides color.

Other traditional ingredients for this recipe include apples,

coconut milk, onions, and leek. If you want to use white rice, stir in ⅓ cup along with the apple; cook until tender.

For a more intense flavor, you can add curry paste instead of curry powder. These pastes are found in the ethnic foods aisle and are very concentrated; use a few teaspoons.

**Yield: Serves 6–8**

## Ingredients

2 onions, chopped

4 cloves garlic, minced

3 carrots, cut into chunks

1 leek, chopped

½ cup uncooked brown rice

5 boneless, skinless chicken thighs, chopped

2 boneless, skinless chicken breast halves

1 teaspoon salt

⅛ teaspoon cayenne pepper

1 tablespoon curry powder

¼ teaspoon allspice

2 tablespoons minced gingerroot

7 cups chicken stock

1 Granny Smith apple, chopped

½ cup coconut milk

½ cup sour cream

1 tablespoon lemon juice

2 tablespoons cornstarch

*Mulligatawny Stew*

- In 5- or 6-quart slow cooker, place onions, garlic, carrots, leek, and rice.

- Sprinkle chicken with salt, pepper, curry powder, and allspice; add to slow cooker. Add gingerroot and chicken stock.

- Cover and cook on low for

6–8 hours or until chicken is thoroughly cooked. Shred chicken breasts and return to slow cooker.

- Add apple; turn slow cooker to high. In bowl, combine remaining ingredients and mix; add to slow cooker. Cover and cook on high for 30–40 minutes.

**Lentil Mulligatawny Soup**
Cook as directed, except omit rice. Add ½ cup dried green lentils in place of the rice. Use 8 boneless, skinless chicken thighs, cubed; omit chicken breasts. Omit curry powder and allspice; use 2 teaspoons red curry paste dissolved in ¼ cup chicken broth. Omit sour cream; increase coconut milk to 1 cup.

**ZOOM**

Coconut milk is not the liquid found inside a fresh coconut. Coconut milk is made by blending coconut with hot water. It is about 20 percent fat. This fat will rise to the surface and form a solid layer in the canned product; use the fat and liquid. Coconut milk is good for you; it has antibacterial agents and healthy fats.

## Layer Ingredients

- To prepare the leek, trim off tough green parts and the root. Cut the leek in half lengthwise.

- Place the leek in a sink of cold water and separate into layers. As the leek grows, it traps sand in between the layers.

- Make sure all the sand and grit are removed, then slice the leek crosswise and chop.

- Prepare the chicken breasts as directed so they cook through, but don't overcook.

## Combine Ingredients

- The chicken will be so tender it should fall apart. To shred it, place on a plate and pull apart using 2 forks.

- Return the chicken and any juices to the slow cooker.

- The apple will cook quickly; you want to make sure it doesn't turn into applesauce, but remains in discrete pieces.

- If the coconut milk has a solid layer on top, that's fine. Add it to the stew and stir a few times to dissolve.

# TURKEY SWEET POTATO STEW

## Sweet potatoes and other root vegetables add color and nutrition to this easy stew

The richness of sweet potato adds wonderful flavor, texture, and nutrition to this easy stew. It's the perfect dish to serve during the holiday season, or any of the cold winter months.

Sweet potatoes have to be peeled before cooking in a stew. Use a swivel-bladed peeler to remove the skin, then cut the hard potatoes into cubes.

Turkey tenderloin is part of the turkey breast. It's very low fat and tender. There may be a tendon running along the tenderloin; just cut through it.

Serve this hearty stew with a spinach salad made with apples and dried cherries, and some crunchy breadsticks.

**Yield: Serves 6–8**

### Ingredients

2 sweet potatoes, peeled and cubed

3 carrots, cut into chunks

1 onion, chopped

4 cloves garlic, minced

2 pounds turkey tenderloin, cubed

1 teaspoon salt

$1/8$ teaspoon pepper

$1/2$ teaspoon cinnamon

$1/8$ teaspoon nutmeg

3 tablespoons flour

6 cups chicken stock

1 teaspoon dried thyme leaves

$1 1/2$ cups frozen peas

*Turkey Sweet Potato Stew*

- In 5- or 6-quart slow cooker, place sweet potatoes, carrots, onion, and garlic.

- Toss turkey pieces with salt, pepper, cinnamon, nutmeg, and flour; add to slow cooker. Add chicken stock and thyme.

- Cover and cook on low for 7–9 hours until sweet potatoes are tender and turkey is done.

- Add peas; cover and cook on high for 20–30 minutes until hot. Stir and serve.

**Turkey Potato Stew**
Use 4 russet potatoes, peeled and cubed, in place of the sweet potatoes. Omit cinnamon and nutmeg; add 1 teaspoon dried basil to the flour mixture. Cook as directed. Omit thyme leaves.

**African Sweet Potato Stew**
Cook as directed, except omit carrots, cinnamon, and nutmeg. Add 1 teaspoon ground cumin and 1 tablespoon grated gingerroot. Omit peas, add ¼ cup peanut butter mixed with ⅓ cup chicken broth; cook on high 15 minutes. Sprinkle with ½ cup chopped peanuts.

*Prepare Ingredients*

- You can prepare the potatoes, carrots, onion, and garlic ahead of time; just cover tightly.

- Be sure that the sweet potatoes and carrots are at the bottom of the slow cooker because they take longer to cook.

- The turkey tenderloin shouldn't have any visible fat. Cut into even 1-inch pieces so the turkey cooks in the right time.

- You can substitute chicken breasts or thighs for the turkey tenderloin; cook 6–7 hours for breasts, 7–8 hours for thighs.

*Toss Turkey with Spices*

- Don't prepare the turkey ahead of time. It should be placed in the slow cooker with the broth when tossed with the flour and spices.

- You can vary the spices used in this recipe. Use allspice and cardamom instead of cinnamon and nutmeg.

- Other ingredients that would work well in this recipe include bell peppers or sliced mushrooms.

- This stew reheats well. Remove from the slow cooker when done and place in shallow container to cool.

# CHICKEN FRUIT STEW
## Dried fruits are a delicious addition to this easy chicken stew

Add some dried fruit to a chicken stew for a delightful change of pace. Dried fruits cook exceptionally well in the slow cooker.

The fruits add a remarkable depth of flavor to this easy stew. Choose high quality fruits with little or no preservatives. You can also use dates, prunes, or dried cranberries or cherries in this recipe.

This combination of flavors and textures is reminiscent of the Middle East, so the spices, cinnamon and cardamom, are from that region as well.

You could make this recipe with chicken breasts; cook them whole and cook for 5–7 hours on low.

Serve the stew over couscous or basmati rice pilaf for the perfect finishing touch.

**Yield: Serves 6**

### Ingredients

2 onions, chopped

4 cloves garlic, minced

1 tablespoon grated gingerroot

2 pounds boneless, skinless chicken thighs, cubed

1/4 cup flour

4 teaspoons curry powder, divided

1 teaspoon salt

1/4 teaspoon cayenne pepper

7 cups chicken broth

1 cup apple juice

1 cup golden raisins

1/2 cup dried currants

1/4 cup chopped dried apricots

1 cup sour cream

1/4 cup pomegranate seeds or chopped cherries

*Chicken Fruit Stew*

- In 5-quart slow cooker, combine onions, garlic, and gingerroot. Toss chicken with flour, 2 teaspoons curry powder, salt, and pepper; add to slow cooker.

- Pour chicken broth and apple juice over; add raisins, currants, and dried apricots.

- Cover and cook on low for 6 hours; stir. Cover and cook on low for another 1–2 hours or until chicken is thoroughly cooked.

- Combine sour cream, 2 teaspoons curry powder, and pomegranate seeds in small bowl. Serve stew and top with sour cream mixture.

**Mexican Chicken Fruit Stew**
Cook recipe as directed, except add 1 tablespoon chili powder to onion mixture. Omit gingerroot, cinnamon, cardamom, raisins, currants, and apricots. Add 2 poblano peppers, chopped, and 1 (8-ounce) can pineapple tidbits. In last 20 minutes, stir in 1 chopped apple and 1 chopped banana.

**Chicken Tagine**
Make recipe as directed, except add ½ cup kalamata olives and ½ cup sliced black olives to onion mixture. Omit gingerroot, cinnamon, cardamom, raisins, and currants. Add 1 teaspoon dried marjoram leaves, ⅛ cup cider vinegar, and ¼ cup brown sugar. Omit sour cream topping.

## *Prepare Chicken*

- Trim excess fat off the chicken thighs. Because they aren't browned before cooking in this recipe, this is a necessary step.

- You can increase the spice level in this dish, or add other warm spices, including nutmeg or allspice.

- Make sure the chicken is evenly coated with the flour. If there's any flour mixture left over, just add it to the slow cooker.

- The fruits will plump in the liquid as they cook, absorbing the other flavors in the dish.

## *Sour Cream Topping*

- The flour that coats the chicken will thicken the stew as the recipe cooks.

- If you'd like a thicker stew, stir in 2 tablespoons cornstarch dissolved in ¼ cup water; cook on high 15 minutes.

- You can make the topping ahead of time and keep it in the refrigerator until you're ready to eat.

- To remove pomegranate seeds, cut fruit in half and hit the rounded side of each half with a spoon.

# RICH TURKEY STEW
## Heavy cream and melted cheese make this stew special

This rich stew is really a meal in a bowl. Classic flavors like bacon, onion, and garlic flavor turkey in a thickened sauce that's full of cheese.

You can use your own favorite cheeses in this dish; shredded Pepper Jack or Havarti would also be delicious. Just be sure that the cheese is evenly shredded, and add it at the end of cooking time.

Bacon drippings are a traditional way to flavor poultry recipes. The flavor will permeate the dish when you cook the onions and garlic in the drippings.

This stew will be even better the second day, if there's any left. Refrigerate it, then place it in a saucepan. Heat on the stove until the soup bubbles, then serve.

**Yield: Serves 6–8**

### Ingredients

5 slices bacon
I onion, chopped
3 cloves garlic, minced
2 cups baby carrots
2 potatoes, peeled and cubed
2-pound turkey tenderloin, cubed
$\frac{1}{4}$ cup flour
I teaspoon salt
$\frac{1}{8}$ teaspoon pepper
I teaspoon dried marjoram
2 cups white sauce
4 cups chicken broth
2 cups frozen green beans
I cup frozen peas
I cup shredded Gouda cheese
$\frac{1}{2}$ cup shredded Muenster cheese

*Rich Turkey Stew*

- Cook bacon until crisp; drain, crumble, and refrigerate. In drippings, cook onion and garlic 5 minutes.

- In 5-quart slow cooker, combine onion, garlic, carrots, and potatoes. Toss turkey with flour, salt, pepper, and marjoram.

- Add turkey to slow cooker with white sauce and broth; stir. Cover and cook on low for 7–9 hours.

- Add green beans and peas; cover and cook on high for 20 minutes. Add cheeses and bacon; cover and cook on high for 20–30 minutes.

**Tex–Mex Turkey Stew**

Cook as directed, except add 2 minced jalapeños with the onion and garlic. Omit bacon; use 2 tablespoons olive oil. Omit potatoes and baby carrots; use 2 cubed sweet potatoes and 3 sliced carrots. Add 2 tablespoons chili powder. Omit peas; use shredded Cheddar cheese in place of Gouda.

**Tuscan Turkey Stew**

Cook as directed, except use turkey bacon. Omit potatoes; use 8-ounce package cremini mushrooms, sliced. Omit marjoram; use ½ teaspoon fennel seed and 1 teaspoon dried Italian seasoning. Add 1 (15-ounce) can cannellini beans in place of peas.

## *Add White Sauce*

- The white sauce can be made ahead of time and frozen. Thaw it in the refrigerator overnight before using.

- The chicken broth can be homemade or purchased. Boxed broths are higher quality than canned.

- Stir gently but thoroughly, so the white sauce is well incorporated with the broth.

- You might want to stir once or twice during cooking time; add another 20 minutes to the time if needed.

## *Add Cheeses*

- Don't shred the cheeses ahead of time; they should be freshly shredded so they don't dry out.

- Packaged shredded cheeses can be used, but they are coated with anti-caking agents that can prevent smooth melting.

- If you can find a preshredded cheese blend that doesn't have any other ingredients, it will work well.

- This recipe won't work well with the keep-warm feature after you add the cheese; serve it immediately.

# GREEK CHICKEN STEW
## Add tender veggies at the end of cooking time so they are perfect

Greek flavors and ingredients are the perfect companions to tender chicken in this easy stew.

Typical Greek ingredients include lentils, olive oil, lemon, oregano, garlic, and olives. Chicken, with its mild flavor, blends very well with these ingredients. Substitute cubed chicken thighs for the breasts; cooking time will be the same.

You can vary the vegetables to your own taste. Use parsnips instead of potatoes; use baby carrots in place of regular carrots, add sliced portobello or shiitake mushrooms in place of the celery, This is an easy way to make a recipe your own.

Serve this hearty stew with a mixed green salad with a creamy herb dressing, some grilled garlic toast, and rice pudding for dessert.

**Yield: Serves 6–8**

### Ingredients

3 potatoes, peeled and cubed

4 carrots, cut into chunks

3 stalks celery, chopped

I onion, chopped

4 cloves garlic, minced

I cup green lentils

2 pounds boneless, skinless chicken breasts

5 cups chicken broth

I cup dry white wine

I teaspoon dried basil

I teaspoon dried oregano

1/2 teaspoon dried thyme

1/2 cup sliced olives

I cup frozen peas

2 tablespoons lemon juice

*Chicken Vegetable Stew*

- In 5-quart slow cooker, combine potatoes, carrots, celery, onion, garlic, and lentils.

- Top with chicken breasts; pour broth and wine over and sprinkle with basil, oregano, and thyme.

- Cover and cook on low for 6–8 hours until chicken is done and vegetables are tender. Remove chicken and shred; set aside.

- Using a potato masher, mash some of the vegetables. Add chicken, olives, peas, and lemon juice; stir well, cover, and cook on high 15 minutes.

**Moroccan Chicken Stew**

Make as directed, except use 2 peeled and cubed sweet potatoes in place of the potatoes. Omit celery, basil, oregano, thyme, and olives. Add ½ teaspoon each turmeric and cinnamon and ⅛ teaspoon cloves. Add 1 (14.5-ounce) can diced tomatoes and 1 (15-ounce) can drained chickpeas.

**French Chicken Stew**

Make as directed, except cook 6 slices bacon; drain and refrigerate. Cook onion and garlic in bacon fat. Omit lentils, oregano, and olives. Add 1 (14.5-ounce) can diced tomatoes, 1 teaspoon dried tarragon, and 12 red new potatoes.

*Prepare Ingredients*

- Pick over the lentils, removing any extraneous material. Rinse them well, then drain and add to the recipe.

- The chicken breasts are cooked whole and shredded later so they don't overcook by the time the vegetables are tender.

- You can omit the wine if you'd like. The alcohol will not cook out of the stew. The flavor isn't crucial to the recipe.

- Substitute apple juice, or just use more chicken broth or water.

*Add Vegetables*

- Mashing and pureeing vegetables is an easy and low-fat way to thicken any stew.

- Turn the slow cooker off before you use the potato masher, for safety reasons.

- You can also remove some of the vegetables and puree them in a food processor or blender, then return to stew.

- When you return the chicken to the slow cooker, add any juices that may have accumulated on the plate.

POULTRY STEWS

# CARNITAS

## Shredded pork flavored with Mexican spices is tender and crisp

Carnitas are made of slowly cooked pork, which is then shredded and then fried to make crispy edges. This full-flavored recipe can be served as is, added to chili or barbecue, or used as a filling for enchiladas or burritos.

This is a great recipe to make ahead of time. Cook the pork completely, shred it, then combine with some of the cooking liquid. Let stand 15 minutes, then freeze.

Let the pork stand in the refrigerator overnight to thaw. Then place in a roasting pan and roast as directed, adding about 10 minutes to the cooking time.

You can make your version of carnitas as mild or spicy as you'd like. Add chile peppers for more heat.

**Yield: Serves 6–8**

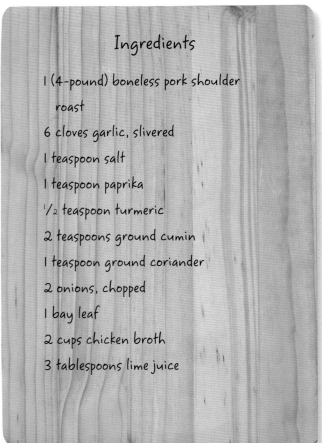

### Ingredients

1 (4-pound) boneless pork shoulder roast

6 cloves garlic, slivered

1 teaspoon salt

1 teaspoon paprika

1/2 teaspoon turmeric

2 teaspoons ground cumin

1 teaspoon ground coriander

2 onions, chopped

1 bay leaf

2 cups chicken broth

3 tablespoons lime juice

*Carnitas*

- Cut the pork into 6 pieces. Cut slits in pork and insert garlic slivers.

- In small bowl, mix salt, paprika, turmeric, cumin, and coriander; rub on pork. Place with onions in 4-quart slow cooker.

- Add bay leaf and chicken broth. Cover; cook on low for 9–10 hours until pork is tender. Shred pork.

- Place pork in large roasting pan; top with 1 cup cooking liquid and lime juice. Stir, then bake at 400 degrees F 20 minutes until edges are crisp.

**Carnitas Enchiladas**
Make the carnitas as directed. Mix 1 (10-ounce) can of enchilada sauce with 1 cup salsa. Place ½ cup of this sauce in 9 x 13-inch pan. Divide carnitas among 12 flour tortillas; add 1 cup shredded Pepper Jack cheese; roll up. Place in pan; add remaining sauce. Bake at 375 degrees F for 35–45 minutes.

**Carnitas Tamales**
Make carnitas as directed. Make tamale dough using a corn flour masa mix. Spread dough on cleaned and soaked cornhusks. Divide pork mixture on top of the dough; fold up and tie with kitchen twine. Place in steamer; steam 40 minutes.

*Shred Pork*

*Brown Pork in Oven*

- Evenly space the garlic slivers in the pork. Press the garlic completely into the pork so it disappears.

- The garlic will flavor the pork and slowly mellow to become sweet as it cooks.

- You can use your own spice blend, or choose a Mexican or Tex-Mex packaged spice blend to season the pork.

- Use 2 forks to shred the pork; it should fall apart very easily as you work.

- You can skip the step of browning the pork in the oven if you'd prefer it to be soft and tender.

- But the crisp edges, contrasting with the tender interior, are part of the appeal of the dish.

- You can make the pork mixture ahead of time, shred it, combine with some liquid, and refrigerate.

- Then when you're ready to eat or make enchiladas, brown the pork in the oven as directed.

# STUFFED MANICOTTI
## This elegant recipe is flavorful and so easy

Cooking pasta in the slow cooker can be problematic. The point between al dente and mushy can occur in minutes, if not seconds. Most recipes tell you to cook pasta in a separate pot and add to the slow cooked recipe at the end of cooking time.

But some pasta will cook fairly well in the slow cooker. Just like brown rice, whole grain pastas stand up better to the long, moist cooking environment. And large pastas, like manicotti or large shells, turn out well.

It's important to only partially cook the shells before draining and filling with the sausage mixture. Don't cook them completely or they will fall apart as you serve the dish.

**Yield: Serves 8**

### Ingredients

1 pound spicy pork sausage

1 onion, chopped

3 cloves garlic, minced

2 cups baby spinach leaves

2 tablespoons tomato paste

1/2 cup chicken broth

1 teaspoon dried oregano

1/8 teaspoon pepper

16 manicotti shells

1 (26-ounce) jar pasta sauce

1 cup shredded mozzarella cheese

1/4 cup grated Parmesan cheese

Stuffed Manicotti

- Bring a large pot of water to a boil. Meanwhile, cook sausage with onion and garlic in skillet; drain.

- Add spinach, tomato paste, broth, oregano, and pepper to skillet; simmer 5 minutes. Cook shells for 5 minutes; drain, rinse with cold water, and drain again.

- Fill shells with pork mixture. Place 1/2 cup pasta sauce in bottom of 5-quart slow cooker. Top with shells.

- Pour pasta sauce over. Cover and cook on low for 7–8 hours. Top with cheeses, let stand until melted.

**Pesto Manicotti**
Make recipe as directed, except omit pork sausage, spinach, tomato paste, and chicken broth. Cook onions in 1 tablespoon olive oil; mix with 1 (16-ounce) package ricotta cheese, 1 (3-ounce) package cream cheese, and 1 (7-ounce) container basil pesto. Stuff shells with this mixture; proceed.

**Tex-Mex Manicotti**
Make recipe as directed, except omit spinach leaves. Add 1 (15-ounce) can refried beans and 1 minced jalapeño to sausage mixture. Add 1 cup salsa to pasta sauce. Top with shredded Pepper Jack cheese and Cotija cheese in place of the mozzarella and Parmesan cheeses.

## *Cook Pork*

- You can usually find bulk pork sausage in the supermarket. It comes without a casing and looks like hamburger.

- If all you can find is sausage in casings, just slit the side of each sausage and remove the meat; discard casings.

- There are lots of different levels of spices in pork sausage. They range from hot to sweet to mild; choose your favorite.

- Work the sausage with a fork as it cooks so it breaks into small pieces.

## *Fill Shells*

- Don't cook the shells ahead of time; they will dry out if not filled immediately.

- The water the shells cook in should be well salted. Some cooks throw in a handful of salt; Italians say the water should be as salty as the sea.

- When the shells have cooked for 5 minutes in the boiling water, rinse them with cold water.

- This will stop the cooking and make the shells easier to handle. Drain well and fill using a small spoon.

PORK & LAMB ENTREES

# STUFFED PORK CHOPS
## Pork chops are stuffed with an apple and raisin filling

Pork chops are an excellent choice for the slow cooker. Chops can be tough if overcooked or cooked in a very dry heat environment. The slow cooker renders them fork tender.

To stuff, pork chops have to be cut at least 1 ¼ inch thick. These might only be available if you ask your butcher. You may have to order them ahead of time. Boneless chops are easier to work with, but bone-in chops have more flavor. If you choose bone-in chops, cook for 8–10 hours on low.

You can stuff pork chops with any type of stuffing; use your favorite. Just don't overstuff them, or they may split during cooking.

**Yield: Serves 6**

### Ingredients

6 (1 ½-inch-thick) boneless pork chops

1 teaspoon salt

⅛ teaspoon pepper

2 tablespoons butter

1 onion, chopped

2 cloves garlic, minced

1 Granny Smith apple, peeled and
  chopped

½ cup dark raisins

1 cup soft fresh breadcrumbs

1 teaspoon dried thyme leaves

1 cup chicken broth, divided

2 cups white sauce

*Apple Stuffed Pork Chops*

- Cut a pocket in each of the pork chops, cutting almost to other side. Sprinkle chops with salt and pepper.

- In small saucepan, cook onion and garlic in butter until tender. Remove from heat; add apple, raisins, breadcrumbs, thyme, and ¼ cup broth.

- Stuff chops with this mixture. Layer into 4- or 5-quart slow cooker.

- In bowl, combine remaining broth and white sauce; pour over chops. Cover and cook on low for 7–9 hours until pork is cooked.

### Cornbread Stuffed Pork Chops

Make recipe as directed, except add 2 cups crumbled cornbread in place of breadcrumbs. Omit apple and raisins; add 4 slices crisply cooked crumbled bacon. You may need to add more chicken broth to the stuffing mixture to make it moist. Cook as directed.

### Vegetable Stuffed Chops

Make recipe as directed, except omit apple and raisins. Add 1 cup frozen corn, thawed, and 1 red bell pepper, chopped, to the stuffing mixture. Omit white sauce; use 1 (15-ounce) can tomato sauce, seasoned with 1 teaspoon dried Italian seasoning.

*Cut Pocket in Chops*

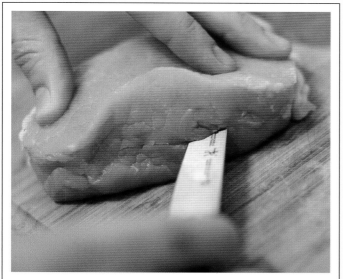

- Use a small, sharp knife to cut the pocket in the chops and work slowly and carefully.

- Be sure that your knife stays parallel to the chops so you don't poke holes or make weak spots in the meat.

- Make the opening as small as you can, and move the knife back and forth to enlarge the pocket.

- Sprinkle the chops inside and out with the salt and pepper. And don't pack the stuffing into the chops.

*Layer Chops in Slow Cooker*

- As you layer the chops and the sauce in the slow cooker, be sure that there is a bit of sauce in between the layers.

- This will help keep the pork moist and will help the chops cook evenly.

- You can flavor the white sauce any way you'd like. Add some more herbs, add some cheese for richness, or add spices.

- To make it easier, use 1 (16-ounce) jar of bottled Alfredo sauce instead of the white sauce.

# BBQ RIBS
## Glazed and tender pork ribs are easy to make in the slow cooker

Most people have only eaten ribs cooked on the grill. They are delicious, but there's nothing as meltingly tender as ribs cooked in the slow cooker.

There are a few steps to take before the ribs are ready to put in the slow cooker. The ribs are very fatty; you have to remove some of that fat.

There are several ways to do this: broil the ribs, bake them in the oven, or boil in water or broth.

Broiling and baking not only remove fat, but also add flavor through browning and caramelization The proteins and sugar in the meat combine to form complex compounds that create rich flavor. Use your favorite barbecue sauce, whether homemade or purchased, and enjoy.

**Yield: Serves 6**

### Ingredients

2 (2-pound) racks baby back ribs

$1/2$ teaspoon salt

$1/4$ teaspoon pepper

1 teaspoon five-spice powder

2 tablespoons olive oil

2 onions, chopped

1 cup barbecue sauce

$1/4$ cup hoisin sauce

3 tablespoons honey

3 tablespoons soy sauce

2 tablespoons Dijon mustard

3 cloves garlic, minced

1 tablespoon minced gingerroot

*Asian Glazed Ribs*

- Preheat oven to 375 degrees F. Cut ribs into 2-rib portions and place in roasting pan. Sprinkle with salt, pepper, and five-spice powder; drizzle with olive oil.

- Roast ribs for 1 hour; remove and drain. Place onions in 4- or 5-quart slow cooker; top with ribs.

- Combine remaining ingredients in bowl and pour over ribs.

- Cover and cook on low for 8–9 hours, or on high for 4–5 hours, until ribs are very tender.

### Classic BBQ Ribs

Make recipe as directed, except omit five-spice powder, hoisin sauce, soy sauce, and gingerroot. Add 1 teaspoon dried oregano and 1 teaspoon dried basil leaves. Add 1 cup ketchup to the sauce mixture. Bake ribs, then cook as directed.

### Spicy BBQ Ribs

Make recipe as directed, except add 2 minced jalapeños to onion mixture. Omit five-spice powder, hoisin sauce, and soy sauce. Add 1 cup hot salsa to the sauce mixture. Bake ribs as directed, then cook in slow cooker with sauce.

*Brown Ribs*

*Add Sauce*

- The ribs are seasoned before they are browned to bring out as much flavor as possible.

- There will be quite a bit of fat in the pan when you roast the ribs; be careful removing it from the oven.

- Do not roast the ribs ahead of time. Never partially cook meat then hold it for later cooking.

- You can place the ribs in large racks; just be sure they fit in the slow cooker.

- Substitute your own favorite homemade barbecue sauce, or use a purchased sauce instead of this recipe if you'd like.

- Create your own sauce by varying the ingredients. Add herbs, more tomato products like salsa, or fresh tomatoes.

- The ribs will be so tender they will probably fall off the bone. Be careful removing them from the slow cooker.

- Serve these ribs with fresh, crisp coleslaw and lots of napkins; they're messy but fun to eat.

# LAMB RAGOUT
## Tender lamb cooks beautifully in the slow cooker

This classic ragout pairs lamb with lots of tender root vegetables and spices.

A ragout is a simple French stew of meat and vegetables, seasoned with herbs and spices. It can be made with any meat, but typically is made from lamb or beef.

The flavors blend and meld beautifully in the slow cooker. If you want to punch up the flavor even more, you can add a few stems of fresh oregano just before serving.

Serve this delicious ragout with hot cooked rice or pasta, and a spinach salad.

**Yield: Serves 6–8**

### Ingredients

2 pounds lamb shoulder, cut into
   2-inch cubes
1 teaspoon salt
1 teaspoon paprika
1 teaspoon cinnamon
1/4 teaspoon pepper
1 teaspoon dried oregano
3 tablespoons flour
2 tablespoons olive oil
2 sweet potatoes, peeled and cubed
1 parsnip, peeled and cubed
2 onions, chopped
4 cloves garlic, minced
1/2 cup dry red wine
2 cups beef broth
1/4 cup chopped parsley

*Middle Eastern Lamb Ragout*

- Toss lamb cubes with salt, paprika, cinnamon, pepper, oregano, and flour. Brown in olive oil in large skillet.

- Place potatoes, parsnip, onions, and garlic in bottom of 4- or 5-quart slow cooker. Add lamb as it browns.

- Add wine to skillet; bring to a boil, scraping up drippings. Add broth and pour over food in slow cooker.

- Cover and cook on low for 8–9 hours or until lamb is very tender. Shred lamb, using fork; stir ragout, sprinkle with parsley, and serve.

## • • • • RECIPE VARIATION • • • •

**French Lamb Ragout**
Make recipe as directed, except use 1 ½ pounds small red potatoes and 1 turnip, peeled and chopped, in place of the sweet potatoes. Omit paprika, cinnamon, and oregano; use 2 teaspoons fresh rosemary leaves.

## ZOOM

Lamb is a very tender meat, especially when properly cooked. The most common cuts include shoulder roast, leg, and loin. Fresh lamb should be firm and have a pink or red color with even, white marbling running through the meat. It may have a coating of fat; leave this on, as it adds flavor. You may need to order lamb from your butcher as it isn't always kept in stock.

## Layer Ingredients

- Leave any visible fat on the lamb as you cut it into cubes. Unlike other red meats, lamb fat is delicate and carries much of the flavor.

- When you brown the lamb, don't cook it too long. Just brown it on 2 sides; this adds color and flavor.

- Prepare the vegetables and place them in the slow cooker before browning the lamb.

- Be sure to thoroughly scrape up the pan drippings with the wine; there's lots of flavor in those brown bits.

## Shred Lamb

- The lamb should fall apart when the recipe is done, but you may need to pull some pieces apart.

- You can use 2 forks to shred the lamb, or your fingers if you're careful.

- Return the lamb and any juices to the ragout and stir to incorporate. If you are adding fresh oregano, stir it in at this time.

- Keep the lamb in fairly large pieces to provide a texture and flavor counterpart to the dish.

PORK & LAMB ENTREES

# LAMB SHANKS

## This classic dish is topped with gremolata, a mixture of lemon and parsley

The lamb shank is a very flavorful cut of meat that contains bone. Shanks can be tough if not cooked correctly; they have to be braised for a long period of time. So the slow cooker is the perfect choice. Pairing the shanks with white beans makes this the perfect one-dish meal.

The lamb shanks you buy in the store should be "cracked."

This means the butcher makes some cuts in the meat so the shanks don't curl up tightly while cooking. You can place garlic cloves in those slits.

Serve this dish with garlic toast to soak up the juices, and a spinach and fruit salad.

**Yield: Serves 4**

### Ingredients

2 cups dried white beans

$1/4$ cup flour

1 teaspoon salt

$1/4$ teaspoon pepper

1 teaspoon dried thyme

1 teaspoon dried marjoram

4 lamb shanks

2 tablespoons olive oil

1 onion, chopped

3 cloves garlic, minced

2 carrots, sliced

2 cups chicken stock

1 cup dry red wine

1 (14.5-ounce) can tomatoes, undrained

gremolata

*Lamb Shanks with White Beans*

- Sort beans; cover with cold water. Let stand overnight. Drain and rinse.

- Combine flour, salt, pepper, thyme, and marjoram; sprinkle over lamb shanks. Brown in oil over medium heat. Add onion to the lamb after lamb is browned; cook 2 minutes.

- Place beans in 4-quart slow cooker. Add lamb, onion, garlic, and carrots; pour stock over. Cover and cook on low for 8–9 hours.

- Add wine and tomatoes; cook, uncovered, on high for 40 minutes. Sprinkle with gremolata and serve.

**Gremolata**
Finely chop ½ cup flat-leaf parsley. In small bowl, place 3 peeled garlic cloves. Add ½ teaspoon salt; work with back of spoon until paste forms. Add 2 teaspoons lemon juice, parsley, and 1 teaspoon lemon zest; mix and refrigerate.

**Greek Lamb Shanks**
Make recipe as directed, except mince together 1 clove garlic and ¼ cup onion; press into slits in lamb. Omit marjoram; add 1 teaspoon dried oregano and ½ teaspoon dried mint. Omit beans; increase onions to 2 and carrots to 4. Cook as directed.

*Brown Lamb*

*Add Stock*

- It's important to brown the lamb well, to add color and flavor to the recipe.

- When browning the lamb, don't move the shanks until they release easily from the pan.

- When they do, turn them and brown on the second side. Cooking the onions will help release drippings.

- These drippings, or brown bits, that are stuck to the pan bottom have a lot of flavor and you don't want to lose them.

- The wine and tomatoes are added after the beans are cooked because their acidity will prevent the beans from softening.

- If you use 2 (15-ounce) cans cannellini beans, drained, instead of dried beans you can add the wine and tomatoes right away.

- The dish is cooked uncovered at the end to help evaporate some of the liquid.

- This also concentrates the flavor of the juices. Serve this dish in a bowl, not a plate.

# FISH AND POTATOES
## Cook potatoes for hours, then steam fish in the slow cooker

Seafood isn't commonly cooked in the slow cooker, and for good reason. Fish fillets, shrimp, salmon steaks, and other shellfish take only minutes to cook, and that just doesn't translate to the slow cooker.

But with a few tricks you can cook seafood to perfection in this appliance. The low, moist heat is really ideal for producing tender, melting fish and seafood.

Cook a base for the fish first. Cook potatoes, root vegetables, or wild rice or other grains first, then add the fish during the last hour or so of cooking time.

The fish will be perfectly cooked, and will pick up some of the other flavors in the dish.

**Yield: Serves 6**

### Ingredients

6 russet potatoes, cubed

1 onion, chopped

3 cloves garlic, minced

1/2 teaspoon salt

1/8 teaspoon pepper

1 teaspoon dried thyme leaves

1/2 cup chicken broth

1/4 cup light cream

1/2 cup shredded provolone cheese

2 pounds fish fillets

1/3 cup Dijon mustard

1/4 cup grated Parmesan cheese

### Cheesy Smashed Potatoes with Fish

- In 4-quart slow cooker, combine potatoes, onion, and garlic. Sprinkle with salt, pepper, and thyme.

- Pour chicken broth over. Cover and cook on high for 4 hours or until potatoes are tender.

- Turn off slow cooker and mash potatoes, leaving some pieces. Stir in light cream and provolone.

- Turn slow cooker to high and add fish fillets. Mix mustard and Parmesan cheese; spread over fish. Cover and cook for 45–60 minutes until fish flakes.

## • • • • • • • • • • • • • • • • • RECIPE VARIATION • • • • • • • • • • • • • • • • •

**Fish and Sweet Potatoes**
Make recipe as directed, except use 4 sweet potatoes, peeled and cubed, in place of the russet potatoes. Add ½ teaspoon cinnamon along with the thyme leaves. Use ½ cup heavy cream in place of the light cream. And spread the fish fillets with ¼ cup Dijon mustard; omit Parmesan cheese.

**Fish with Fluffy Mashed Potatoes**
Make recipe as directed, except reduce chicken broth to ½ cup. Peel the potatoes before cubing them. When potatoes are done, add ¼ cup softened butter and mash until smooth. Beat in cream, then top with fish fillets and Dijon-Parmesan mixture. Omit provolone cheese.

*Potatoes in Slow Cooker*

- Make sure that the potatoes are all the same size so they cook at the same time.

- You want the potato pieces to be fairly large, about 1 inch or so in width, because this is a rustic dish.

- Leave the skins on for more nutrition and fiber and an even more rustic dish!

- Mash the potatoes using a potato masher, a large spoon, or other handheld tool. For safety, turn off the slow cooker while you work.

*Add Topping*

- You can spread the topping individually on each fish fillet, or just pour it over the top of the fish in the slow cooker.

- The topping will help keep the fish moist, and gives the dish a pretty look.

- Use other types of mustard if you'd like; grainy mustard or a coarse mustard with visible seeds give a nice look.

- Sprinkle the dish with chopped parsley or some fresh thyme sprigs when done to add a pop of color.

# POACHED SALMON

## Salmon steaks, which are sturdy and thick, cook well on low in a few hours

Poached fish has been slowly simmered in a pan. The poaching liquid never comes to a boil; in fact, the French say the liquid is "smiling." But you can also poach fish in a slow cooker, with very little liquid. Low, moist heat, rather than a lot of liquid, achieves the poached effect. And that describes the slow cooker environment to a T.

Still, you have to keep an eye on the fish. When testing the fish, lift off the first layer with a large spatula and set aside. Test the fish in the middle of the stack. If the flesh flakes easily when a fork is inserted and twisted, it's done.

**Yield: Serves 6**

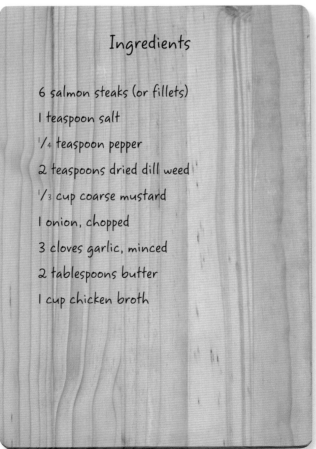

### Ingredients

6 salmon steaks (or fillets)

1 teaspoon salt

1/4 teaspoon pepper

2 teaspoons dried dill weed

1/3 cup coarse mustard

1 onion, chopped

3 cloves garlic, minced

2 tablespoons butter

1 cup chicken broth

*Dill Poached Salmon*

- Sprinkle salmon with salt, pepper, and dill weed. Spread thinly with mustard. Cook onion and garlic in butter until tender in small saucepan.

- Place 5 crumpled foil balls in the bottom of the slow cooker, or use a wire rack.

- Top with 2 salmon steaks and sprinkle with some onion and garlic; repeat layers twice.

- Pour chicken broth over all. Cover and cook on low for 3 ½–4 ½ hours or until salmon flakes when tested with fork.

········· YELLOW ●LIGHT ·········

The salmon steak is made by cutting 1-inch-thick pieces directly through the center of the fish. This cut has bones. The bones radiate along the thin "legs" of the steak, from the center bone. Tell your guests this so they can avoid the bones as they eat.

···· ● RECIPE VARIATION ● ····

**Marinated Poached Salmon Steaks**
For marinade, combine 2 tablespoons soy sauce, 3 tablespoons hoisin sauce, 2 tablespoons cider vinegar, 1 tablespoon vegetable oil, and 3 cloves minced garlic. Pour over salmon; marinate in the refrigerator 1–3 hours. Layer with onion and garlic mixture; top with broth and cook as directed.

## Layer Salmon

- It's important to have some of the onion and garlic mixture between the salmon steaks so they cook evenly.

- If you just plopped the salmon into the slow cooker, the mass would cook like a single piece of fish.

- And that would mean that the salmon steaks around the edges and on the bottom and top of the stack would overcook by the time the middle was done.

- So carefully layer those steaks with the vegetables for best results.

## How to Test Doneness

- There are 2 ways to test doneness. You can insert a fork directly into the flesh of the fish, and twist.

- When the salmon is done, it will flake. That means it will easily separate into long, thin fibers.

- Or you can test the salmon by temperature. Use an instant-read meat thermometer in the center of a steak.

- When done, the salmon will register 140–145 degrees F. Remove the salmon from the slow cooker immediately.

# SEAFOOD STEW
## Seafood and shellfish combine to make this delicious stew

Seafood stew is cooked like fish fillets and shellfish. The fish is added at the end of cooking time for perfect results.

When you cook a seafood stew on the stove, you do the same thing. The base of the stew—in other words, the vegetables and seasonings—cook until tender and blended, then you add the fish.

You can add any seafood to any slow cooker soup or stew recipe, as long as you follow these basic rules. Cut the fish fillets into cubes and cook 30–40 minutes on high. Shrimp and scallops will cook on high for 15–20 minutes. And whole fillets cook for about an hour on high heat.

Serve this hearty dish with a mixed green salad tossed with apples and pears.

**Yield: Serves 6**

### Ingredients

3 tablespoons olive oil
1 onion, chopped
4 cloves garlic, minced
2 tablespoons grated gingerroot
1 (8-ounce) package sliced mushrooms
2 stalks celery, chopped
1/4 cup minced celery leaves
2 tablespoons soy sauce
1/8 teaspoon pepper
1/2 teaspoon five-spice powder
1 (14.5-ounce) can diced tomatoes, undrained
1 cup white wine
5 cups seafood broth or clam juice
3 cups water
2 salmon steaks
1 cup bay scallops
1 cup medium raw shrimp

*Asian Seafood Stew*

- In 6-quart slow cooker, combine olive oil, onion, garlic, shallot, gingerroot, mushrooms, celery, and celery leaves.

- Add soy sauce, pepper, and five-spice powder; pour tomatoes, wine, broth, and water over. Cover and cook on low 7–8 hours.

- Stir soup. Cut salmon into 1-inch pieces; add to soup. Cover and cook on low for 20 minutes.

- Add scallops and shrimp. Cover and cook on low for 15–20 minutes or until shrimp and scallops are done.

## • • • • • • • • • • • • • • • RECIPE VARIATION • • • • • • • • • • • • • • •

**Italian Seafood Stew**
Cook onion and garlic in olive oil; omit ginger, celery leaves, soy sauce, and five-spice powder, Add 1 teaspoon dried thyme, ½ teaspoon dried oregano, and 1 teaspoon lemon rind. Omit salmon steaks; add cleaned mussels with shrimp and scallops.

**Greek Seafood Stew**
Cook onion and garlic as directed; omit ginger, celery and leaves, soy sauce, and five-spice powder. Add 1 chopped leek, 1 cup chopped fennel, 1 teaspoon dried oregano, and 1 bay leaf. Substitute white fish fillets for salmon. Stir in 2 tablespoons lemon juice and ¼ cup chopped parsley before serving.

### *Cook Soup Base*

- A good soup base uses lots of fresh vegetables and good olive oil.

- As they cook, the vegetables release their flavor into the stock or broth, flavoring the whole soup.

- You can use your favorite vegetables for this stew.

- Add sliced or baby carrots, leeks, or fresh chopped tomatoes.

- The soup base can cook for a longer period of time without overcooking. Cook for 8–9 hours with no problem.

### *Prepare Seafood*

- To prepare the salmon steaks, cut off the skin, or peel it off using a sharp knife.

- Remove the bones and feel the flesh with your fingers. There may be tiny bones, called pin bones, in the flesh.

- Remove these bones with tweezers and discard, then cut the salmon into chunks.

- The shrimp can be peeled or unpeeled, depending on if you want an elegant or rustic dish.

# JAMBALAYA

## Spicy sausage and tender shrimp cook in a velvety tomato sauce

Jambalaya is a festive dish—a combination of highly seasoned vegetables and lots of seafood. The original came from Louisiana, a blend of French, Spanish, and Creole influences.

This dish is one of the original one-pot meals, served over rice. Classic jambalaya combines sausages, chicken, tomatoes, and spices, but there are countless variations.

You can make your jambalaya as mild, hot, or smoky as you'd like. Add smoked crisply cooked bacon, Andouille or boudin sausage, or any type of seafood.

Serve jambalaya with lots of hot cooked rice to soak up all the delicious juices. All you need with this dish is a simple salad, either green or fruit, and some nice white wine.

**Yield: Serves 6**

### Ingredients

8 ounces smoked sausage, sliced
2 tablespoons butter
2 onions, chopped
4 cloves garlic, minced
1 teaspoon salt
$1/8$ teaspoon cayenne pepper
2 tablespoons flour
1 bay leaf
3 stalks celery, chopped
1 green bell pepper, chopped
1 red bell pepper, chopped
1 cup uncooked long-grain brown rice
1 1/2 cups chicken broth
2 (14.5-ounce) cans diced tomatoes, undrained
3 tablespoons tomato paste
1 cup clam juice
1 cup dry white wine
1 1/2 pounds raw medium shrimp

*Shrimp Jambalaya*

- In large saucepan, cook sausage until browned; drain, and drain fat from skillet.

- Add butter; cook onion and garlic until tender. Add salt, pepper, and flour; cook until flour begins to brown.

- Add bay leaf, celery, peppers, rice, and chicken broth; stir thoroughly. Pour into 4- or 5-quart slow cooker; add sausage.

- Add tomatoes, tomato paste, clam juice, and wine. Cover; cook on low 6–8 hours. Add shrimp; cook on high 15–20 minutes until shrimp is pink. Remove bay leaf.

## • • • • • • • • • • • • • RECIPE VARIATION • • • • • • • • • • • • •

**Mixed Seafood Jambalaya**
Make jambalaya as directed, except start with ½ pound smoked bacon, cooked crisp. Drain and crumble the bacon; drain pan but don't wipe. Add butter; cook onions and continue with the recipe. Use 1 pound shrimp, 1 pound mussels, and 1 pound clams during last 20 minutes.

**Rice for Jambalaya**
You can add cooked rice directly to the Jambalaya during the last 5 minutes of cooking time so it absorbs some of the liquid. Or cook white rice in chicken or seafood broth in a 1:2 ratio. You can add herbs to the rice for green rice, or saffron for yellow rice.

*Cook Vegetables*

*Add Shrimp*

- If you have a slow cooker with a stovetop-proof lining made of metal, cook the bacon and vegetables in that for less cleanup.

- Using the same container for cooking the sausage and for finishing the dish also ensures you don't lose a drop of flavor.

- Vary the proportion and combination of vegetables as you'd like. Add mushrooms, carrots, or fennel.

- The "holy trinity" of onion, celery, and green bell pepper is traditional in jambalaya.

- You can add the shrimp peeled or unpeeled. Peeling the shrimp makes the jambalaya easier to eat.

- But using unpeeled shrimp is very pretty and looks rustic.

- To peel shrimp, remove the legs and pull the shell from the shrimp. If the vein is visible (a dark line), remove it.

- To remove the vein, make a shallow cut down the back and rinse, or remove it by hand.

# SALMON WITH PILAF

## A rice pilaf cooks in the slow cooker, then is topped with salmon fillets

This dish is perfect for entertaining. Not only do you get perfectly cooked, tender, and flavorful salmon fillets, but a creamy and cheesy wild and brown rice pilaf to serve with it.

Wild rice and brown rice are the types that cook best in the slow cooker. Long-grain white rice will become mushy, and short-grain rice will be too sticky.

A rice pilaf consists of rice with other vegetables. Sometimes a sauce is added, and the pilaf is highly seasoned.

To serve, remove the salmon carefully with a large spatula to a serving plate; cover with foil. Remove the rice and pile in a bowl. Serve with dinner rolls and a fruit salad.

**Yield: Serves 6**

### Ingredients

2 shallots, minced

2 cloves garlic, minced

2 tablespoons butter

1 cup long-grain brown rice

1 1/2 cups wild rice

1 teaspoon dried marjoram leaves

1 teaspoon salt

1/8 teaspoon pepper

1 (8-ounce) package mushrooms, sliced

3 cups chicken broth

1 1/2 cups white sauce

1 cup shredded Swiss cheese

6 salmon fillets

1/3 cup grated Parmesan cheese

2 tablespoons chopped fresh parsley

1/4 cup ground almonds

*Salmon with Cheesy Rice Pilaf*

- Cook shallot and garlic in butter over medium-low heat until soft.

- Add both kinds of rice; cook and stir for 3 minutes. Place in 4-quart slow cooker. Add marjoram, salt, pepper, and mushrooms.

- Pour chicken broth and white sauce into skillet; simmer. Pour into slow cooker; cover; cook on high 3–4 1/2 hours until rice is tender.

- Add Swiss cheese to pilaf. Mix Parmesan, parsley, and almonds; sprinkle on salmon. Place salmon on pilaf; cover; cook on high 20–30 minutes until done.

## • • • • • • • • • • • • • • • RECIPE VARIATION • • • • • • • • • • • • • • •

**Salmon with Wild Rice Pilaf**
Make recipe as directed, except use 2 ½ cups wild rice instead of combination of wild and brown rice. Substitute 1 teaspoon dried thyme leaves for the marjoram, and use an 8-ounce package of cremini mushrooms, sliced. Sprinkle salmon with a combination of parsley and ½ cup green onions.

**Salmon with Brown Rice Pilaf**
Make recipe as directed, except use 2 ½ cups long-grain brown rice instead of the combination of wild and brown rice. Substitute 1 teaspoon dried oregano leaves for the marjoram. Add 1 cup sliced carrots. Top the salmon with a combination of chopped cilantro and Romano cheese.

### Cook Pilaf

- Look for wild rice that was naturally harvested, with very long grains. Some rice is mechanically harvested.

- This is fine, but some American Indians still harvest the rice by hand. This rice is not much more expensive, and supports a hallowed way of life.

- If you use grains that are short or broken, the finished pilaf will be mushy.

- Gently stir the pilaf before adding the salmon. Add more white sauce if the mixture seems dry.

### Add Salmon

- Try to arrange the salmon in a single layer, or overlap just a little bit, so it cooks evenly.

- If you'd prefer to use steaks instead of fillets, increase the cooking time to 50–60 minutes.

- Watch the cooking time carefully and remove the salmon when it flakes. Check for doneness at 20 minutes.

- For a more casual dish, when the salmon is done stir it into the rice mixture for a salmon pilaf.

# BACCALA STEW

## This old-fashioned stew is made with salt, or dried cod for lots of flavor

Baccala is salt cod, an unusual dried and salted fish that becomes very tender when soaked and cooked.

You may need to order baccala (also spelled *bacalhau*) from your butcher or an international foods store; it's not a common ingredient. And you must follow soaking and rinsing times exactly or the dish will be too salty.

Baccala stew can be made in many variations. Use your favorite vegetables, or take a chance and try something different: a combination of olives, prunes, and cauliflower in place of the tomatoes and potatoes. Serve with crisp garlic toast, a fresh fruit salad, and some red wine to savor.

**Yield: Serves 6**

### Ingredients

I pound dried salted cod

2 onions, chopped

3 cloves garlic, minced

5 russet potatoes, peeled and cubed

2 red tomatoes, peeled seeded, and
    diced

I (8-ounce) can tomato sauce

2 tablespoons flour

$1/8$ teaspoon pepper

I cup white wine

3 cups seafood broth

$1/2$ cup sliced green olives

I tablespoon fresh thyme leaves

*Baccala Stew*

- Place cod in large bowl; cover with water. Refrigerate for 12–18 hours, changing water 3 times.

- When ready to cook, remove the skin and pick out bones with tweezers. Cut into chunks.

- Place onions, garlic, and potatoes in 4-quart slow cooker. Top with fish and tomatoes. Mix tomato sauce, flour, pepper, and wine in bowl; pour over fish.

- Add broth. Cover and cook on low for 6–8 hours until vegetables are tender. Add olives and thyme; stir.

130

Baccala (or *bacalhau*) is dried and salted cod. It's used in Portuguese cooking, and was a staple during the winter months. When you choose baccala, make sure that the piece is uniformly thick and the flesh is pliable, not hard. Soak for 12 hours, changing the water 3 times.

## • • • • • RECIPE VARIATION • • • • •

**Classic Baccala Stew**
Make recipe as directed, except use 12 small red potatoes in place of the russet potatoes. Add 4 prunes, chopped, and 1 head cauliflower, cut into florets. Omit tomatoes and tomato sauce; add 1 (14.5-ounce) can diced tomatoes, undrained. Cook recipe as directed.

### Prepare Baccala

- Make sure that you completely change the water when soaking the baccala.

- The fish is too salty to eat as is, and even after a simple soaking in water it will be too salty.

- To make sure that the fish isn't too salty, you can cook a small piece in a bit of butter until flaky, then try it.

- If it's still salty, change the water again and soak for another 1–2 hours.

### Add Other Ingredients

- The tomatoes must be peeled because the tomato skins can have an unpleasant texture when cooked for a long period of time.

- You can use other types of olives. Authentic olives would be kalamata, or wrinkled oil-cured olives.

- Be careful with the olive amount; the stew is already salty. Taste before adding.

- You can add other fresh herbs at the end; some chopped parsley or cilantro would be nice.

# CHILI WITH BEANS

## True chili doesn't use beans, but this hybrid version is rich and delicious

Chili with beans might not be authentic, but it is very satisfying. And the inexpensive beans add nutrition and fiber.

Using canned beans in the slow cooker is much easier than using dried. Dried beans can be tricky to cook, especially when salt and tomatoes are used in the recipe. These ingredients stop the beans from softening properly. But canned beans are very high in salt, so have to be drained and rinsed before using.

This is a fairly mild chili. Jalapeño peppers are hot, but on the mild end of the chile heat range. For more heat, use habañero chiles or Scotch bonnets. Season to taste!

**Yield: Serves 6**

### Ingredients

1 pound beef bottom round, cubed
2 tablespoons flour
1 teaspoon salt
$1/8$ teaspoon cayenne pepper
2 tablespoons olive oil
2 onions, chopped
3 cloves garlic, minced
1–2 jalapeño chiles, minced
1 (6-ounce) can tomato paste, divided
2 (14.5-ounce) cans diced tomatoes, undrained
1 (8-ounce) can tomato sauce
1 cup beef broth
2 tablespoons Dijon mustard
2 tablespoons chili powder
1 teaspoon ground cumin
2 (15-ounce) cans kidney beans, drained

*Tex-Mex Chili with Beans*

- Toss beef with flour, salt, and pepper. Brown in olive oil in large skillet; drain and place in 4- or 5-quart slow cooker.

- Add onions, garlic, and jalapeños to drippings remaining in skillet; cook and stir for 1 minute. Add 2 tablespoons tomato paste;

- let brown for 3–4 minutes.

- Pour 1 can diced tomatoes into skillet and bring to simmer, scraping up drippings. Add to slow cooker along with remaining ingredients.

- Cover and cook on low for 8–9 hours or until chili is thick and blended.

**Ground Beef Chili**
Make as directed, except use 1 pound ground beef in place of the bottom round. Omit flour; reduce salt to ½ teaspoon. Brown the ground beef with the onions and garlic; drain and combine with remaining ingredients. Cook as directed.

**Beefier Chili**
Make recipe as directed, except use 2 pounds of the beef bottom round, chuck steak, or sirloin tip, or a combination of these cuts. Add another cup of beef broth; keep other ingredients the same, except add 1 (4-ounce) can diced green chiles, undrained.

*Brown Beef*

- As the beef browns, the flour will cook too. This releases the starch in the flour, which will help thicken the chili.

- Letting the tomato paste brown for a few minutes also adds great depth of flavor to the mixture.

- Don't let the tomato paste burn; you're looking for a dark brown color.

- Then scrape up the drippings with the juice from the diced tomatoes and mix everything together in the slow cooker.

*Stir Chili*

- If necessary, you can thicken the chili with a cornstarch slurry. About 2 tablespoons cornstarch to ¼ cup water or beer is perfect.

- Or you can thicken the chili by cooking it on high for 20–30 minutes with the lid removed.

- Mashing some of the beans will thicken the chili by releasing starch. Do this about 30 minutes before serving.

- Sprinkle the chili with shredded cheese; top with sour cream, crushed tortilla chips, or guacamole.

# CLASSIC BEEF CHILI
## Classic chili includes chunks of tender beef in a red sauce

While most people know that true chili is made without beans, many don't know that true chili is also made without tomatoes. The red color of this kind of chili comes from dried red chiles.

The chiles are soaked in water and chopped, or just crushed and added to the mixture. They will soften in the long cooking time. You can find these chiles in the ethnic foods aisle of your supermarket, or in Mexican markets.

Use an inexpensive cut of beef for this recipe. Chuck steak, sirloin tip, or top or bottom round are good choices. These meats benefit from the moist environment and long slow cooking time. The meat should fall apart when done.

**Yield: Serves 6**

## Ingredients

2 pounds bottom round steak

2 tablespoons chili powder

1 teaspoon cumin

1 teaspoon salt

1/4 teaspoon pepper

3 tablespoons flour

1 teaspoon dried oregano leaves

4 slices bacon

2 onions, chopped

4 cloves garlic, minced

2 jalapeño chiles, minced

2 dried ancho chiles, crushed

1 cup water

4 cups beef broth

*A Bowl of Red*

- Cut steak into 2-inch cubes; trim excess fat. Toss with chili powder, cumin, salt, pepper, flour, and oregano.

- In large skillet, cook bacon until crisp; remove, drain, crumble, and refrigerate. Brown beef cubes in drippings.

- Place beef in 4-quart slow cooker. Cook onions and garlic in drippings until tender; add to slow cooker.

- Add all remaining ingredients. Cover and cook on low for 8–9 hours until chili is thick and beef is very tender; stir in bacon and serve.

## •••• RECIPE VARIATION ••••

**Ground Beef Chili**
Make recipe as directed, except use 2 pounds of lean ground beef in place of the bottom round steak. Omit the bacon; cook the ground beef with onion and garlic, drain, and add to slow cooker. Reduce the chili powder to 1 tablespoon; add 1 teaspoon ground dried ancho chiles.

**ZOOM**

There is chili powder, and there is ground chile powder. Chili powder is a combination of ground chiles, cayenne pepper, cumin, paprika, and oregano or garlic powder. Ground chile powder is made of just the dried chile, finely ground. Both of these powders are hot and spicy, but their flavors do vary. Buy several kinds and experiment to find your favorites.

### *Brown Beef*

- The beef is cut into large cubes so, after it falls apart in the chili, you'll still be able to see it and bite into a chunk of meat.

- When the beef is browned in the bacon drippings, it will pick up that smoky flavor.

- Some chili recipes call for adding liquid smoke or smoke seasonings. Use smoky bacon instead for a more authentic flavor.

- The onions and garlic add water to the pan to help release the drippings and brown bits.

### *Combine Ingredients*

- Add the bacon at the end of cooking time so it keeps its texture. You can stir it in at the beginning; it will melt into the chili.

- Make sure that the dried and crushed chiles are covered with liquid as they cook.

- The chiles will rehydrate and add great flavor along with heat to the chili.

- Top this chili with some sour cream mixed with chopped tomatoes and avocados for a cooling contrast.

# WHITE CHILI
## White chili uses chicken or turkey along with green chiles

Not all chilis have to be tomato-based. When they don't include tomatoes or red chiles, these soups are called white or green chili. These hearty soups are made with chicken or pork, completing the "white" theme. They can be just as spicy as red chili.

White beans used in white or green chili include butter beans, cannellini beans, pinto beans, navy beans, black-eyed peas, and small white beans—either dried or canned.

Chili can be thickened by adding a cornstarch slurry, coating the meat in flour, or pureeing or mashing some of the beans. Thickness and texture are up to you.

Serve chili with cornbread or tortilla chips, and some cold Mexican beer.

**Yield: Serves 6**

### Ingredients

6 boneless, skinless chicken thighs, cubed

2 tablespoons flour

1 teaspoon salt

$1/4$ teaspoon pepper

$1/2$ teaspoon dried thyme

$1/2$ teaspoon dried basil

2 onions, chopped

5 cloves garlic, minced

2 green bell peppers, chopped

2 jalapeño peppers, minced

1 (15-ounce) can pinto beans, drained

2 (15-ounce) can cannellini beans, drained

4 cups chicken broth

2 tablespoons cornstarch

1 (4-ounce) can chopped green chiles, undrained

*White Chicken Chili*

- Toss chicken with flour, salt, pepper, thyme, and basil. Place onions and garlic in 4- or 5-quart slow cooker.

- Top with chicken; add green bell peppers, jalapeño peppers, pinto beans, and 1 can cannellini beans.

- Puree second can of

cannellini beans and add to slow cooker along with broth. Cover and cook on low for 7–8 hours.

- In small bowl, combine cornstarch and green chiles; stir into slow cooker. Cover and cook on high for 20–30 minutes until thickened.

**Green Pork Chili**
Make recipe as directed, except substitute 1 pound boneless pork chops, cut into 1-inch cubes, for the chicken thighs. Instead of the pinto beans, add 1 cup green enchilada sauce and 1 cup green salsa. Finish the chili with 2 tablespoons lime juice and ½ cup chopped fresh cilantro.

**Creamy White Chicken Chili**
Make chili as directed, except use 4 whole boneless, skinless chicken breasts instead of the thighs. Do not puree beans. To thicken chili, combine 2 tablespoons cornstarch with 1 cup light cream instead of the green chiles. Cook on high 20–30 minutes until thickened. Top with chopped fresh cilantro.

*CHILIS*

## Prepare Chicken

- For more heat, add 1–2 teaspoons ground chile powder to the mixture used to coat the chicken.

- You can brown the chicken in some olive oil or butter before adding it to the slow cooker for more flavor.

- If you want to use chicken breasts in this recipe, do not cube them; keep them whole and shred after cooking.

- Reduce the cooking time to 5–7 hours if you use chicken breasts so they don't overcook.

## Layer Food in Slow Cooker

- It's important to layer the food as directed. The onions take longest to cook, so have to be placed at the bottom of the slow cooker.

- You may not need to add the cornstarch mixture if you think the chili is thick enough.

- You can stay with the green and white theme and garnish the chili with sour cream and chopped avocados.

- Or to add a pop of color, texture, and flavor, top with fresh chopped tomatoes, green onion, and cilantro.

# FOUR PEPPER CHILI
## Vegetarian chili is rich, thick, and delicious

Chili is a perfect choice for a hearty vegetarian soup. All of the peppers and onions add lots of flavor and heat, and beans add protein, fiber, B vitamins, and texture.

Chile peppers can be added as is, just chopped, minced, diced, or sliced. But for more flavor and a silky texture, roast the chiles and remove the skin.

This is easy to do, and takes just a few extra minutes. You can buy chiles already broiled and skinned, but these don't have as much flavor.

Use your favorite combination of chiles, other vegetables, and beans in vegetarian chili. And for topping, cheeses, guacamole, salsa, and tortilla chips are good choices.

**Yield: Serves 6**

## Ingredients

2 onions, chopped
4 cloves garlic, minced
1 jalapeño pepper, minced
1 red bell pepper, cut in half
1 green bell pepper, cut in half
1 poblano chile pepper, cut in half
1 (15-ounce) can black beans, drained
1 (15-ounce) can red beans, drained
1 (15-ounce) can white beans, drained
2 cups vegetable broth
2 tablespoons chili powder
1 teaspoon salt
1/4 teaspoon pepper
1 teaspoon dried oregano
1 teaspoon dried marjoram
1 bay leaf

*Four Pepper Chili*

- Place onion and garlic in 4- or 5-quart slow cooker. Preheat broiler.

- Place peppers on broiler rack, skin side up. Broil for 7–8 minutes until skin browns. Remove and wrap in foil; let steam 5 minutes. Remove and discard skins.

- Chop peppers and add to slow cooker along with all remaining ingredients.

- Cover and cook on low for 7–8 hours until chili is thickened. Remove bay leaf and thicken with cornstarch slurry, if needed; serve.

**Dried Bean Chili**

Make recipe as directed, except use ¾ cup each dried red beans, black beans, and white beans in place of the canned beans. Soak beans overnight and place in bottom of slow cooker; top with remaining ingredients. Cook on low for 8–9 hours.

**Vegetarian Crumble Chili**

Make chili as directed, except add 1 (12-ounce) package of frozen vegetarian meat substitute crumbles to the slow cooker. This product is safe to cook from the frozen state. Omit the white beans and the marjoram.

*Broil Chiles*

*Remove Blackened Skin*

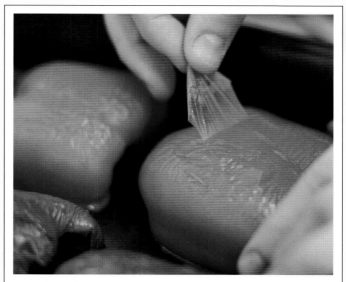

- When you broil or cook chiles over high heat, the skin blackens and wrinkles and the flesh starts to cook.

- This process gives the peppers a smoky flavor that adds greatly to the chili.

- Rearrange the peppers often while broiling. The skin should turn dark brown or even black.

- But you want to make sure just the skin is black, not the flesh. Then place the chiles in a paper bag to steam.

- As the chiles steam, the skin loosens from the flesh and becomes easy to peel away.

- Peel using your fingers or tweezers. Remove as much of the skin as you can; you don't have to remove all of it.

- Never rinse chiles that have been roasted and peeled; you'll rinse away all the flavor you built.

- When the chiles are cool enough to handle, discard the skin, remove seeds, then slice or chop according to the recipe.

# BLACK BEAN CHILI

## Kidney beans, while classic, aren't the only legume used in chili recipes

Black beans, also called turtle beans, are shiny and black on the surface, but brown or red inside. They look like the back of a turtle shell, which is how they got their name.

Black beans are very nutty, with a perfect creamy texture. They pair beautifully with other grains like wild rice or barley to add more flavor and nutrition to the chili.

In chili, canned beans just work better than dried. Dried beans won't soften in the presence of tomatoes, and tomatoes are an integral part of most chili recipes. Look for low-salt and flavored black beans in the supermarket.

Top black bean chili with sour cream and shredded cheese.

**Yield: Serves 6**

## Ingredients

1 cup wild rice, rinsed

2 onions, chopped

3 cloves garlic, minced

1 jalapeño pepper, minced

3 (15-ounce) cans black beans, drained

2 (14.5-ounce) cans diced tomatoes, undrained

1 (8-ounce) can tomato sauce

3 cups water

1 tablespoon chili powder

1 teaspoon dried basil leaves

1 teaspoon dried marjoram leaves

1 bay leaf

*Black Bean Wild Rice Chili*

- Place wild rice in bottom of 4- or 5-quart slow cooker. Top with onions, garlic, and jalapeño.

- Rinse black beans and drain again. Add to slow cooker along with remaining ingredients.

- Cover and cook on low for 7–9 hours, stirring halfway through cooking time, until wild rice is tender.

- Remove bay leaf and thicken chili with cornstarch slurry if desired. Serve with sour cream and chopped chives.

**Barley Black Bean Chili**

Make recipe as directed, except add 1 cup medium pearl barley in place of the wild rice. Omit the tomato sauce and add 1 cup beef or chicken broth, or water for a vegetarian chili. Omit basil leaves; add 1 teaspoon dried oregano leaves.

**Super Spicy Black Bean Chili**

Make recipe as directed. Add 1 minced habanero pepper and 1 (4-ounce) can diced green chiles, undrained, to the slow cooker. Add 1 roasted and peeled poblano pepper, and increase chili powder to 2 tablespoons. Add 2 teaspoons dried ancho chile powder with other ingredients.

## *Rinse Black Beans*

- To rinse black beans, open the can and pour the contents directly into a sieve or colander placed in the sink.

- Run cold water over the beans, gently stirring them with your fingers or shaking the colander.

- You want to remove the thick, sweet liquid the beans are packed in.

- You can add a small amount of that sweet liquid to thicken the chili, but more than ¼ cup isn't desirable.

## *Stir Chili*

- Stir the chili only once during cooking time. Remember, every time you lift the lid you should add 20 minutes to the cooking time.

- Stir quickly but gently, and be sure to scrape the sides of the slow cooker.

- A heatproof rubber spatula or wooden spoon are good tools to use. This will clean the sides and mix all the ingredients.

- Stir the chili once again when it's done, just before you serve it, to mix all the ingredients and flavors.

# BEEF AND BEAN CHILI
## Ground beef makes an inexpensive and hearty chili

The least expensive and heartiest of all the chilis, this recipe uses a special ingredient: seasoned canned beans. In the supermarket, you'll find all kinds of seasoned canned beans, ranging from mild ranch-style to super hot chile beans.

Add these beans, liquid and all, to the slow cooker. Don't drain this type of bean, because the liquid carries ingredients like chiles and garlic and provides lots of flavor.

Think about using other forms of meat: pork sausage like hot Italian or linguica, exotic sausage like andouille or mortadella. Remove the sausage from its casing and break up, then brown with the onions and garlic.

Enjoy this easy chili with a green salad and tortilla chips.
**Yield: Serves 6**

### Ingredients

I pound ground beef

I onion, chopped

2 cloves garlic, minced

I (4-ounce) can chopped green chiles, undrained

I (8-ounce) jar salsa

2 (15-ounce) cans kidney beans, drained

I (15-ounce) can ranch-style chili beans, undrained

I tablespoon chili powder

1/2 teaspoon ground cumin

1/2 teaspoon pepper

2 cups beef broth

I tablespoon cornstarch

1/2 cup tomato juice

*Thick Beef and Bean Chili*

- In large skillet, brown ground beef with onion and garlic until beef is done; drain and add to 4-quart slow cooker.

- Add all remaining ingredients except for the cornstarch and tomato juice.

- Cover and cook on low for 8–9 hours, or on high for 4–5 hours, until chili is blended.

- In small bowl, combine cornstarch with tomato juice; stir into slow cooker. Cover and cook on high for 20 minutes; serve.

**· · · · RECIPE VARIATION · · · ·**

**Mixed Bean and Beef Chili**

Make recipe as directed, except use 2 (15-ounce) cans kidney beans in sauce, and 1 (15-ounce) can pinto beans in sauce in place of the kidney beans and ranch-style chili beans. You could also use spicy pinto beans or chili beans with jalapeño and red pepper.

*GREEN ● LIGHT*

Keep a good supply of canned beans in your pantry and you'll be able to make a chili at a moment's notice. Nothing's easier than opening some cans, pouring them into the slow cooker, adding some spices, and turning it on. You can prepare dinner in 5–10 minutes!

## *Brown Ground Beef*

- You can brown the ground beef ahead of time, as long as it's fully cooked before you refrigerate it.

- In fact, when there's a sale on ground beef, stock up and have a marathon cooking session.

- Cook ground beef with onions and garlic, then package into freezer containers.

- You can use this mixture to start a multitude of recipes, including chili and spaghetti sauce.

## *Add Cornstarch Slurry*

- A cornstarch slurry is the best way to thicken this type of chili.

- Use care when making the slurry. Be sure that the cornstarch is completely dissolved in the water before adding to the chili.

- And stir the chili thoroughly while you're adding the slurry. You don't want to come upon a congealed lump of cornstarch!

- If the chili gets too thick, just add some more broth or tomato juice to it.

# QUINOA STEW
## Quinoa is a delicious ancient and nutritious grain

Vegetable stews cooked in your slow cooker are among the healthiest meals on the planet. The sealed slow cooking environment traps all of the vitamins, and the low, slow heat prevents the formation of harmful compounds that can form when food is cooked at a high heat.

Quinoa has some special properties that must be noted. It is gluten-free, so is a good choice for people with celiac disease or wheat allergies. And it is a great source of other vitamins, like zinc, potassium, and B vitamins.

These tiny, round seeds become tender when cooked, but retain a slightly crunchy coating for a nice texture.

Enjoy this savory stew using this exotic grain; serve with a cold fruit salad.

**Yield: Serves 6–8**

### Ingredients

1 onion, chopped

3 cloves garlic, minced

1 cup uncooked quinoa, rinsed

3 carrots, sliced

1 (15-ounce) can red beans, drained

5 cups vegetable broth

1 cup water

1 teaspoon ground cumin

1 teaspoon salt

$1/8$ teaspoon pepper

$1/2$ teaspoon dried marjoram

2 cups frozen corn, thawed

*Quinoa Vegetable Stew*

- In 4-quart slow cooker, combine onion, garlic, thoroughly rinsed quinoa, and carrots.

- Top with rinsed and drained red beans, broth, water, cumin, salt, pepper, and marjoram.

- Cover and cook on low for 7–8 hours or until quinoa and vegetables are tender.

- Stir in frozen corn. Cook on high for 20–30 minutes until stew is hot and blended.

Quinoa (pronounced keen-wah), is an ancient grain that is a complete source of high quality protein. Most grains are missing one or more amino acids your body needs so they must be combined; not so with quinoa. It was a staple of the Inca Indians and has been harvested for hundreds of years.

## • • • • RECIPE VARIATION • • • •

**Curried Quinoa Stew**
Make recipe as directed, except add 1 tablespoon curry powder and 1 tablespoon grated gingerroot to onion mixture. Omit red beans; add 1 red bell pepper, chopped, and 1 cup chopped celery. Stir ½ cup mango chutney into recipe just before serving.

### Rinse Quinoa

- It's important to rinse quinoa before you use it because it has a coating called saponin that is bitter.

- The coating is easily removed by a thorough rinsing. Do this every time you use quinoa.

- To tell if the saponin is all rinsed off, place the quinoa in the slow cooker and add water; swish a bit.

- If you do not see suds, the saponin is removed and you can proceed with the recipe.

### Add Vegetables

- Find quinoa in health food stores and in the natural foods aisle of the supermarket.

- Add more vegetables to this stew if you'd like. Chopped bell peppers, zucchini, summer squash, or mushrooms would be good additions.

- You'll know the quinoa is done when you bite into it. There will be a slightly crunchy coating, with a tender center.

- Make sure that the corn is completely heated before you serve the stew.

# BEAN STEWS
## Dried beans cook perfectly in the slow cooker along with seasonings and veggies

Cooking dried beans so they are evenly tender can be a challenge. Here's the trick: avoid ingredients that prevent softening, like salty foods and acidic ingredients.

Salty foods include salt, olives, capers, fermented black beans, bacon, and smoked sausages. High-acid foods include tomatoes, citrus juices, sour cream, buttermilk, and wine.

Soaking the beans is an important step. The beans should be soaked overnight, or you can boil the beans for a few minutes then let them stand for 1–2 hours; cook as directed.

Be sure that the beans are completely covered with liquid in the slow cooker so they cook evenly.

**Yield: Serves 6**

### Ingredients

1 cup dried navy beans

1 cup dried black beans

1 cup dried pinto beans

1 onion, chopped

4 cloves garlic, minced

1 teaspoon celery salt

1 teaspoon dried oregano

$1/8$ teaspoon pepper

3 carrots, sliced

2 potatoes, peeled and diced

8 cups vegetable broth

1 cup frozen corn, thawed

1 (14.5-ounce) can diced tomatoes, undrained

*Many Bean Stew*

- Sort beans to remove extraneous material and rinse well. Place in large pot; cover with cold water.

- Bring to a boil; boil for 2 minutes, then cover, remove from heat, and let stand for 2 hours.

- Drain and place in 5- or 6-quart slow cooker along with remaining ingredients except corn and tomatoes.

- Cover and cook on low for 8–10 hours until beans are tender. Mash some of the beans. Add corn and tomatoes; cook on high for 20 minutes.

**Mediterranean Bean Stew**
Make recipe as directed, except use lima beans in place of pinto beans. Omit oregano; add 1 teaspoon dried thyme leaves. Add 1 chopped red bell pepper with the beans. Omit corn; add ⅓ cup sliced green olives.

**Tex-Mex Bean Stew**
Make recipe as directed, except increase onions to 2. Add 2 minced jalapeño peppers along with the onions and garlic. Omit frozen corn; add 1 (15-ounce) jar of baby corn, drained, instead. Stir ½ cup light cream into stew before serving.

## Sort Beans

- Sort over beans to remove any twigs, leaves, or bits of dirt that processing left behind.

- Beans are, after all, a natural product and processing doesn't remove every bit of extraneous material.

- Rinse the beans well to remove dust or dirt; change that water for soaking.

- You can often find prepared bean mixes that are already sorted and blended. Just substitute, cup for cup, in any recipe.

## Boil Beans

- If you choose to boil the beans for 1–2 minutes, make sure the water comes to a complete boil.

- This means the water is bubbling furiously, and the bubbling doesn't subside when the mixture is stirred.

- If you'd rather soak the beans, just cover them with cold water, cover the bowl, and let stand overnight.

- In the morning, drain the beans, rinse again, and use as the recipe directs.

# VEGETABLE RAGOUT
## Hard winter squash adds color, flavor, and nutrition to a veggie stew

The French term ragout, or in Italian, ragu, means a stew or sauce that is heavy with slow-cooked vegetables. This type of food is perfect for the slow cooker.

This is where root vegetables shine. Think about using less common types of vegetables, like turnips, rutabagas, and parsnips, in these recipes.

A ragout is a very comforting dish, inexpensive and warming on cold winter days. You can serve it as a stew, or it can be ladled over hot cooked rice, barley, or pasta, or served over mashed potatoes.

Flavor the ragout well using dried herbs during cooking, and stir in fresh herbs just before serving for a pop of flavor.

**Yield: Serves 6–8**

### Ingredients

1 butternut squash, peeled, seeded, and cubed
2 onions, chopped
4 cloves garlic, minced
4 carrots, sliced
1 (8-ounce) package cremini mushrooms, sliced
1 (14-ounce) can artichoke hearts, drained
1 teaspoon salt
1/4 teaspoon pepper
1 teaspoon dried thyme
1 teaspoon dried oregano
5 cups vegetable broth
2 tablespoons lemon juice
1/2 cup chopped parsley
1/2 cup chopped cilantro
1/2 cup grated Romano cheese

*Vegetable Ragout*

- Layer vegetables in order in 5- or 6-quart slow cooker. Sprinkle with salt, pepper, thyme, and oregano.

- Pour broth over all. Cover and cook on low for 8–10 hours until vegetables are tender.

- You can also cook this on high for 4–5 hours. For a thicker ragout, partially mash some of the vegetables about 30 minutes before serving.

- Add lemon juice just before serving. Serve topped with mixture of parsley, cilantro, and Romano cheese.

## RECIPE VARIATION

**Root Vegetable Ragout**
Make recipe as directed, except add 1 peeled, cubed sweet potato and 2 peeled, cubed russet potatoes. Omit mushrooms and artichoke hearts. Add 1 (15-ounce) can drained white beans with the vegetables. Serve over hot cooked rice.

**Greek Vegetable Ragout**
Make recipe as directed, except omit mushrooms. Add another can of artichoke hearts, and add 2 cups cauliflower florets. Omit thyme; add 1 teaspoon dried marjoram leaves. Stir in ½ cup kalamata olives at end; use feta cheese in parsley mixture.

*Prepare Squash*

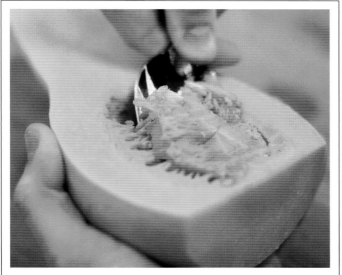

- To prepare squash, cut it in half using a chef's knife. Be careful with this process; hold the knife with both hands so you don't cut yourself.

- Then use a metal spoon to scrape out the seeds and membranes from the cavity.

- At this point, you can peel the squash. Then cut it into strips, and cut those strips into chunks.

- Any squash, whether butternut, acorn, or buttercup, is prepared the same way.

*Mix Herb Topping*

- When you use sturdy herbs like parsley and cilantro, you can prepare the herb topping ahead of time.

- You could repeat the flavors in the dish and choose fresh oregano and thyme leaves.

- But beware: fresh oregano is very strong, so only use

- about 2 tablespoons of it. Thyme is milder, so use ¼ to ⅓ cup.

- Pull the leaves from the stems and coarsely chop with a chef's knife. Refrigerate until ready to serve.

# PUMPKIN STEW

## A fresh pumpkin is easy to prepare and cook in this colorful stew

Pumpkins are the essence of fall. Their color, texture, and flavor are evocative of the cooler months, when we start craving heartier and more filling foods.

If you've never had pumpkin in a soup or a stew, you're in for a treat. Pumpkin's smooth texture, rich flavor, and beautiful color make a spectacular stew. Look for sugar pumpkins, not the big pumpkins you carve for jack o'lanterns. These smaller pumpkins are sweeter with a less dense flesh.

Once you've learned how to work with pumpkins, the sky's the limit. Make a pumpkin bisque or a spicy pumpkin soup with the flavors of fall and winter.

Serve these rich stews and soups with bread or scones and soft spinach salads.

**Yield: Serves 6–8**

### Ingredients

2-pound sugar pumpkin, seeded, peeled, and cubed

2 onions, chopped

4 cloves garlic, minced

1 red bell pepper, chopped

1 teaspoon salt

1/8 teaspoons pepper

1 teaspoon dried thyme

1 teaspoon dried marjoram

1 teaspoon dried basil

5 cups vegetable broth

1 tablespoon lemon juice

1 cup light cream or milk

2 tablespoons cornstarch

2 teaspoons fresh thyme

1/4 cup chopped parsley

*Herbed Pumpkin Stew*

- Layer pumpkin, onions, garlic, and bell pepper in 5- or 6-quart slow cooker.

- Sprinkle with salt, pepper, and dried herbs. Pour vegetable broth over all. Cover and cook on low for 8–10 hours until pumpkin is tender.

- Partially mash some of the pumpkin and stir in the lemon juice.

- Mix cream and cornstarch and stir into stew with fresh thyme and parsley. Cover and cook on high for 15–20 minutes.

**Pumpkin Bisque**
Make recipe as directed, except don't add red bell pepper to slow cooker. Cook as directed. Then turn off slow cooker; mash vegetables until smooth. Turn slow cooker to high. Add bell pepper and cream slurry; cook 30–40 minutes on high.

**Curried Pumpkin Stew**
Make recipe as directed, except add 1 cup chopped celery along with the red bell pepper. Omit thyme and marjoram; add 1 tablespoon curry powder and ½ teaspoon cinnamon. Cook as directed, but omit thyme and parsley; garnish with mango chutney.

## *Prepare Pumpkin*

- Choose a pumpkin that's heavy for its size, smooth, and firm, with no soft spots.

- To prepare pumpkin, cut into quarters then scoop out seeds. Peel the pumpkin with a swivel-bladed vegetable peeler.

- Then cut the pumpkin into lengths and chunks. You can reserve the seeds if you'd like.

- Wash the seeds and let dry overnight. Toss with oil, spread on a baking sheet, and then toast in 275 degree F oven for 70–80 minutes, stirring every 20 minutes.

## *Layer Ingredients*

- Be sure that the pumpkin is cut into evenly sized cubes so it cooks thoroughly.

- You could add other vegetables to this recipe: sliced mushrooms or carrots would be good.

- Many recipes for pumpkin stew include meats. You could brown a pound of cubed beef stew meat and add it along with the pumpkin.

- Or choose chicken thighs or breasts, or cubed pork chops or pork shoulder. Don't brown these foods; just add them to the slow cooker.

VEGETABLE STEWS

# POTATO KALE STEW
## Wild rice and barley combine for a delicious and nutritious stew

Potato stew is one of the most nutritious and least expensive stews you can make. And it's so easy with your slow cooker.

The best potatoes to use in stews include russets, sweet potatoes, and Yukon Gold potatoes. Red potatoes are too waxy and won't melt into the stew the way the other varieties will.

To give the stew some deep flavor and gorgeous color, along with another texture, add sturdy greens to the stew toward the end of cooking time.

Greens that stand up to the slow cooker's environment include mustard greens, kale, turnip greens, and chard. These strong-flavored greens add a punch of flavor to the mild potato mixture. Garnish with chopped chives or parsley.

**Yield: Serves 6**

### Ingredients

2 tablespoons butter

2 onions, chopped

4 cloves garlic, minced

1 pound russet potatoes, cubed

1 pound Yukon Gold potatoes, cubed

5 cups vegetable broth

1 teaspoon salt

1/8 teaspoon pepper

1/2 teaspoon caraway seeds

1/8 teaspoon nutmeg

1-pound bunch kale, chopped

2 tablespoons cornstarch

1/2 cup light cream or milk

1/4 cup chopped coriander

*Potato Kale Stew*

- Melt butter in medium skillet. Add onions and garlic; cook and stir 4 minutes.

- Place potatoes in 4-quart slow cooker; top with onion mixture. Add broth, salt, pepper, caraway, and nutmeg.

- Cover and cook on low for 7–9 hours until potatoes are tender. Partially mash potatoes.

- Add kale to slow cooker; cover and cook on low 30 minutes. Combine cornstarch with cream; stir into slow cooker. Cover; cook on high 15 minutes. Sprinkle with coriander.

152

**Creamy Vegetable Potato Stew**

Make recipe as directed, except peel the potatoes before you cube and add to the slow cooker. Add 1 cup sliced celery and omit the nutmeg and caraway seeds. Omit the kale. Add 1 cup light cream mixed with 2 tablespoons cornstarch at the end; stir in 1 cup shredded Havarti cheese.

**Tex-Mex Potato Stew**

Make recipe as directed, except add 2 minced jalapeño peppers with the onions. Omit caraway seeds, nutmeg, and kale. Add 1 teaspoon dried oregano, 1 teaspoon dried basil, and 2 tablespoons chili powder. Stir in 1 cup shredded Pepper Jack cheese at end.

*Chop Kale*

*Add Broth*

- Kale is a member of the cabbage family, with all of the health benefits that implies.

- It has powerful antioxidant compounds, including beta-carotene, vitamin K, and vitamin C.

- Kale should be dark green, with firm leaves, and no browned, soft, or wet spots.

- To prepare, swish in a sink full of cool water, then shake off. Chop the leaves roughly, discarding thick stems and ends. Other dark greens are prepared the same way.

- If you don't peel the potatoes, the soup will be more rustic and have an earthier flavor. Most of the potato's nutrients are found right under the skin. The soup will also have more fiber.

- Peel the potatoes for a more elegant soup or a creamier finish.

- For a richer stew, you can use chicken or beef broth in place of the vegetable broth.

- Top the soup with chopped parsley, gremolata, or shredded cheese.

VEGETABLE STEWS

# ROOT VEGETABLE STEW

## Wheat berries become chewy and nutty in this hearty stew

Root vegetables have sustained populations for generations, and for good reason. They are filling, hearty, easy to store and use, and combine into sublime stews and soups.

Root vegetables include onions, garlic, carrots, potatoes, sweet potatoes, parsnips, turnips, and rutabagas. Store in a cool, dark place. Prepare them by peeling and cutting out any rough spots or eyes, then cut into slices and cube or chop.

Fresh herbs, including oregano, thyme, basil, marjoram, or rosemary, are great complements to root vegetables. Choose your favorite.

Serve these stews with scones or breadsticks hot from the oven and a chopped fruit or vegetable salad.

**Yield: Serves 6**

### Ingredients

1 cup wheat berries, rinsed

1 onion, chopped

2 cloves garlic, minced

1 (8-ounce) package mushrooms, sliced

3 carrots, sliced

6 cups vegetable broth

1 teaspoon salt

$1/8$ teaspoon pepper

2 teaspoons minced fresh rosemary leaves

1 bay leaf

*Wheat Berry Vegetable Stew*

- Place wheat berries, onion, garlic, mushrooms, and carrots in a 4- or 5-quart slow cooker.

- Top with vegetable broth and add salt, pepper, rosemary, and bay leaf.

- Cover and cook on low for 8–10 hours or on high for 4–5 hours until wheat berries are tender.

- Remove bay leaf. Cover and cook on low for 30–40 minutes longer until soup is hot and blended. You can partially mash some of the root vegetables if you'd like.

**Roasted Root Vegetable Stew**
Toss all the root vegetables with the olive oil and spread in single layer on a large baking sheet. Roast in the oven at 400 degrees F for 15 minutes. Add all vegetables to slow cooker; omit wheat berries. Add broth; cook as directed.

**Creamy Root Vegetable Stew**
Make recipe as directed. When done, remove bay leaf and puree vegetables using an immersion blender or potato masher. Add ½ cup light cream along with 1 cup white cheddar cheese tossed with 1 tablespoon cornstarch. Cover and cook on high 20–30 minutes longer.

*Prepare Wheat Berries*

*Layer in Slow Cooker*

- Wheat berries are actually the entire kernel of wheat. The hull has been removed so the wheat will cook.

- They're easy to prepare; just rinse and add to the recipe. Their texture will become nutty while retaining some crunch.

- You can find wheat berries in health food stores and co-ops, and also in bulk bins in regular supermarkets.

- Store them in airtight containers in a cool, dark place; a glass jar is ideal. Label with date of purchase.

- Make sure that the wheat berries are in the bottom of the slow cooker and are completely covered with liquid.

- The berries are very nutritious and add a great texture to the soup.

- Peel all the root vegetables, cut out any eyes or soft spots, and cut into cubes of equal size.

- You could use other root vegetables, including rutabagas and turnips, in this easy stew.

**VEGETABLE STEWS**

# CORN

## Corn is delicious baked into a soft and moist spoon bread

Side dishes are where your slow cooker really shines. No matter what kind of main dish you're planning, you can find a side dish recipe that beautifully complements it and cooks all by it itself in your slow cooker.

Most hearty vegetables cook well in the slow cooker, but have to be placed at the bottom of the insert. More tender vegetables such as corn and mushrooms also work well;

however they should be handled a bit differently.

Corn is a whole grain that is available in many different forms. Frozen corn is usually used in the slow cooker. It keeps its texture when cooked frozen and thaws and cooks perfectly in a relatively short time.

**Yield: Serves 6**

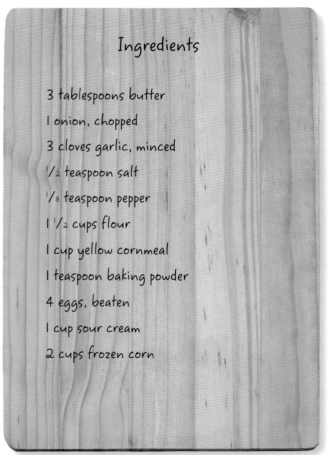

### Ingredients

3 tablespoons butter

1 onion, chopped

3 cloves garlic, minced

$1/2$ teaspoon salt

$1/8$ teaspoon pepper

$1 1/2$ cups flour

1 cup yellow cornmeal

1 teaspoon baking powder

4 eggs, beaten

1 cup sour cream

2 cups frozen corn

*Corn Spoon Bread*

- In small saucepan, melt butter on medium heat. Add onion and garlic; cook until tender, about 6 minutes.

- Sprinkle with salt and pepper; set aside. In large bowl, combine flour, cornmeal, and baking powder; mix well.

- Add eggs and sour cream; stir until combined. Fold in onion mixture and frozen corn.

- Pour into greased 3-quart slow cooker. Partially cover and cook on high 2–3 hours until knife inserted in center come out clean. Spoon from slow cooker to serve.

156

### Scalloped Corn

Cook 1 chopped onion in ¼ cup butter. Add 4 cups frozen corn; remove from heat. Add 1 chopped red bell pepper, 1 cup sour cream, 2 beaten eggs, 1 teaspoon dried thyme, 3 tablespoons flour, ¼ cup cornmeal, and ½ cup cracker crumbs. Cover and cook on high 2–3 hours.

### Creamed Corn

Cook 1 chopped onion and 1 clove minced garlic in 3 tablespoons butter. Add 1 (8-ounce) package cream cheese, cubed; 2 cups white sauce or 1 (16-ounce) jar Alfredo sauce; 8 cups frozen corn; and 1 cup shredded cheddar cheese. Place in 5-quart slow cooker; cook on low 3 hours, stirring twice.

*Make Batter*

*Fold in Corn*

- It's important to cook the onion and garlic before adding to the batter because it won't cook surrounded by batter.

- Stir the dry ingredients together using a wire whisk, then beat in the eggs and sour cream.

- Don't make the batter ahead of time; the baking powder will react with the liquid too soon.

- You can add other vegetables to this mixture. Precook mushrooms until brown, or add chopped, seeded tomatoes.

- You can use thawed corn in this recipe, just drain it before adding it to the batter; you don't want to add too much water.

- You can use fresh corn cut off the cob instead of the frozen corn if you'd like.

- Husk the corn and place one end in the hole in the middle of a bundt pan. Cut down the cob; the kernels will fall into the pan.

- Then scrape the cob with your knife to remove any bits of corn. Serve this recipe hot from the slow cooker.

VEGETABLE SIDES

# CARROTS

## Carrots become sweet and tender when cooked in the slow cooker

Regular carrots and baby carrots cook very well in the slow cooker. These root vegetables become tender and sweet when cooked for a longer period of time.

When using regular carrots, peel them first. Use a swivel-bladed vegetable peeler and remove all of the dull skin. Then cut off the tips and slice the carrot into ½-inch slices.

Baby carrots don't need any special preparation; just pour them right into the slow cooker, add the other ingredients, and turn it on.

It's fun to make carrots using lots of different foods and flavors. They can be sweet, savory, sweet-and-sour, or hot and spicy. Use your imagination to create your own special recipe.

**Yield: Serves 6**

## Ingredients

2 tablespoons butter

1 onion, chopped

3 cloves garlic, minced

8 carrots, sliced

1 (8-ounce) can crushed pineapple, undrained

3 tablespoons tomato paste

½ cup water

1 teaspoon salt

⅛ teaspoon pepper

⅓ cup sugar

⅓ cup apple cider vinegar

1 tablespoon mustard

### Sweet and Sour Carrots

- In small saucepan, melt butter and cook onion and garlic until tender, about 6 minutes.

- Add carrots and pineapple and transfer to 3-quart slow cooker.

- Add tomato paste and water to saucepan; cook and stir until blended and pour into slow cooker. Add remaining ingredients and stir.

- Cover and cook on low for 6–7 hours or until carrots are tender. Serve hot or cold.

**Honey Glazed Carrots**
Make recipe as directed, except increase butter to 3 tablespoons and omit pineapple, tomato paste, sugar, vinegar, and mustard. Add ⅓ cup honey; reduce water to ½ cup. Cook as directed. During last 30 minutes, cook on high with lid off to glaze carrots.

**Spicy Baby Carrots**
Make recipe as directed, except use 2 (16-ounce) bags baby carrots instead of the whole carrots. Omit pineapple, tomato paste, sugar, and vinegar. Add 2 minced jalapeño peppers with the onions. Reduce water to ½ cup; add ½ cup salsa; cook as directed.

*Prepare Vegetables*

- When buying carrots, look for a bright orange color and firm texture. The carrots should feel heavy for their size.

- There shouldn't be any soft or brown spots on the carrots, or scars or tough areas. Baby carrots are completely prepared.

- If you're buying top-on carrots, with greens attached, the greens should not be wilted.

- The carrot greens are edible; wash, chop, and stir into the dish at the end, or use in salads.

*Add Tomato Paste*

- The tomato paste adds a rich flavor, some pretty color, and lots of nutrition to this already nutritious dish.

- If you choose to use baby carrots instead, use 2 (16-ounce) bags. Rinse the carrots well and drain, then add to the slow cooker.

- To make this recipe simpler, use a bottled sweet and sour sauce instead of the tomato paste on down.

- You can find sweet and sour sauce in the ethnic or Asian foods aisle of your supermarket.

VEGETABLE SIDES

# BEETS
## Beets take on a new twist in the slow cooker

Many people look askance at beets. But they are a delicious vegetable, with a rich, earthy, and sweet taste. Preparing them seems challenging, but it's easy.

There are three kinds of beets: sugar beets, used to make granulated sugar, fodder beets that are used as animal food, and the red beets we eat.

The general rule is that the smaller the beet, the sweeter.

Large beets take longer to cook, and always need to be peeled before use. Baby beets are tender, with a thinner skin, so they are just scrubbed before using.

You can make a beet dish, or just cook beets in the slow cooker to use for other recipes.

**Yield: Serves 6–8**

### Ingredients

20 baby beets, scrubbed

1 onion, chopped

1 cup orange juice

2 cloves garlic, minced

1 teaspoon salt

$1/8$ teaspoon pepper

2 tablespoons honey

6 cups chopped Swiss chard

2 tablespoons butter

*Beets with Swiss Chard*

- Scrub the baby beets and cut off any rough spots with knife; no need to peel.

- Combine in 3- or 4-quart slow cooker with onion, orange juice, garlic, salt, pepper, and honey.

- Cover and cook on low for 6–7 hours or until beets are almost tender. Add chard and butter.

- Cover and cook on low for 1–2 hours longer or until beets and chard are tender. Serve.

**ZOOM**

There are all kinds of varieties of beets! If all you've ever seen are the deep red globes, look for candy cane beets, which are striped with color; white beets, which are very mild; and golden beets, which are a beautiful gold color and are mildly sweet.

## • • • • RECIPE VARIATION • • • •

**Harvard Beets**

Harvard beets, a classic sweet and sour recipe, are very simple. Peel 5 large beets and cut into ½-inch slices. Place in 3 ½-quart slow cooker. In bowl, combine ⅓ cup sugar, 1 tablespoon flour, 1 tablespoon cornstarch, ⅓ cup vinegar, ¼ cup water, salt, and pepper; pour over beets. Cover; cook on low 8–9 hours.

## Scrub Beets

## Swiss Chard

- Scrub the beets using a vegetable brush. Cut off and reserve the greens, if attached.

- If the beets come with green tops, you can wash and chop them and add along with the chard.

- Carefully look at the beets; if there are any soft spots or bruises, cut them out. Baby beets shouldn't need peeling.

- You could leave out the onion and garlic if you like; just add more beets!

- Swiss chard is sometimes known as the "bottomless beet" because it looks so much like beet greens.

- Chard, like many dark sturdy greens, tastes better after frost has hit the garden. It's often one of the last harvested vegetables.

- To prepare, immerse the greens in a sink full of cool water to remove all the grit.

- Shake off excess water and coarsely chop the chard. You can prepare it ahead of time.

VEGETABLE SIDES

# CLASSIC STUFFING

## For Thanksgiving or other holidays, make stuffing in your slow cooker

Well, technically this is called "dressing." A bread and vegetable mixture that's cooked inside poultry is stuffing; that same mixture, cooked in the oven or slow cooker, is dressing.

Whatever you call it, this is a delicious and easy way to prepare this standard holiday side dish. And since there's never enough stuffing, double your recipe and cook part in the bird and part in the slow cooker.

If you have a favorite stuffing recipe, convert it to the slow cooker. Just reduce the liquid by half, make sure any meat you add is fully cooked first, and fill the slow cooker one-half to three-quarters full. Cook for at least 6 hours on low.

**Yield: Serves 8–10**

### Ingredients

6 slices oatmeal bread
6 slices whole wheat bread
2 onions, chopped
2 cloves garlic, minced
1 (8-ounce) package mushrooms, sliced
1/2 cup butter
3 stalks celery, chopped
2 eggs, beaten
1 cup chicken or vegetable broth
1 teaspoon salt
1/8 teaspoon pepper
1 teaspoon dried thyme leaves
1 teaspoon paprika
1/2 teaspoon dried sage leaves
1/4 cup chopped parsley

*Classic Bread Stuffing*

- Lightly toast the bread, not to brown it, but so it is slightly dry. Cut into cubes.

- Cook onion, garlic, and mushrooms in butter in medium saucepan until tender.

- Combine in 4-quart slow cooker with bread and celery. Mix eggs, chicken broth, and all seasonings in bowl; pour into slow cooker.

- Stir gently to evenly coat. Cover and cook on low for 6–8 hours, stirring once during cooking, until stuffing is hot and blended.

## ···· GREEN ● LIGHT ··········

Not only is it easier to cook your stuffing or dressing in the slow cooker, but it is safer too. When stuffing made with eggs or meat is cooked inside a bird, it's difficult to make sure that the stuffing cooks thoroughly all the way through; and there is lots of bacteria in the bird.

## ···· RECIPE VARIATION ····

**Sage Stuffing**
Prepare as directed, except increase garlic to 4 cloves. Use cremini mushrooms in place of button mushrooms. Omit thyme and paprika and use 1 teaspoon dried sage leaves and 2 tablespoons chopped fresh sage leaves. Cook as directed.

## *Prepare Ingredients*

- The slow cooker is almost as moist as the inside of a turkey! No evaporation takes place.

- So don't make the stuffing too wet. The vegetables will release liquid into the bread mixture.

- The bread is toasted to remove moisture so it will absorb the flavors in the recipe.

- Beat the egg and broth mixture well so it will evenly coat the bread and the vegetables. Use your favorite herbs and vegetables.

## *Toss Ingredients*

- Toss the bread mixture as you add the egg mixture. Toss gently but thoroughly so all the food is coated.

- There shouldn't be any standing liquid in the bottom of the slow cooker; the dressing should absorb it all.

- For lightly toasted edges, first cook on high for 1 hour, then reduce heat to low and cook 5–6 hours.

- If you'd like, add ¾ pound cooked and drained pork sausage to the mixture with the bread.

VEGETABLE SIDES

# ROOT VEGETABLES

## These vegetables become tender and sweet in the slow cooker

Root vegetables and the slow cooker were made for each other. All of these vegetables cook well using low heat, a moist environment, and long time periods.

These foods have lots of natural sugars. The roots are storage systems for the plant, and store the plant's energy as sugar. As the vegetables cook, the sugars become more prominent, concentrate, and develop.

Vary the root vegetables, using sweet potatoes, turnips, rutabagas, squash, carrots, and other types of potatoes.

You can also season them with herbs, hot peppers, salsa, or cheeses. Serve with roasted or grilled meats, casseroles, or as a vegetarian main dish.

**Yield: Serves 6–8**

### Ingredients

1 onion, chopped

3 cloves garlic, minced

3 carrots, cut into chunks

1 parsnip, peeled and cubed

1 turnip, peeled and cubed

2 sweet potatoes, peeled and cubed

3 russet potatoes, peeled and cubed

1/2 cup water

1 teaspoon salt

1/8 teaspoon pepper

1/4 cup honey

2 tablespoons brown sugar

2 tablespoons butter

1 tablespoon cornstarch

*Glazed Root Vegetables*

- Combine onion, garlic, carrots, parsnip, turnip, sweet potatoes, and russet potatoes in 4- or 5-quart slow cooker.

- Add water, salt, and pepper and stir. Cover and cook on low for 7–9 hours or until vegetables are tender.

- In bowl, combine honey, brown sugar, butter, and cornstarch and mix well. Pour into slow cooker.

- Cover and cook on high for 45–60 minutes or until vegetables are glazed and tender.

**Moroccan Tagine**
Make recipe as directed, except add 1 teaspoon turmeric, 1 teaspoon cinnamon, ¼ teaspoon cayenne pepper, and 1 teaspoon cumin. Add 1 cup golden raisins and ½ cup dried currants. Omit honey and brown sugar. Sprinkle finished dish with parsley and cilantro.

**Apple Root Vegetables**
Make recipe as directed, except use 1 cup apple juice instead of ½ cup water. Add ½ cup applesauce with the apple juice. Omit brown sugar; add 1 teaspoon dried thyme and 1 teaspoon dried marjoram leaves.

*Prepare Vegetables*

*Pour Glaze Over*

- When you choose root vegetables, look for firm produce with no soft or wet spots.

- The vegetables should feel heavy and solid. They will look "rough," especially the rutabaga and parsnip; that's okay.

- Peel them until you get to the moist interior. Discard the peel or use it in your compost pile.

- Cut all of the vegetables to the same size so they cook evenly. Fill the slow cooker ¾ full.

- You can flavor the glaze any way you'd like. Use the basic ingredients: honey, butter, and cornstarch.

- Then add heat with jalapeño or habañero peppers, or with chili powder or ground chiles.

- Double the glaze for a holiday casserole, or flavor it with cinnamon, allspice, nutmeg, and cardamom.

- You can make the glaze ahead of time; cover it and store in the refrigerator. Stir before adding to the food.

VEGETABLE SIDES

# UPDATED STUFFING
## Use unusual ingredients for a new twist on stuffing

One of the fun things about stuffing or dressing is that it's such an adaptable recipe. You can use just about any ingredient, as long as you include some kind of bread, some kinds of vegetables or fruit, and liquid to moisten.

There are many delicious and different recipes for stuffing in cookbooks and on the Web. Use unusual breads, like challah, cornbread, muffins, or flatbread.

Use meats and seafood like sausage, bacon, oysters, shrimp, or gizzards. Make sure the meats are fully cooked before adding to the stuffing.

And the fruit and vegetable combinations are limitless. Fresh fruits, dried fruits, dried mushrooms, and all vegetables are fair game. Dried and fresh herbs provide additional flavor.

**Yield: Serves 8–10**

## Ingredients

2 onions, chopped

2 tablespoons butter

2 Granny Smith apples, peeled and chopped

1 pan cornbread, cut into cubes

1/2 cup dried cranberries

1/2 cup fresh cranberries, cut in half

1/2 cup golden raisins

1/3 cup butter

1 cup chicken stock

1 teaspoon dried thyme leaves

1 teaspoon salt

1/4 teaspoon pepper

### Onion Cranberry Stuffing

- Cook onions in 2 tablespoons butter until tender, about 6 minutes. Remove to large bowl. Add apples and toss.

- Add cornbread, dried and fresh cranberries, and golden raisins; toss gently.

- In small saucepan, melt 1/3 cup butter. Stir in stock, thyme, salt, and pepper and drizzle over stuffing; toss lightly.

- Place in 4- or 5-quart slow cooker. Cover and cook on low for 6–8 hours, stirring once during cooking time, until stuffing is hot.

### Cornbread

Combine 1 cup cornmeal, 1 cup flour, ½ teaspoon salt, ½ teaspoon baking soda, ¼ cup sugar. Cut in ⅓ cup butter. Stir in 2 eggs, ¼ cup heavy cream, and ⅔ cup buttermilk; spread in greased 9-inch pan. Bake at 375 degrees F for 35–40 minutes until toothpick inserted in center comes out clean. Cool.

### Pumpkin Stuffing

Crumble 8 pumpkin muffins from the bakery. Add the onion and apple mixture; add 2 cloves minced garlic. Omit fresh and dried cranberries; add ½ cup dried cherries and ½ cup applesauce. Make butter mixture as directed; cook as directed.

## *Precook Vegetables*

## *Mix Ingredients*

- Because there is so much food in the slow cooker, and the mixture is fairly dense, vegetables won't cook through.

- They have to be sautéed, baked, or microwaved before being added to the bread mixture.

- This is an opportunity to add more flavor, too; let the onions caramelize, or add bell peppers or chile peppers.

- Fruits like apples and pears will soften in the slow cooker without precooking.

- The gentle, low heat cooks the stuffing without drying it out, and blends the flavors.

- At the end of cooking time, taste the stuffing. If it needs more moisture, add more butter or chicken stock.

- If it is wet or mushy, turn the heat to high and cook for 30–40 minutes with the lid off.

- If you're making this for the holidays, you can keep the stuffing warm on low for 1–2 hours after it's done.

# BAKED BEANS
## Classic baked beans are easily made in the slow cooker

Baked beans is among the oldest recipes in America. It is very inexpensive, easy to make, and has to cook for a long time. The slow cooker is the perfect way to make it.

In New England, the beans are served with brown bread. Not only is this traditional, it also provides complete protein. Beans eaten with grains provide all of the amino acids your body needs. And the combination tastes wonderful.

You can make your beans vegetarian, with no meat, or start by cooking bacon or salt pork until crisp; add at the end of cooking time.

Serve your baked beans as a side dish or a vegetarian main dish.

**Yield: Serves 6–8**

### Ingredients

1 pound dried navy beans

2 onions, chopped

4 cloves garlic, minced

3 tablespoons butter

6 cups water

1/3 cup brown sugar

1/4 cup maple syrup

2 tablespoons molasses

2 tablespoons Dijon mustard

1/2 cup chopped Canadian bacon, if desired

1 cup ketchup

1/2 cup chili sauce

3 tablespoons tomato paste

1 teaspoon salt

1/4 teaspoon pepper

*Rich Baked Beans*

- Sort the beans to remove extraneous material, rinse, and drain. Place in large pot; cover with water, and soak overnight.

- The next day, cook onion and garlic in butter for 4–5 minutes. Add to 4-quart slow cooker with beans and water.

- Cover; cook on low for 8–9 hours until beans are almost tender. Drain, saving liquid.

- Stir in remaining ingredients, including enough liquid to make everything moist, cover, and cook on high for 1–2 hours; stir well and serve.

168

### Brown Bread

Mix 2 cups whole wheat flour, ½ cup flour, ½ cup corn-meal, ¼ cup brown sugar, 1 teaspoon baking soda, and ¼ teaspoon salt. Add 1 egg, ¾ cup molasses, 1 cup butter-milk, and ½ cup water; mix. Stir in 1 cup raisins. Bake in 2 greased 5 x 3-inch baking pans at 350 degrees F for 40–45 minutes.

### Bacon Baked Beans

Make recipe as directed, except when ready to cook, cook ½ pound regular bacon until crisp. Drain, crumble, and refrigerate. Drain fat from pan; don't wipe out. Add butter to pan; cook onions and garlic 4–5 minutes. Omit Canadian bacon. Cook as directed; stir in bacon with ketchup.

## Soak Beans

- Most beans you buy nowa-days are fairly clean. They used to be full of dirt, twigs, and leaves.

- Modern harvesting and cleaning methods have reduced that material. Still, it's a good idea to sort over the beans.

- Remove any beans that feel very light or are broken, shriveled, or wrinkled.

- For a shortcut, you can boil the beans 2 minutes, then let stand 2 hours instead of soaking overnight.

## Stir in Acidic Ingredients

- Salt and acidic ingredients will prevent the beans from becoming tender.

- These ingredients should be added at the end of cooking time, when the beans are almost soft.

- If you live in an area that has hard water, add a pinch of baking soda to the soaking water; this will compensate for the low pH of the water.

- And if you have very hard water, use bottled water to cook the beans. Or add another pinch of baking soda.

BEANS & GRAINS

# QUINOA PILAF

## This ancient seed is nutty and delicious when slow cooked

When you say "pilaf," most people think of rice. But a pilaf can be made from any grain. Quinoa, that ancient seed that has recently come back into popularity, makes an excellent pilaf cooked in the slow cooker.

Quinoa is known as a super grain, even though it's a seed. It provides complete protein: it contains every amino acid your body needs for good health. It's also gluten-free, so is a great choice for those who can't eat wheat.

Quinoa has a nutty, mild flavor with a tender inside and slightly crunchy exterior. It pairs well with just about any vegetable. Use your favorite combination, or make a classic pilaf with just the quinoa and onions and garlic.

**Yield: Serves 6**

### Ingredients

2 cups quinoa, rinsed

1 onion, chopped

2 cloves garlic, minced

2 tablespoons butter

2 cups vegetable broth

2 cups water

1 teaspoon salt

$\frac{1}{8}$ teaspoon pepper

1 teaspoon dried marjoram

1 (15-ounce) can garbanzo beans, drained

$\frac{1}{4}$ cup chopped flat leaf parsley

2 tablespoons chopped cilantro

*Quinoa Pilaf*

- Rinse quinoa very well to remove bitter coating. Place in 3 ½-quart slow cooker.

- Cook onion and garlic in butter until tender; add to slow cooker along with broth, water, salt, pepper, marjoram, and garbanzo beans.

- Cover and cook on low for 2–3 hours or until quinoa is tender.

- Stir in parsley and cilantro; cover and cook on low for 20–30 minutes. Stir again and serve.

**Spicy Quinoa Pilaf**
Make recipe as directed, except add 1 minced jalapeño pepper and 1 chopped poblano pepper along with the onions and garlic. Omit marjoram, garbanzo beans, and parsley. Add 1 red bell pepper and 1 cup salsa to the slow cooker. And increase cilantro to ⅓ cup.

**Vegetable Quinoa Pilaf**
Make recipe as directed, except cook 1 (8-ounce) package mushrooms, sliced, 1 green bell pepper, and 1 cup chopped zucchini with onions. Omit garbanzo beans. Add 1 teaspoon dried thyme along with the marjoram. Stir in ½ cup Parmesan cheese before serving.

*Add Quinoa*

- Make sure that the quinoa is thoroughly rinsed before using to remove its bitter coating.

- Rinse until the water runs clean and doesn't foam. For a slightly different texture, toast the quinoa before adding to the slow cooker.

- Dry the quinoa in kitchen towels, then add to 1 tablespoon olive oil. Toast for 2–3 minutes over medium heat.

- Then proceed as directed with the recipe. This makes quinoa slightly crunchier.

*Stir Quinoa*

- Stir the mixture thoroughly, both before cooking and before serving.

- You want to evenly mix the ingredients in the slow cooker. They all cook at the same time, so layering isn't necessary.

- Add other vegetables, like carrots, or potatoes.

- But since the cooking time is short, make sure they are almost cooked before adding.

- Dice these ingredients and sauté or microwave until almost tender, then add to the slow cooker.

# BEAN CASSOULET

## A vegetable cassoulet is a great side dish or vegetarian main dish

Cassoulet is a complex recipe made of beans, onions, garlic, and usually several types of meat. But this recipe is also delicious made without any meat at all, and very healthy too.

Cassoulet is originally from France. The dish is named after a deep, round pot called a *cassole*, in which the dish is cooked. The recipes can get very complicated, using duck, partridge, pork, and mutton. The dish has very humble origins, having been made by peasants hundreds of years ago.

And the dish traditionally uses only white beans, although many versions using mixed beans appear in cookbooks.

Serve your cassoulet with a spinach salad and some crisp toasted garlic bread.

**Yield: Serves 6–8**

*Vegetarian Bean Cassoulet*

### Ingredients

2 cups dried lima beans

2 cups dried black beans

2 onions, chopped

4 cloves garlic, minced

2 stalks celery, chopped

2 cups baby carrots, cut in half crosswise

3 cups vegetable broth

3 cups water

1 bay leaf

1 teaspoon dried thyme leaves

1 teaspoon dried basil leaves

1 (14.5-ounce) can diced tomatoes, undrained

2 tablespoons cornstarch

3 tablespoons tomato paste

1/2 teaspoon salt

- Sort beans and rinse; drain and cover with cold water. Soak overnight.

- The next day, drain; place in 4-quart slow cooker with onions, garlic, celery, carrots, broth, water, bay leaf, thyme, and basil.

- Cover and cook on low for 8–9 hours or until beans are almost tender. In small bowl, mix tomatoes, cornstarch, tomato paste, and salt.

- Stir into slow cooker; cover and cook on high for 45–55 minutes until cassoulet is bubbling. Remove bay leaf, stir, and serve.

**Lima Bean Cassoulet**
Make recipe as directed, except use all lima beans. Brown 1 pound garlic sausage; drain and add to slow cooker along with beans. Omit baby carrots and thyme; add 1 teaspoon oregano. Cook 1 cup breadcrumbs in 2 tablespoons butter until crisp; top cassoulet.

**Classic Cassoulet**
Make recipe as directed, except reduce beans to 1 cup each. Add 1 pound sweet Italian sausage, browned and sliced, and 1 pound cubed chicken thighs to the slow cooker. Add ½ cup dry red wine with the tomatoes. Cook as directed. Cook 1 cup breadcrumbs in 2 tablespoons butter until crisp; top cassoulet.

## *Sort Beans*

- Sort the beans well, discarding any that are shriveled or broken.

- You can boil the beans for 2 minutes, then let stand for 2 hours instead of soaking overnight.

- Since most cassoulet is baked in the oven for a long period of time, it develops a crunchy crust.

- This can be approximated in the slow cooker by browning coarse breadcrumbs in butter, then adding just before serving.

## *Combine Tomato Mixture*

- As with all dried bean dishes, add tomatoes and other acidic ingredients like lemon juice at the end of cooking.

- Acid reacts with proteins in the bean's coating, slowing down the absorption of water.

- The beans will be firm, not soft and tender, even after hours of cooking if there is too much acid.

- After you add the tomato mixture, the beans can be cooked for 2–3 hours more to develop flavors; the beans will not get mushy.

# BARLEY WHEAT BERRY CASSEROLE

## Whole grains like wheat berries are perfect for the slow cooker

Wheat berries are actually the whole kernel of the grain. Just the hull, or tough outer coating, has been removed, so the berries are very high in fiber and B vitamins.

Their nutty taste and slightly crunchy texture are the perfect foil for barley. Barley is also nutty tasting, and becomes almost creamy when cooked for a long time.

These grains mix well with just about any ingredient—from meat to vegetables to fruits to herbs to cheese. Using these proportions of grains to liquid, you can create many new, delicious, and healthy recipes.

Serve this casserole as a side dish for grilled meats, or as a main dish, with a green salad and some cornbread.

**Yield: Serves 6**

## Ingredients

1 ½ cups wheat berries

1 cup barley

2 onions, chopped

3 cups apple juice

1 cup water

1 teaspoon salt

¼ teaspoon pepper

½ cup golden raisins

½ cup dried currants

½ cup dried cherries

½ cup chopped dried apricots

2 tablespoons lemon juice

*Fruity Barley Wheat Berry Casserole*

- Rinse wheat berries and barley and place in 3 ½-quart slow cooker.

- Add all remaining ingredients in order listed, except lemon juice.

- Cover and cook on low for 8–9 hours, or on high for 4–5 hours, until wheat berries and barley are tender and dried fruits are plump.

- Stir in lemon juice; cover and cook on low for 20 minutes. Stir gently and serve.

**Wheat Berry Breakfast**

Rinse 1 ½ cups wheat berries and place in 3-quart slow cooker. Add 1 cup water, 2 cups apple juice, and 1 cup orange juice. Stir in ¼ cup sugar, 1 teaspoon vanilla, ½ cup dried currants, and ½ cup dried cherries. Cover and cook on low 7–8 hours.

**Spicy Wheat Berry Casserole**

Prepare recipe as directed, except increase wheat berries to 2 cups. Omit barley, apple juice, raisins, currants, cherries, apricots, and lemon juice. Use 4 cups vegetable broth. Add 1 chopped onion, 3 cloves garlic, 2 minced jalapeño peppers, 1 tablespoon chili powder, and ¼ cup minced sun-dried tomatoes in oil.

*Combine Ingredients*

- The wheat berries, because they are a whole grain and minimally processed, should be rinsed before using.

- You're just rinsing away the dust left over from processing, plus any dirt or sand.

- You can use any combination of dried fruits that you'd like; just keep the proportions of wheat and barley to fruit the same.

- If you're cooking on high, stir the mixture once during cooking time so nothing sticks.

*Add Lemon Juice*

- Stir in the lemon juice at the end to add a pop of flavor. You could also add orange or lime juice.

- As with beans, other whole grains cook better when not in a high-acid environment, so the citrus juice is added at the end of cooking time.

- Barley is a high-fiber food. More importantly, it has soluble fiber, which removes cholesterol from your body.

- You should eat whole grains like barley or wheat berries 6 times a week.

# ASIAN RICE AND LENTILS
## Rice and lentils provide complete protein in a delicious dish

Rice and the slow cooker isn't exactly the ideal combination. It's very easy for white rice to overcook and become mushy.

Brown rice, because it has only the hull removed and still contains the bran and germ, absorbs liquid more slowly, so it does cook well in the slow cooker.

Featuring rice combined with lentils, this dish provides complete protein to the vegetarian. And the flavors and textures are wonderful. Flavor this combination any way you'd like. Asian flavorings are a natural, but you can also use the flavors of Greece, Mexico, France, Spain, or Morocco.

Serve as a side dish to roast chicken, or as a vegetarian main dish with a nice spinach salad.

**Yield: Serves 6**

### Ingredients

2 cups red lentils

2 tablespoons butter

1 onion, chopped

2 cloves garlic, minced

1 tablespoon grated gingerroot

1 cup long-grain brown rice

2 tablespoons soy sauce

4 cups vegetable broth

2 cups water

1 tablespoon rice vinegar

*Curried Rice and Lentils*

- Rinse lentils and place in 4-quart slow cooker. Melt butter in skillet and cook onion and garlic for 5 minutes.

- Add gingerroot and rice; cook and stir for 3–4 minutes longer. Place in slow cooker.

- Add soy sauce, vegetable broth, and water. Cover and cook on low for 7–9 hours until lentils and rice are tender.

- Stir in rice vinegar, fluff mixture with fork, and serve immediately.

Lentils are also known as daal or pulses. They are legumes, or the fruit of a plant in the family Fabaceae. Other legumes include peas, beans, and peanuts. Lentils cook fairly quickly, so don't need the presoaking dried beans do. They are nutty and delicious, and cook well in the slow cooker.

## • • • • RECIPE VARIATION • • • •

**Tex-Mex Rice and Lentils**
Make recipe as directed, except add 2 minced jalapeño peppers with the onions and garlic. Omit gingerroot, soy sauce, and rice vinegar. Add 1 cup salsa with the vegetable broth and water. Stir in 1 cup shredded Pepper Jack cheese at the end of cooking time.

### Cook Rice in Skillet

- One way to make rice successfully in the slow cooker is to toast it in a dry pan or in butter or olive oil.

- This firms up the rice coating, which helps delay the absorption of liquid.

- This step also adds a nice nutty taste to the dish, and helps the rice absorb other flavors in the recipe.

- Look for low-sodium soy sauce for a milder flavor. Choose regular soy sauce for more flavor.

### Fluff Mixture with Fork

- Most rice mixtures benefit from fluffing with a fork just before serving.

- This helps distribute the starch so the grains of rice don't stick together. It also introduces air into the mixture.

- You could add lots of vegetables to this dish. Add mushrooms; cook with the onions and garlic until tender.

- Or add bell peppers, zucchini, sliced summer squash, or tomatoes. Chop all vegetables to about the same size before adding.

# BARLEY MUSHROOM CASSEROLE
## This classic combination can be flavored so many ways

There's something about the combination of barley with mushrooms that's very satisfying. The nutty barley, which is still slightly chewy even after hours of cooking, blends well with the earthy, sweet tenderness of mushrooms.

This dish can be served as a vegetarian main dish, perhaps with a fresh fruit salad and some breadsticks, or as a side dish to roast chicken or a beef tenderloin cooked on the grill.

Take some time to browse through your supermarket's produce aisle to look at what's new. Ingredients that were difficult to find even 5 years ago, like shiitake or morel mushrooms, are now available almost everywhere. Use your favorite mushrooms and herbs in this easy dish.

**Yield: Serves 6**

## Ingredients

1 cup barley

2 tablespoons butter

1 (8-ounce) package cremini mushrooms, sliced

1 (8-ounce) package shiitake mushrooms, sliced

1 onion, chopped

3 cloves garlic, minced

2 cups vegetable broth

1 teaspoon dried thyme

1/8 teaspoon white pepper

1/3 cup chopped parsley

*Barley Mushroom Casserole*

- Place barley in 3 ½-quart slow cooker. Melt butter in large skillet. Add mushrooms; cook and stir 4–5 minutes. Remove to slow cooker.

- Add onion and garlic to skillet; cook and stir 4 minutes. Add to slow cooker.

- Add broth, thyme, and pepper. Cover and cook on low for 4–6 hours until barley is tender.

- Fluff with fork, top with parsley, and serve.

**Barley Risotto**

Cook 1 chopped onion and 3 cloves garlic in 2 tablespoons butter. Add to 4-quart slow cooker with 1 cup each pearl barley, shredded carrots, and finely chopped mushrooms. Add 3 cups vegetable broth. Cook on high 2–3 hours, stirring twice, until thick. Stir in ½ cup Parmesan cheese.

**Barley Vegetable Casserole**

Make recipe as directed, except add 1 chopped green bell pepper, 1 chopped red bell pepper, and 1 cup chopped zucchini. Omit shiitake mushrooms. Add 1 cup diced carrots. Cook recipe as directed, except stir in ½ cup grated Romano cheese before serving.

*Prepare Mushrooms*

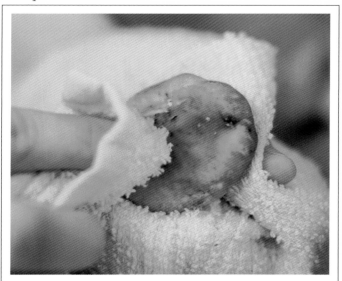

- To prepare mushrooms, wipe off with a damp cloth. Don't immerse them in water or they will get tough.

- The mushrooms may also absorb water during washing, which will make the dish too runny.

- Don't worry about the dirt on mushrooms; it's sterilized dirt. Just brush it off or gently wipe.

- Fresh mushrooms have a lot of water, which they release during cooking, so they must be browned before adding to slow cooker recipes.

*Combine Ingredients*

- You could use any type of broth or stock you'd like. For a heartier dish, use beef broth.

- Other herbs that would be delicious in this recipe include basil, rosemary, sage, or marjoram.

- Those herbs complement the earthy flavor of the mushrooms and the mildness of the barley.

- For a heartier dish, stir in ½ to 1 cup of shredded cheese just before serving. Let stand 5 minutes and serve.

# RISOTTO

## The classic Italian dish is made with ease in the slow cooker

Risotto seems like a simple dish, and it's easy to make, but you have to follow some rules to make a true risotto.

The rice you use is important. Look for Arborio rice, which is a short-grain rice from Italy. This rice is high in the starch amylopectin, which is a branched molecule that makes the liquid creamy when it's released from the grain.

The rice is usually stirred constantly when making risotto.

This disturbs the outer coat, letting the rice release more starch. This is where the slow cooker shines: the longer cooking time eliminates the need for constant stirring.

Finally, let the risotto stand with the heat off for 5 minutes to thicken a bit and finish cooking. Then enjoy!

**Yield: Serves 6**

### Ingredients

I onion, finely chopped

2 cloves garlic, minced

2 tablespoons olive oil

2 cups Arborio rice

5 cups chicken broth

$1/2$ cup dry white wine

I teaspoon salt

$1/8$ teaspoon white pepper

2 tablespoons butter

$1/2$ cup grated Parmesan cheese

*Classic Risotto*

- Cook onion and garlic in olive oil until tender. Add rice; cook and stir for 4 minutes. Place in 3- or 4-quart slow cooker.

- Add broth, wine, salt, and pepper. Cover and cook on high for 2–3 hours, until rice is tender, stirring once during cooking time.

- Add the butter and cheese. Turn off slow cooker and let stand for 5 minutes.

- Uncover, stir risotto. If risotto is runny, let stand uncovered for 10 minutes, then stir and serve.

## • • • • • • • • • • • • • • • RECIPE VARIATION • • • • • • • • • • • • • • •

**Vegetable Risotto**
Make recipe as directed, except add 2 thinly sliced car-
rots and 1 red bell pepper to olive oil; cook with onions.
Use 4 cups vegetable broth in place of the chicken broth.
Add 1 teaspoon dried thyme leaves with the rice. Cook as
directed; add 1 ½ cups baby spinach leaves with butter.

**Spicy Risotto**
Make recipe as directed, except add 2 minced jalapeño
peppers with the onions and garlic. Add 1 tablespoon
chili powder, 1 minced chipotle pepper, and 1 tablespoon
adobo sauce with the broth. Increase cheese to 1 cup; use
Cotija cheese instead of Parmesan.

### *Toss Rice with Olive Oil*

- The rice needs to be cooked with the olive oil to slow down the cooking process slightly.

- This step also increases the flavor of the rice, adds a nutty touch to the dish, and helps incorporate the onion and garlic flavors.

- During the long cooking time (regular risotto takes about 30 minutes to cook) the rice releases lots of starch.

- This naturally thickens the risotto. Stirring the rice once during cooking time helps this process along.

### *Add Butter and Cheese*

- Butter and cheese stirred in at the end is a classic finish for risotto.

- It adds creaminess and more flavor to the dish. Don't substitute margarine; the butter flavor is essential.

- Parmesan cheese is the classic finish to risotto. You

could also use Romano or Asiago cheese for a bit more flavor.

- At this point you could also stir in fresh herbs. A table-spoon of fresh thyme leaves is traditional.

# RICE PILAF
## Rice pilaf is the perfect side dish for many meat dishes

Rice pilaf can be as simple as cooked rice mixed with some cheese, or it can be complicated, with lots of vegetables, a white sauce, and herbs.

This classic dish is easy to dress up for a special occasion. And with a little help, it cooks beautifully in the slow cooker. Use brown rice, season the mixture well, and add your favorite vegetables and fruits for perfect results.

Rice is one of those foods that blend well with the flavors and ingredients from every cuisine. And it's used in most cuisines. It's an inexpensive grain that can be healthy when you choose brown, red, or wild varieties. Enjoy these easy recipes.

**Yield: Serves 6**

### Ingredients

2 links chorizo sausage, chopped
1 tablespoon olive oil
2 tablespoons butter
1 onion, chopped
3 cloves garlic, minced
2 cups long-grain brown rice
1/2 cup tomato juice
1 red bell pepper, chopped
3 stalks celery, chopped
4 plum tomatoes, chopped
3 1/2 cups chicken or vegetable broth
1 bay leaf
1 teaspoon dried thyme leaves
1/2 teaspoon dried oregano leaves
1/4 teaspoon pepper

*Creole Rice Pilaf*

- Cook sausage in medium skillet until done. Remove sausage and drain. Drain pan, but do not wipe out.

- Add olive oil and butter to pan. Cook onion and garlic for 4 minutes. Add rice; cook for 3 minutes.

- Add tomato juice and bring to a simmer, stirring to remove pan drippings. Place in 4-quart slow cooker along with all remaining ingredients.

- Cover and cook on low for 5–7 hours or until rice is tender. Remove bay leaf and serve.

# • • • • • • • • • • • • • • RECIPE VARIATION • • • • • • • • • • • • • • •

**Creamy Rice Pilaf**
Prepare recipe as directed, except add 1 cup white sauce to the slow cooker. Omit sausages, tomato juice, plum tomatoes, oregano, and bay leaf. Add 1 teaspoon dried basil leaves. Stir in 1 cup shredded Swiss cheese at the end of cooking time.

**Fruited Rice Pilaf**
Make recipe as directed, except use apple juice in place of the chicken or vegetable broth. Omit sausage, tomato juice, bell pepper, tomatoes, bay leaf, and oregano. Add ½ cup each dried currants, raisins, cherries, and cranberries. Add ½ teaspoon salt along with the pepper; cook as directed.

## *Cook Vegetables*

- Onion and garlic almost always need to be fully cooked until tender before adding to rice mixtures.

- The low heat required for cooking rice just won't cook these foods through and they'll be too harsh tasting.

- Softer vegetables like bell peppers, mushrooms, zucchini, and celery will cook well without sautéing.

- In fact, in rice pilaf mixtures these vegetables will still retain a bit of crunch, lending nice texture to the dish.

## *Stir Pilaf*

- It's important that all of the food in a pilaf cooks evenly and at the same time.

- You do need to stir the pilaf just once in the slow cooker. Do it quickly, so you lose as little heat as possible.

- Stirring also makes sure that there aren't any clumps of undercooked or overcooked rice in the pilaf.

- When the pilaf is done, you can keep it on warm for 1–2 hours until the rest of dinner is ready.

# MIXED RICE PILAF

## Different types of rice make a flavorful and interesting pilaf

Mixing rice together in a pilaf creates an interesting dish with lots of flavor, color, and texture. If you really look at the different varieties of rice, you'll be amazed at the quantity and range.

There are more than 40,000 varieties of rice cultivated in the world. These include pecan rice, red rice, Jasmine rice, black rice, glutinous rice, and baby basmati rice. All of them have distinct textures, colors, and flavors.

When you make a mixed rice pilaf, choose rice that cooks in about the same time. If you want to use 2 kinds of rice with different cooking times, just parboil the longer-cooking variety, then combine everything in the slow cooker.

**Yield: Serves 6**

### Ingredients

1 tablespoon olive oil
2 tablespoons butter
1 onion, chopped
2 cloves garlic, minced
1 (8-ounce) package cremini mushrooms, sliced
1 teaspoon salt
1/4 teaspoon pepper
1 teaspoon dried thyme leaves
1 cup wild rice
1 cup long-grain brown rice
3 1/2 cups vegetable broth
1 cup white sauce
1/2 cup grated Romano cheese
1/4 cup chopped parsley

*Mixed Rice Pilaf*

- In large saucepan, melt olive oil and butter; cook onion, garlic, and mushrooms until tender, about 6–7 minutes.

- Add salt, pepper, thyme, and both types of rice; cook and stir for 4 minutes. Pour into 4-quart slow cooker.

- Add broth; stir, then cover and cook on low for 5–6 hours until rice is almost tender. Stir in white sauce.

- Cover and cook on low for 1–2 hours longer until rice is tender. Stir in cheese and parsley and serve.

184

## • • • • RECIPE VARIATION • • • •

**Tex-Mex Rice Pilaf**

Make recipe as directed, except add 1 minced haba-ñero pepper to the onion mixture. Add 3 cloves minced garlic and use brown Texmati rice in place of the long-grain brown rice. Omit white sauce; use 1 cup salsa. Stir in 1 cup shredded Pepper Jack cheese at end of cooking.

### ZOOM

Pilaf, also known as pilau or pulao, is defined as a recipe in which rice or wheat is browned in oil first, then cooked in broth or stock. This dish is served often in Middle Eastern, Latin American, and Caribbean cuisines. It was invented in the Persian empire hundreds of years ago.

### *Sauté Vegetables*

- Make sure that you stir almost constantly when cooking the rice. You don't want it to burn; just toast.

- Try different types of onions and mushrooms in this dish. Green onions make a nice change of pace, as do sweet red onions.

- There are lots of varieties of fresh and dried mushrooms in the marketplace, like shiitake and morel.

- Soak dried mushrooms in hot water, then cut off the stems, chop, and add to the pilaf for intense flavor.

### *Stir in White Sauce*

- The white sauce adds a creamy texture to this dish as it envelops the rice and vegetables.

- You can substitute 1 (10-ounce) container of refrigerated Alfredo sauce for the white sauce if you'd like.

- The cheese adds great flavor and even more creaminess to the pilaf. Make sure to shred it right before adding to the slow cooker so it doesn't dry out.

- Use your favorite cheese; experiment with flavored varieties like Havarti with dill or horseradish Jack.

# WILD RICE CASSEROLE
## Wild rice becomes tender and nutty cooked in the slow cooker

Wild rice is not a rice, but a seed of a water grass, Zizania aquatica. It's the state grain of Minnesota. Traditionally, the rice is harvested by American Indians as they glide through reedy lakes in canoes. Once harvested, it must be cured by parching in a fire or high heat.

You can still find wild rice harvested this way. Much of the nation's wild rice is grown on farms, but nothing compares to

the flavor and texture of wild rice harvested by hand.

The texture of wild rice is quite chewy. It can be cooked to either of two end points: chewy but tender, or popped. Popped rice has literally exploded, and is very tender.

Enjoy these easy recipes for wild rice.

**Yield: Serves 6–8**

### Ingredients

2 tablespoons butter

2 shallots, minced

2 cups wild rice

I teaspoon salt

I teaspoon dried thyme leaves

2 cups pineapple juice

I cup apple juice

I cup pear nectar

1/2 cup golden raisins

1/2 cup dried cherries

1/2 cup dried cranberries

1/2 cup chopped dried apricots

1/2 cup slivered almonds

*Fruity Wild Rice Casserole*

- In small skillet, melt butter; cook shallots until tender, about 4 minutes.

- Combine all ingredients except almonds in 4-quart slow cooker. Stir, cover, and cook on low for 6–8 hours until rice is tender.

- Toast the almonds in a small skillet over low heat until fragrant and light brown.

- Stir almonds into pilaf and serve immediately.

## • • • • • • • • • • • • • • • • • RECIPE VARIATION • • • • • • • • • • • • • • • •

**Vegetable Wild Rice Casserole**
Make recipe as directed, except cook 1 chopped onion and 3 cloves garlic in butter. Use 4 cups vegetable broth in place of the fruit juices. Omit shallots, raisins, cherries, cranberries, apricots, and almonds. Add 1 chopped red bell pepper and 1 (8- ounce) package sliced mushrooms.

**North Woods Wild Rice Casserole**
Make recipe as directed, except add 2 cups sliced button mushrooms and 1 cup dried, reconstituted morel mushrooms, chopped, to the shallot mixture. Add 2 cloves minced garlic. Use vegetable broth in place of the fruit juices; omit all dried fruit. Omit almonds; add 1 cup shredded Havarti cheese.

*Stir Ingredients*

- Make sure that the wild rice is completely covered with liquid in the slow cooker. You may need to add more.

- It's important to stir the ingredients in the slow cooker once during cooking time.

- If you cook the casserole for 8–10 hours, the wild rice may pop. It will curl up and become very tender.

- The dish can be kept hot on keep-warm for 1–2 hours after it's finished cooking.

*Toast Almonds*

- To toast almonds or any nuts, place them in a single layer in a dry saucepan.

- Cook over low heat, stirring or tossing the nuts frequently, until they turn darker brown.

- The nuts will also smell fragrant, as the oils in the nuts are developed. You can also microwave the nuts for 4–5 minutes on high per cup.

- Always cool toasted nuts before chopping them, or they can become greasy or mushy.

# VEGETABLE RICE PILAF
## This delicious recipe could be a vegetarian main dish

The more vegetables the better! Rice and vegetables are a natural combination, and the slow cooker is the ideal appliance to cook them.

This pilaf can be served as a vegetarian main dish. The combination of rice and lots of vegetables provides complete protein in a delicious package.

Other ingredients add to the texture and flavor of these dishes. Chopped nuts should be stirred in just before serving so they retain their crunch. Fresh herbs add a pop of flavor when added right at the end. And cheeses add an incomparable flavor and creaminess to any pilaf recipe.

Use your favorite ingredients and flavor combinations to create your own special rice pilaf recipe.

**Yield: Serves 6**

## Ingredients

2 tablespoons olive oil
1 onion, chopped
3 cloves garlic, minced
1 red bell pepper, chopped
1 green bell pepper, chopped
2 teaspoons chili powder
1 teaspoon paprika
1 teaspoon salt
1/4 teaspoon pepper
2 cups long-grain brown or wehani rice
1 (14.5-ounce) can diced tomatoes, undrained
1/4 cup chopped sun-dried tomatoes, not in oil
1/2 cup chopped kalamata olives
3 cups vegetable broth
1/2 cup sliced almonds
2 tablespoons butter
2/3 cup shredded Manchego cheese

*Spanish Vegetable Rice Pilaf*

- In large skillet, heat olive oil over medium heat. Add onion and garlic; cook and stir for 4 minutes.

- Place in 3 1/2-quart slow cooker along with all remaining ingredients except almonds, butter, and cheese.

- Stir well, then cover and cook on low for 6–8 hours or until rice is tender.

- Cook almonds in butter until light brown. Stir cheese into pilaf, sprinkle with almonds; cover and let stand for 5 minutes, and serve.

······· GREEN ● LIGHT ·········

Don't be afraid to experiment with different types of rice. There are lots of different varieties within the rice categories. For instance, in long-grain brown rice you can find basmati rice, Jasmati rice, and wehani. Mix and match the rice varieties in these recipes.

· · · · · RECIPE VARIATION · · · ·

**Greek Vegetable Rice Pilaf**
Make recipe as directed, except add 1 teaspoon dried oregano and 2 tablespoons lemon juice to slow cooker. Omit chili powder, paprika, and almonds. Add ½ cup sliced green olives along with the kalamata olives, and stir in ½ cup feta cheese just before serving.

## Sauté Vegetables

- Cook onions and garlic until tender so they become soft and sweet in the pilaf.

- The sun-dried tomatoes in this recipe are dried, but not packed in oil. They absorb some of the broth as the pilaf cooks.

- The texture of the sun-dried tomatoes will be tender but slightly chewy when the recipe is done.

- The almonds are cooked in butter to add even more flavor. Nuts toasted in butter are rich tasting and crisp.

## Mix Ingredients

- Stir the ingredients in the slow cooker well, both before cooking and after, just before serving.

- It's a good idea to spray the inside of the slow cooker insert with nonstick cooking spray before adding ingredients.

- This makes cleanup easier, and also prevents the pilaf from sticking to the sides and burning.

- Serve this pilaf as a main dish with a spinach salad and a fruit salad, along with breadsticks for crunch.

# CHICKEN RISOTTO
## Add chicken, and risotto becomes an easy main dish

Risotto is an excellent and elegant side dish, and is made with ease in the slow cooker. Adding meat to this dish turns it into a hearty main dish.

Chicken is the perfect addition to risotto. Its mild taste, velvety texture, and low cost turn risotto into a meal fit for company.

You can use chicken breasts or thighs in this recipe. Cook the breasts whole on top of the risotto; cube the chicken thighs, because they take longer to cook.

Make sure that your chicken broth is nice and rich. If you aren't using homemade stock, boxed stock is a good substitute that adds long-cooked flavor to the recipe. Serve with roasted carrots and a fruit salad.

**Yield: Serves 6**

## Ingredients

- 2 tablespoons butter
- 1 tablespoon olive oil
- 2 onions, chopped
- 2 cloves garlic, minced
- 2 cups Arborio rice
- 4 cups chicken broth
- ½ teaspoon saffron or turmeric
- ½ teaspoon salt
- ⅛ teaspoon white pepper
- 1 teaspoon dried oregano
- 4 boneless, skinless chicken breast halves
- ½ cup grated Parmesan cheese
- ½ cup crumbled feta cheese
- 2 tablespoons lemon juice

*Greek Chicken Risotto*

- In large saucepan, melt butter and olive oil over medium heat. Cook onions and garlic for 5 minutes.

- Place in 4-quart slow cooker and add rice, chicken broth, saffron, salt, pepper, and oregano; mix well.

- Top with chicken breasts. Cover and cook on high for 2 ½–3 hours until rice is tender and chicken is cooked.

- Remove chicken and cube. Stir into risotto along with cheeses and lemon juice. Cover and cook on high for 10–20 minutes.

## • RECIPE VARIATION •

**Tex-Mex Chicken Risotto**
Make recipe as directed, except add 1 (4-ounce) can chopped green chiles, drained. Omit saffron and feta cheese. Add 1 tablespoon chili powder to onion mixture along with 1 chopped green bell pepper. Stir in 1 cup shredded Pepper Jack cheese with the Parmesan cheese.

**Creamy Chicken Risotto**
Make recipe as directed, except add ½ cup heavy cream with the cubed chicken at the end of cooking time. Omit saffron, oregano, feta, and lemon juice; use 1 teaspoon dried thyme. Stir in 1 cup shredded Gouda cheese and 2 tablespoons butter at end of cooking time.

*Cook Onions*

- For more flavor, you can caramelize the onion and garlic mixture before assembling the risotto.

- Just let it keep cooking in the butter and olive oil mixture. Cook on medium-low heat for 15–25 minutes.

- The onion mixture will start to turn brown. This means that the sugar in the onions is beginning to caramelize.

- The caramelized onions add lots of rich flavor to the risotto. The onions will almost dissolve during the long cooking time.

*Cube Chicken*

- While you're cubing the chicken, keep the lid on the risotto so it stays hot.

- If you're using chicken thighs, you can shred them, or just stir them into the rice mixture.

- Immediately stir the chicken back into the

- risotto along with cheeses and lemon juice so it stays hot.

- This final cooking time lets the starch released by the rice thicken up a bit so the risotto has the perfect texture.

# SALT ROASTED POTATOES

## Salt flavors the potatoes and shields them from heat so they cook to perfection

Potatoes are one of the perfect foods to cook in the slow cooker. And there are lots of ways to do this.

One of the more unusual methods is to cook the potatoes completely buried in kosher salt. This shields the potatoes from the direct heat and the results are spectacular. The flesh becomes buttery and the skin very tender.

This recipe is a great idea for a large party. The potatoes will stay hot in the salt mixture even when the slow cooker is turned off. And you can reuse the salt up to 10 times; just chip it away, let cool, and store.

**Yield: Serves 6**

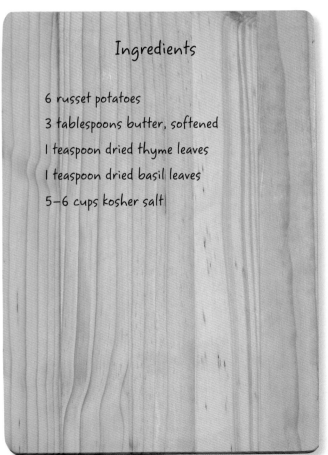

## Ingredients

6 russet potatoes

3 tablespoons butter, softened

1 teaspoon dried thyme leaves

1 teaspoon dried basil leaves

5–6 cups kosher salt

*Salt Roasted Potatoes*

- Scrub potatoes well, then dry thoroughly with kitchen towels and paper towels.

- Prick the potatoes several times each with a fork. Rub all over with butter, then sprinkle with mixture of thyme and basil; rub in well.

- Pour 2 cups of salt in the bottom of a 4- or 5-quart slow cooker; add a few potatoes.

- Pour salt in, adding potatoes, layering them evenly. Cover potatoes with salt. Cover and cook on high for 2–3 hours until potatoes are tender.

## · · · · · YELLOW ● LIGHT · · · · ·

The potatoes don't absorb much of the salt in this recipe. They shouldn't taste salty. The tender skin is one of the best parts of the potato, but if you are concerned about sodium intake, just don't eat the skin. Don't use a salt substitute in this recipe; it just won't work.

## · · · · RECIPE VARIATION · · · ·

**Bacon Roasted Potatoes**
Make recipe as directed, except substitute 3 tablespoons bacon fat for the butter. Omit thyme and basil leaves; add ⅛ teaspoon pepper and 1 teaspoon dried marjoram leaves to the potatoes before layering in the slow cooker.

### Layer Salt and Potatoes

- Snuggle the potatoes into the salt. You can add as many potatoes as you can fit into the slow cooker.

- But still keep the ½ to ¾ fill ratio in mind. Make sure the potatoes are completely covered with salt.

- You can use gourmet varieties of salt. Sea salt and gray salt, while more expensive, have more flavor than kosher or regular salt.

- You can bake russet, Yukon Gold, white, or red potatoes using this method.

### Remove Cooked Potatoes

- The potatoes will stay warm in their salt casing, with the slow cooker turned off, until you're ready to serve them.

- These potatoes will be slightly higher in sodium content than regular baked potatoes, but not overly high.

- Break through the crust carefully with a knife and remove potatoes with a large spoon or tongs keeping them intact.

- Brush off excess salt and serve them with butter, sour cream, and chives for an excellent side dish.

# SWEET POTATO CASSEROLE
## This classic recipe is ideal for the slow cooker

Sweet potatoes are another fabulous food to cook in the slow cooker. They are the best holiday side dish, cooked with lots of sweet and savory ingredients.

Sweet potatoes are also known as yams, but they are not true yams. A yam is a tuber of a tropical vine and has a different flavor and texture.

Sweet potatoes are among the most nutritious vegetables on the planet. They are packed with vitamin A, as evidenced by their deep orange color. The Center for Science in the Public Interest has ranked them number one in nutrition of all vegetables. And they're delicious!

Whether your dish is sweet or savory, sweet potatoes are the perfect side dish.

**Yield: Serves 6–8**

### Ingredients

2 tablespoons butter
2 onions, chopped
1 tablespoon curry powder
4 sweet potatoes, peeled and cubed
$1/4$ cup butter
2 tablespoons flour
1 teaspoon salt
1 cup apple cider
$1/2$ cup orange juice
$1/3$ cup brown sugar
$1/8$ teaspoon nutmeg
$1/2$ teaspoon cinnamon
2 teaspoons vanilla
$1/2$ cup golden raisins
$1/2$ cup dried cranberries
$1/2$ cup chopped pecans
1 cup granola
2 tablespoons butter, melted

*Curried Sweet Potato Casserole*

- Melt 2 tablespoons butter in large saucepan and cook onions until brown, 8 minutes; add curry powder.

- Combine onion mixture and sweet potatoes in 4-quart slow cooker. Melt ¼ cup butter in same saucepan; cook flour and salt until bubbly.

- Add cider and orange juice; bring to a simmer. Add brown sugar, nutmeg, cinnamon, vanilla, raisins, and cranberries; pour into slow cooker.

- Mix pecans, granola, and 2 tablespoons melted butter; sprinkle over top. Cover; cook on low 6–8 hours.

**Spicy Sweet Potato Casserole**
Make recipe as directed, except add 2 cloves minced garlic to onions. Omit cider, orange juice, brown sugar, cinnamon, nutmeg, fruits, nuts, and granola. Add 1 chopped red bell pepper, 1 tablespoon chili powder, 1 teaspoon cumin, and 4-ounce can chopped green chiles. Sprinkle with 1 cup crushed nacho chips just before serving.

**Simple Sweet Potato Casserole**
Make recipe as directed, except increase sweet potatoes to 6. Omit everything after orange juice. Add 1 cup raisins, ½ cup brown sugar, 1 teaspoon cinnamon, and ¼ teaspoon nutmeg. Cook as directed; drizzle with ¼ cup maple syrup.

## *Cook Onions and Curry Powder*

- Curry powder is almost always cooked before eating. The complex of spices has much better flavor when heated.

- Curry powder isn't a spice; it's a combination of up to 20 spices. You can make your own, or experiment with the blends in the supermarket.

- Turmeric or saffron in the curry powder adds a nice yellow color to the dish.

- Use your favorite dried fruits in this recipe. Try mixed dried fruits, dried cherries, dried currants, or chopped apricots.

## *Prepare Sweet Potatoes*

- Sweet potatoes look kind of rough in their raw state. You need to remove the skin before cooking.

- Use a swivel-bladed vegetable peeler, or a sharp paring knife to remove the skin.

- Cut off the ends and remove any eyes or soft spots, then cube the sweet potatoes.

- You can use homemade or purchased granola; just be sure to choose one that's nice and crunchy so it retains some texture after cooking.

# RED POTATOES

## Red potatoes are delicious cooked with lots of cheeses

Red potatoes are usually used in potato salad. But when cooked in a creamy, cheesy sauce, they become true comfort food.

There are several types of red potatoes in the market. The large, waxy red potatoes are better used for potato salad because they keep their shape when cooked.

Tiny, or new, red potatoes are perfect cooked in the slow cooker. They stay whole, but become creamy inside and tender outside.

You can add lots of vegetables to these potatoes. Bell peppers, mushrooms, and celery are all good additions. But like beans, potatoes aren't a good match with tomatoes; the acidity of tomatoes will keep the potatoes firm.

**Yield: Serves 6**

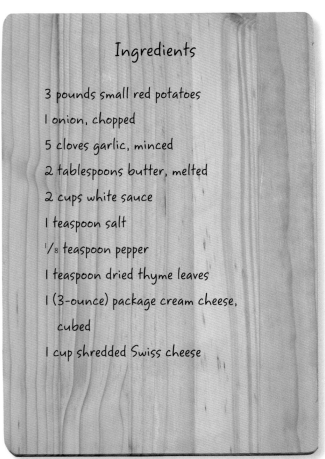

### Ingredients

3 pounds small red potatoes

1 onion, chopped

5 cloves garlic, minced

2 tablespoons butter, melted

2 cups white sauce

1 teaspoon salt

$1/8$ teaspoon pepper

1 teaspoon dried thyme leaves

1 (3-ounce) package cream cheese, cubed

1 cup shredded Swiss cheese

*Cheesy Red Potatoes*

- Scrub potatoes. If any are larger than 1 inch, either cut in half or quarter so pieces are about the same size.

- Add to 4-quart slow cooker with onion, garlic, butter, white sauce, salt, pepper, and thyme; mix.

- Cover and cook on low for 6–8 hours until potatoes are tender. Add cream cheese and partially mash potatoes, leaving some whole.

- Stir in Swiss cheese. Cover and cook on low for 1 hour longer, then stir and serve.

# RECIPE VARIATION

**Bacon Red Potatoes**
Make recipe as directed, except cook 1 pound bacon; drain, and crumble. Drain fat from pan; add onion and garlic; cook until tender. Omit white sauce and cream cheese. Add bacon to slow cooker along with ⅓ cup vegetable broth. Don't mash potatoes.

**Simple Italian Red Potatoes**
Make recipe as directed, using tiny 1-inch whole red potatoes. Omit white sauce, cream cheese, and Swiss cheese. Add 1 teaspoon dried oregano leaves and 1 teaspoon dried basil leaves to potatoes. Stir in ½ cup grated Parmesan cheese at end.

## Prepare Potatoes

- New or baby potatoes are delicate, so handle them gently. Rinse them off and dry before proceeding.

- They may only need a bit of scrubbing with a soft vegetable brush under running water.

- Cut off any brown or tough pieces of skin, and any eyes. Then just add to the slow cooker.

- The potatoes should be around the same size. If some are larger, cut to make the same size.

## Mash Potatoes

- To mash potatoes, you can use a potato masher or a mixer.

- Don't use an immersion blender. Like a regular blender or food processor, it will over-process the potatoes and they will be gluey.

- You can mash the potatoes smooth, or leave some whole for a rustic texture. The peels add color, nutrition, and texture.

- Throw in a bunch of fresh herbs at the end for a pop of flavor and color.

# ROASTED POTATOES

## Potatoes become creamy and silky when roasted in the slow cooker

Technically, these potatoes aren't roasted. Roasting is a dry heat cooking method, and the slow cooker is a wet heat cooking method.

Still, the slow cooker turns out potatoes with creamy, velvety flesh and a fabulous flavor, which is the point.

You can just pile potatoes in the slow cooker and cook them as is. But adding other ingredients is easy and makes

the potatoes much more special.

Cut potatoes in half, slice them thickly into planks, or cut into chunks. Then toss with butter or olive oil, vegetables, and herbs, and roast to perfection in your slow cooker.

With just a few minutes of work you'll have a side dish worthy of a perfectly grilled steak or salmon.

**Yield: Serves 6**

### Ingredients

6 large russet potatoes

3 tablespoons butter

1 tablespoon olive oil

4 cloves garlic, minced

1 teaspoon salt

1/8 teaspoon pepper

1 teaspoon dried oregano

1 teaspoon dried marjoram

1/2 cup vegetable broth

*Roasted Potatoes*

- Scrub potatoes and dry. Cut each in half lengthwise. In small pan, melt butter with olive oil over medium heat.

- Add garlic; cook and stir until fragrant. Remove from heat and add salt, pepper, oregano, and marjoram.

- Layer potatoes in 4- or 5-quart slow cooker, drizzling each layer with butter mixture. Pour vegetable broth over.

- Cover and cook on low for 5–7 hours or until potatoes are tender. Carefully remove from slow cooker and serve.

### Hasselback Potatoes

Scrub each potato, then place in a large spoon. Slice the potato, cutting down to the spoon, crosswise into ⅛-inch slices. The bottom of the potato should be uncut. Make herb mixture as directed; drizzle over potatoes. Layer and cook in slow cooker as directed; omit vegetable broth.

### Roasted Cubed Potatoes

Make recipe as directed, except cut the potatoes into 1 ½-inch chunks, leaving a bit of peel on each potato. Or you can peel the potatoes and cut into chunks. Reduce vegetable broth to ¼ cup. Before serving, sprinkle ⅓ cup Romano cheese over potatoes; toss to coat and serve.

*Cut Potatoes*

- When you cut potatoes in half, sometimes you'll find a brown or black spot in the very center.

- This is just an indication of low calcium while the potatoes grew. While unsightly, this spot isn't dangerous.

- You can just cut out the spot and throw it away, or use other potatoes. Save the discarded potato for another use.

- The potatoes you buy should be firm and heavy for their size, with no wet or soft spots.

*Layer in Slow Cooker*

- Try to layer the potatoes evenly in the slow cooker. As they cook, you can rearrange them halfway through cooking time.

- The potatoes may be very tender and fall apart when done, no matter how carefully you lift them from the slow cooker.

- That's okay – just break them up with a spoon and serve them as smashed potatoes.

- If they do break apart, take advantage of the situation and throw in some shredded cheese.

# MASHED POTATOES

## Make mashed potatoes and keep them warm in the slow cooker

Creamy, smooth, and fluffy mashed potatoes are one of the best parts of the holidays. And they're easy to make in the slow cooker. Best of all, you can keep the mashed potatoes perfectly hot and moist in the slow cooker while you're finishing the rest of the meal.

For the best mashed potatoes, make sure that the potatoes are thoroughly cooked. They must be completely tender,

with no firm areas. Then, add the butter or other fat when you first start mashing. This helps coat some of the starch in fat so the potatoes don't become gluey. Finally, add warm milk, cream, or broth to the potatoes to keep them warm.

**Yield: Serves 8–10**

### Ingredients

4 pounds Yukon Gold potatoes, peeled and cubed

2 onions, chopped

6 cloves garlic, minced

1 cup vegetable broth

1/2 cup butter

1/2 cup sour cream

1/2 cup light cream

1 teaspoon dried thyme leaves

1 teaspoon dried chives

1 teaspoon salt

1/4 teaspoon white pepper

*Creamy Mashed Potatoes*

- In 5- or 6-quart slow cooker, combine potatoes, onion, and garlic. Pour vegetable broth into slow cooker.

- Cover and cook on low for 6–7 hours until potatoes are very tender. Drain liquid.

- Add butter; mash potatoes coarsely. Add remaining ingredients and mash potatoes thoroughly.

- Cover and cook on low for 2–3 hours, or keep-warm for 3–4 hours. Stir before serving.

**Smashed Potatoes**
Make recipe as directed, except don't peel the potatoes before cooking. Scrub the skins well before cutting into cubes. Reduce the garlic to 2 cloves. When mashing the potatoes, don't mash completely; leave some chunks of potato visible.

**Cheesy Mashed Potatoes**
Make potatoes as directed, except use 4 pounds russet potatoes, peeled and cubed, in place of the Yukon Gold potatoes. Ten minutes before serving, stir in 2 cups shredded white cheddar cheese and ½ cup grated Parmesan cheese.

## Cook Potatoes

- The potatoes should be cut to the same size so they cook evenly and at the same time.

- If you'd like, you can omit the onions and garlic completely for plain mashed potatoes.

- For a more mild onion and garlic flavor, sauté the onion and garlic in half of the butter before mixing with the potatoes.

- You can also caramelize the onion and garlic before adding to the slow cooker; sauté for 20–25 minutes.

## Mash Potatoes

- Mash potatoes using a potato masher or a large fork. Don't use an immersion blender.

- You can keep these potatoes hot in the slow cooker, on low or keep-warm setting, for 2–3 hours before serving.

- This is a huge advantage when you're serving a crowd at a holiday dinner.

- If you want potatoes to serve more people, fill another slow cooker with a second batch rather than just increasing the amount.

# SCALLOPED POTATOES

## This classic side dish is so easy to make in the slow cooker

To scallop a vegetable means to slice it thinly and cook it in a white sauce, with or without cheese.

Potatoes are the vegetable most often scalloped. The term is often confused with "au gratin," which means cooked with a cheese or bread crust. Scalloped potatoes can be made au gratin by topping with buttered breadcrumbs or cheese.

These potatoes have to be cooked in a white sauce, which stabilizes the sauce and adds structure to the dish. Making a white sauce isn't difficult; it just requires patience and a wire whisk.

Enjoy these easy scalloped potatoes; serve with meatloaf and a green salad for a comfort food meal.

**Yield: Serves 6**

### Ingredients

¹/₃ cup butter

1 onion, finely chopped

¹/₃ cup flour

1 teaspoon salt

¹/₄ teaspoon white pepper

2 cups whole milk

¹/₂ cup vegetable broth

¹/₂ cup grated Parmesan cheese

8 russet potatoes, peeled and sliced ¹/₄ inch thick

*Scalloped Potatoes*

- In large saucepan, melt butter over medium heat. Add onion; cook and stir until very tender, about 7 minutes.

- Add flour, salt, and pepper; cook and stir 3 minutes. Add milk and broth.

- Cook and stir the sauce, using a wire whisk, for 8–9 minutes until sauce thickens slightly. Remove from heat and stir in Parmesan cheese.

- Layer potatoes with sauce in 4-quart slow cooker. Cover and cook on low for 6–8 hours or until potatoes are tender.

**Tex-Mex Scalloped Potatoes**
Make potatoes as directed, except cook 2 minced jalapeño peppers and 3 cloves minced garlic with the onion. Add 1 tablespoon chili powder and 1 teaspoon cumin with the flour and salt. Substitute 1 cup Cotija cheese for the Parmesan.

**Scalloped Potatoes au Gratin**
Make recipe as directed, except add 3 cloves minced garlic with the onion. Cook for 7 hours, then sauté 1 ½ cups soft breadcrumbs in ¼ cup butter until crisp. Sprinkle over the potatoes; cook, uncovered, for 20 minutes longer on high; serve.

*Make White Sauce*

*Layer Potatoes in Slow Cooker*

- The flour has to cook in the butter for a few minutes to help open up the starch granules.

- The starch will absorb some of the liquid and form a branched structure that thickens the sauce.

- It's important to stir the white sauce constantly as it cooks, so it thickens evenly and no lumps form.

- You can make the white sauce ahead of time; refrigerate it, covered, then reheat just before layering with the potatoes.

- Make sure that there is some white sauce on all of the potatoes. There shouldn't be any potatoes without sauce.

- If you'd like to include other tender vegetables in this dish, like bell peppers, layer them with the potatoes.

- Mushrooms should be cooked with the onions until they turn brown, or they'll add too much liquid.

- Think about adding other ingredients to these classic potatoes. Some crisply cooked bacon would be delicious, as would different types of cheese.

# STEWED FRUIT

## This old-fashioned recipe is updated by using the slow cooker

Dried fruit is a good choice for the slow cooker. The fruit plumps in the moist heat as it absorbs the cooking liquid.

Dried fruit is good for you, too. It is high in iron, fiber, and antioxidants, and low in fat. These fruits have a greater nutrient density than their fresh counterparts.

Dried fruits include dried figs, plums (also known as prunes), cherries, apricots, dates, raisins, currants, and cranberries. You can find them in the baking supplies aisle of your supermarket.

You can serve this fruit as is, or pour it over ice cream, pound cake, or even your breakfast oatmeal. Enjoy this healthy treat, flavored many ways.

**Yield: Serves 6–8**

## Ingredients

1 tablespoon curry powder

2 tablespoons butter

1 cup dark raisins

1 cup golden raisins

1 cup chopped dried apricots

$1/2$ cup dried currants

1 cup dried cranberries

1 cup dried apple slices

2 cups apple juice

2 cups water

$1/3$ cup sugar

1 cinnamon stick

$1/8$ teaspoon freshly grated nutmeg

1 pinch salt

*Curried Stewed Mixed Fruit*

- In small saucepan, cook curry powder in butter for 2 minutes; set aside.

- Combine all remaining ingredients in 3- or 4-quart slow cooker. Add curry mixture; stir well.

- Cover and cook on low for 7–9 hours or until fruit is softened and liquid has slightly thickened.

- Remove cinnamon stick and discard. Serve fruit hot or cold over pancakes or waffles.

**Vanilla Stewed Fruit**
Prepare recipe as directed, except add 1 vanilla bean. Cut open the bean and scrape out the seeds. Add seeds to the liquid, and add the pod to the fruit. Omit butter and curry powder. Remove cinnamon stick and vanilla pod before serving.

**Citrus Stewed Fruit**
Make recipe as directed, except substitute 1 cup chopped dried prunes for the dried apples, and use 1 cup dried cherries in place of the currants. Reduce water to 1 cup; add 1 cup orange juice, 1 teaspoon grated orange zest, and 2 tablespoons lemon juice.

*Cook Curry Powder*

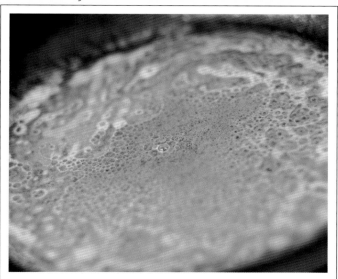

*Prepare Fruit*

- Cook curry powder in butter before adding to the fruits to bring out its flavor.

- Curry powder Is a complex blend of many spices. Heating releases some aromatic oils, which intensifies the flavor.

- Cook the curry powder in butter over low heat just for a few minutes; don't let it burn.

- In place of curry powder, you could add 1 teaspoon cinnamon and ¼ teaspoon cardamom; omit cinnamon stick.

- All of the fruit can be cut to the same size, or you can leave the fruits whole for a different look.

- Since the fruits cook for such a long time, even fruits like whole apricots or prunes will plump and absorb liquid.

- Use any combination of dried fruits that you'd like; just keep the proportion of fruit to liquid the same.

- This recipe can be served warm or cold. If serving cold, stir before use to mix the fruits and the liquid.

# BREAD PUDDING
## The slow cooker is the ideal environment for making bread pudding

Bread pudding is the ultimate in comfort food. It's made from stale or toasted bread, layered with a sweetened custard of eggs, milk, and anything from dried fruits to chocolate.

For a pudding that has a nice crust, place a knife between the lid and the slow cooker insert during the last 30–40 minutes of cooking time. This helps evaporate some of the moisture and creates a crust.

The amount of bread you add to the pudding can vary depending on how dry it is. The mixture should be well moistened, but not overly wet. If there are dry areas, add a bit more milk or cream.

Serve your bread pudding hot with hard sauce or ice cream melting over it.

**Yield: Serves 8–10**

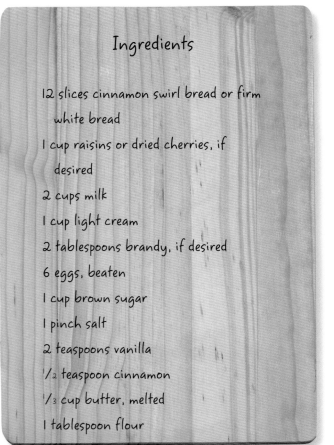

## Ingredients

12 slices cinnamon swirl bread or firm
    white bread

1 cup raisins or dried cherries, if
    desired

2 cups milk

1 cup light cream

2 tablespoons brandy, if desired

6 eggs, beaten

1 cup brown sugar

1 pinch salt

2 teaspoons vanilla

1/2 teaspoon cinnamon

1/3 cup butter, melted

1 tablespoon flour

*Bread Pudding*

- Let bread stand out overnight, uncovered, to dry. Then cut into cubes.

- Place in 5- or 6-quart slow cooker with raisins. In large bowl, combine milk, cream, brandy, eggs, brown sugar, salt, vanilla, cinnamon, butter, and flour; mix well.

- Pour into slow cooker. Push bread cubes down into slow cooker until bread absorbs most of the liquid.

- Cover and cook on high for 2–2 1/2 hours or until pudding is puffed and set. Serve with hard sauce.

**Hard Sauce**

In bowl combine ⅓ cup softened butter with ⅓ cup powdered sugar and 1 teaspoon vanilla; beat until smooth. Stir in 1 tablespoon brandy, if desired. Cover and keep refrigerated until serving time. Spoon on warm dessert and let melt.

**Caramel Cherry Bread Pudding**

Make recipe as directed, except use dried cherries. Increase brown sugar to 1 ½ cups and increase cinnamon to 2 teaspoons. Drizzle top with ¼ cup honey before cooking. Serve with hard sauce made with ⅓ cup brown sugar instead of the powdered sugar.

*Prepare Bread*

*Add Custard and Cook*

- The bread should be dry to the touch, so the final pudding is firm and not mushy.

- The pudding will expand as it cooks, so fill the slow cooker only ⅔ full.

- You can use other types of bread, or a combination of breads. French bread, challah, egg bread, or fruit breads all work.

- Use other dried fruits too, if you'd like. Dried cranberries would be a nice choice for the holidays.

- It's best to cook bread pudding on high because of the delicate nature of the custard.

- The custard should cook fairly quickly as it is absorbed by the bread.

- The pudding is done when the edges look brown and start to pull away from the sides of the slow cooker.

- If the pudding is done but you're not ready to eat, turn it to keep-warm and place some paper towels under the lid to catch condensation.

# POACHED FRUIT
## Hard fruits like apples and pears poach nicely in the slow cooker

Poached fruits are another classic dessert that is made for the slow cooker. Choose firm fruits, preferably stone fruits like peaches or plums, or fall fruit like apples or pears.

Whether you peel your fruits for poaching or leave them unpeeled is a matter of personal choice. If you choose to leave the peel on, you'll need to remove a thin strip of the peel at the top of the fruit so the skin doesn't split in the heat.

Fruit can be poached in fruit juices, wine, or sweetened water. The poaching process turns hard fruits juicy and tender, and adds a wonderful flavor.

Serve with some ice cream or hard sauce for the perfect finish.

**Yield: Serves 4**

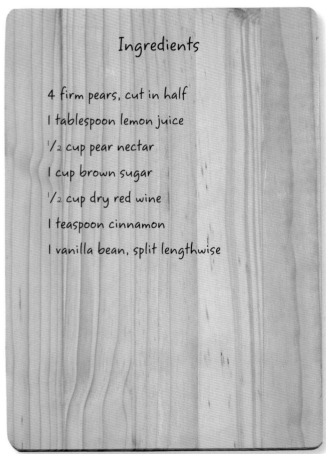

### Ingredients

4 firm pears, cut in half

1 tablespoon lemon juice

½ cup pear nectar

1 cup brown sugar

½ cup dry red wine

1 teaspoon cinnamon

1 vanilla bean, split lengthwise

*Cinnamon Poached Pears*

- Gently remove core from each pear; leave stem attached. Sprinkle with lemon juice.

- In saucepan, combine remaining ingredients and bring to a simmer.

- Place pears, cut side up, in 4-quart slow cooker. Slowly pour sauce over to coat well.

- Cover and cook on low for 2 ½–3 ½ hours or until pears are tender when pierced with fork. Remove vanilla bean; serve pears with sauce.

**Poached Apples**
Make recipe as directed, except use 6 firm apples, peeled, cored, and cut into quarters. Substitute ½ cup apple juice for the pear nectar. Omit dry red wine; use ½ cup water instead. Serve over ice cream or pound cake.

**Poached Peaches**
Use firm peaches with no soft spots. Cut peaches in half; remove pits. Leave skin on. Place in slow cooker. In bowl, mix ½ cup dry white wine, ½ cup water, ⅓ cup sugar, and 2 teaspoons vanilla. Pour over peaches. Cover; cook on low 2–3 hours.

*Core Pears*

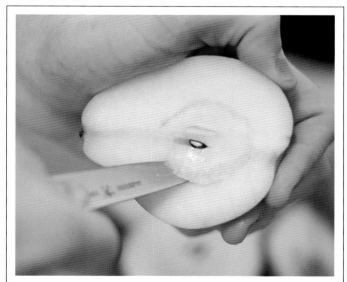

*Make Sauce*

- Choose firm fruit for this type of recipe. It's a good use for slightly unripe fruit.

- Coring any fruit can be a little bit tricky. You can use an apple corer or a sharp knife. Work gently.

- Since the fruit isn't stuffed, core whole fruit from the bottom so the stem stays attached; that makes the fruit look pretty.

- To prevent enzymatic browning, sprinkle the cut sides of the fruit with lemon juice as you work.

- When making the sauce, be sure to simmer until the mixture combines and is smooth.

- Poached fruit can be served warm or cold. If serving cold, refrigerate in the poaching liquid.

- Spoon the liquid over the fruit from time to time until it is very cold to coat it with a glaze.

- Serve the fruit upright in a dessert dish and pour some of the poaching liquid over and around the fruit.

# RICE PUDDING

## Creamy rice pudding is a classic comfort food

Rice pudding is comforting and delicious, and very easy to make in the slow cooker. This is one time when white rice is a good choice. It will cook until the grains almost dissolve, making a thick and creamy pudding.

If you like your rice pudding very thick, you can use medium- or short-grain rice. Stir in any type of dried fruit, or add bits of chocolate.

This recipe is very tolerant. If it's too thick, stir in some more milk; if too thin, cook on high for 20–30 minutes with the lid off.

Serve hot or cold, with some softly whipped sweetened heavy cream or a drizzle of caramel or chocolate sauce.

**Yield: Serves 6**

### Ingredients

I cup long-grain white rice

½ cup golden raisins, if desired

¾ cup sugar

3 cups milk

I cup apple juice

I pinch salt

½ teaspoon cinnamon

⅛ teaspoon nutmeg

¼ cup butter

*Rice Pudding*

- Combine all ingredients in 3 ½-quart slow cooker and stir well to combine.

- Cover and cook on high for 2 ½–3 hours or until rice is tender, stirring once during cooking time.

- Turn off slow cooker and let stand 15 minutes. Add more milk if too thick; cook uncovered on high 20–30 minutes if too thin.

- You can serve this warm, or remove from slow cooker and chill 3–4 hours before serving. If chilled, stir pudding before serving.

**Curried Rice Pudding**
Make recipe as directed, using ¾ cup brown sugar in place of the granulated sugar. Cut milk to 2 cups; increase apple juice to 2 cups. Add 1 tablespoon curry powder with the cinnamon and nutmeg. If using raisins, use dark raisins instead of golden.

**Arborio Rice Pudding**
Make recipe as directed, except substitute 1 cup Arborio rice in place of the long-grain white rice. Omit apple juice; increase milk to 5 cups. Cover and cook on low for 5–7 hours until thick. Stir in 2 teaspoons vanilla and serve.

*Mix Ingredients*

*Stir Pudding*

- Some recipes tell you to rinse the rice before cooking, but that isn't necessary.

- Rinsing washes away surface starch, and in rice pudding, we want as much starch as we can get.

- Spray the slow cooker insert with nonstick cooking spray containing flour for no sticking and best results.

- You could also use a slow cooker cooking bag for the easiest cleanup. Just serve the pudding and throw the bag away.

- As the rice cooks, it will expand while absorbing liquid. For an evenly cooked dish, stir once during cooking time.

- Make sure that you scrape the bottom and the sides of the slow cooker when you stir, so nothing sticks and burns.

- Serve the rice pudding with a simple sauce made by pureeing 1 (10-ounce) package thawed frozen raspberries.

- Or use a purchased ice cream topping. Toasted nuts or granola are also a nice finish.

CLASSIC DESSERTS

# FRUIT CRISP
## Granola is the secret ingredient to a candy-like topping

Fruit crisps are made from fruits topped with a crumble of flour, sugar, oatmeal, and nuts. When baked in the oven, the topping becomes crisp. In the slow cooker, the topping becomes more like candy—thick, chewy, and sweet.

Use the same apples for fruit crisp that you'd use for poaching. They will keep their shape and become tender and juicy cooked in the slow cooker.

Granola helps add a bit of crunch to the topping. You can use homemade or purchased granola; look for types with large and very crunchy clusters or oats and sugar.

These crisps are best served hot or warm, right out of the slow cooker. Top with hard sauce, ice cream, or softly whipped heavy cream.

**Yield: Serves 6–8**

### Ingredients

4 Granny Smith apples

3 Bosc pears

2 tablespoons lemon juice

1/2 cup flour

2/3 cup brown sugar

1 1/2 cups granola

1 cup quick oatmeal

1 teaspoon cinnamon

1/2 cup butter, melted

1/2 cup toffee bits

*Toffee Fruit Crisp*

- Peel and core fruits and cut into 1-inch chunks. Toss with lemon juice and place in 3 ½-quart slow cooker.

- In large bowl, combine flour, brown sugar, granola, oatmeal, and cinnamon and mix well. Stir in butter until crumbly.

- Add toffee bits and sprinkle evenly over fruit in slow cooker to coat.

- Cover and cook on low for 4–6 hours or until fruit is tender and topping is bubbly and hot.

**Apple Fruit Crisp**
Make recipe as directed, except use 8 Granny Smith apples, peeled and sliced; omit pears. Sprinkle apples with ½ cup brown sugar before topping. Omit toffee bits; add 1 cup chopped walnuts to topping mixture. Cook on low for 5–6 hours until apples are tender. Serve with vanilla ice cream.

**Pear Fruit Crisp**
Make recipe as directed, except use 7 Bosc pears, peeled and sliced; omit apples. Sprinkle pears with ½ cup granulated sugar before adding topping. Add ¼ teaspoon nutmeg to topping mixture; omit toffee bits. Add ½ cup chopped pecans to topping.

## Prepare Fruits

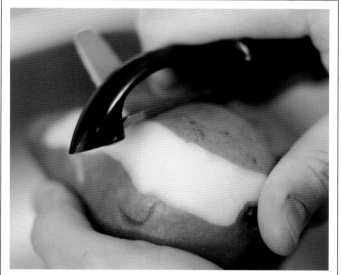

- Peel and toss the fruits with lemon juice so they don't turn brown before you add the topping.

- You can sprinkle the fruits with ⅓ to ½ cup sugar, either brown or granulated, for a sweeter dessert.

- Or drizzle the fruit with a caramel ice-cream topping or honey, then add the granola topping.

- Or add dried fruits, like raisins, dried currants, dried cherries, or dried cranberries, for more flavor and color.

## Mix Toppings

- Mix the flour, brown sugar, oatmeal, and granola well before adding the butter.

- Mix in the butter using your fingers until the mixture is crumbly. When you hold some in your hand and push together, it should hold a shape.

- If you like a lot of topping, you can increase the topping proportion.

- Still, make sure that the slow cooker is filled ⅔ to ¾ full for best results.

# STUFFED FRUIT

## Hard fruits, like apples and pears, pair beautifully with a sweet stuffing

Stuffed fruit is an excellent dessert for the slow cooker. Use the same fruits that you'd use for poaching or in fruit crisps because they hold their shape in the low, slow heat.

Stuff fruit with anything from nuts to sugar mixtures to dried fruits or candy. There are several ways to stuff fruit.

You can core the whole fruit from the top or the bottom and fill the cavity, or cut the fruit in half, cut out the core, then fill and place the halves back together.

Or you can cut the fruit in half, remove the core, and fill; then layer, rounded side down, in the slow cooker. Enjoy with ice cream.

**Yield: Serves 6**

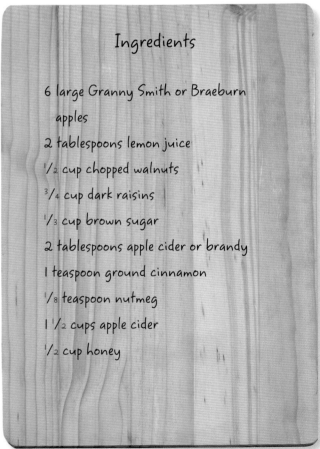

### Ingredients

6 large Granny Smith or Braeburn apples

2 tablespoons lemon juice

1/2 cup chopped walnuts

3/4 cup dark raisins

1/3 cup brown sugar

2 tablespoons apple cider or brandy

1 teaspoon ground cinnamon

1/8 teaspoon nutmeg

1 1/2 cups apple cider

1/2 cup honey

*Stuffed Apples*

- Carefully remove core from each apple starting at the top. Leave the bottom ¼ inch untouched.

- Peel a small strip from the top of each apple. Sprinkle with lemon juice.

- Mix walnuts, raisins, brown sugar, 2 tablespoons apple cider, cinnamon, and nutmeg; overfill apples with mixture.

- Place apples in single layer in 4-quart slow cooker. Mix 1 ½ cups apple cider and honey; pour over and around apples. Cover and cook on low for 4–5 hours until apples are tender.

## RECIPE VARIATION

**Stuffed Pears**
Core 6 pears, leaving the bottom skin intact, and remove ½ inch of the peel from the top of the apples. Fill with a mixture of ½ cup dried cranberries, ½ cup brown sugar, 1 teaspoon cinnamon, and ½ cup pecans. Place in slow cooker; add 1 cup cranberry juice. Cover; cook on low 5–6 hours.

## RED LIGHT

To check an older slow cooker for safety, fill it with water and let cook, covered, on low for 8 hours. The water temperature should be 185 degrees F or higher. If the temperature is any lower, discard the slow cooker.

### Prepare Filling

- You can use any warm spices in this filling. Warm spices include cinnamon, nutmeg, allspice, cloves, and cardamom.

- Try different nut and fruit combinations in your stuffed fruit. In fact, stuff each apple with something different.

- You could use chopped cashews with dried cranberries, or chopped pecans with white chocolate and dried cherries.

- Use your imagination; you could also mix apples and pears and vary the stuffing to create a fruit buffet.

### Fill Apples

- Overfill the apples. This means fill them higher than the core; just heap the filling on top.

- The filling will sink into the apples as it cooks, so you want to add more than you think you'll need.

- If there's any leftover filling, just sprinkle on top of the apples in the slow cooker.

- Serve these apples hot or warm from the slow cooker, with hard sauce, vanilla ice cream, or whipped cream.

# CHOCOLATE PUDDING CAKE

## The slow cooker bakes a velvety cake topped with creamy pudding

Ah, chocolate. The ultimate dessert, chocolate has been used in everything from puddings to cakes. It can be used very successfully in the slow cooker, but with a few caveats.

Chocolate burns at around 180 to 190 degrees F, so even on low you do run the risk of chocolate burning.

Prevent this by keeping an eye on it, stirring when the recipe directs, and checking the dish at the earliest cooking time.

When chocolate is enveloped in a cake batter, the burning point goes up, so it's safer in the slow cooker on low. And when you use a baking pan, the metal shields the batter from the slow cooker's heat.

Use the best chocolate you can afford and enjoy these comforting and indulgent recipes.

**Yield: Serves 6**

### Ingredients

1 ¼ cups flour
¾ cup brown sugar
¼ cup cocoa
1 teaspoon baking powder
½ teaspoon baking soda
¼ teaspoon salt
⅔ cup milk
3 tablespoons butter, melted
1 teaspoon vanilla
1 cup semisweet chocolate chips
3 tablespoons cocoa
½ cup brown sugar
2 tablespoons honey
1 ¼ cups water

*Chocolate Fudge Pudding Cake*

- Grease 2-quart baking dish with unsalted butter. In bowl, mix flour, ¾ cup brown sugar, ¼ cup cocoa, baking powder, baking soda, and salt.

- Add milk, butter, and vanilla; mix until combined. Pour into baking dish; top with chocolate chips.

- In saucepan, combine 3 tablespoons cocoa, ½ cup brown sugar, honey, and water; bring to a boil.

- Pour over batter in pan. Place on rack in 5-quart slow cooker. Cover and cook on high 3–4 hours or until edges are set.

**White and Dark Chocolate Pudding Cake**
Make recipe as directed, except increase cocoa in cake to ⅓ cup. Reduce semisweet chocolate chips to ½ cup; add ½ cup white chocolate chips. Proceed as directed. After cake has baked for 3 hours, sprinkle top with ½ cup white chocolate chips.

**Chocolate Caramel Pudding Cake**
Make cake as directed, except increase cocoa in cake to ⅓ cup. Unwrap 10 caramels and cut into quarters. Push caramels partway into batter in pan. Instead of honey in topping, use 3 tablespoons caramel ice-cream topping.

*Mix Cake Batter*

*Place Pan in Slow Cooker*

- Mix the batter with a wire whisk to ensure there are no lumps. Make the batter right before you bake the cake.

- Baking powder and baking soda are different. Baking powder is made from baking soda and cream of tartar.

- Both are necessary to the cake. The baking soda raises the pH of the batter so it rises evenly.

- Baking powder has an expiration date on its package; follow it to the letter. Baking soda does not expire.

- Be sure to grease the pan with unsalted butter. Salted butter can cause the cake to stick to the pan.

- The cake pan has to be placed on a rack in the slow cooker so the heat circulates around it as it cooks.

- Because this cake has a moist pudding layer, you don't need to add a layer of paper towels under the lid.

- Serve the cake with some vanilla or chocolate ice cream for a wonderful treat.

# FONDUE
## Make and serve a rich and creamy fondue in the slow cooker

Fondue is a Swiss dish. It can be made from cheese, when it's served as a main course, or from chocolate, for a rich and decadent dessert.

The slow cooker is ideal for fondue making because you can cook the fondue and serve it in one pot. Fondue pots, with their canned heat source of Sterno, can burn the chocolate as you're eating it. The slow cooker's low heat, or keep-warm feature, prevents this and keeps the chocolate at the ideal temperature for dipping.

Use your imagination when thinking of dippers for this dessert. Cake squares and fruit are the obvious choices; cookies, candy bars, and snack cakes are delicious, too.

**Yield: Serves 6–8**

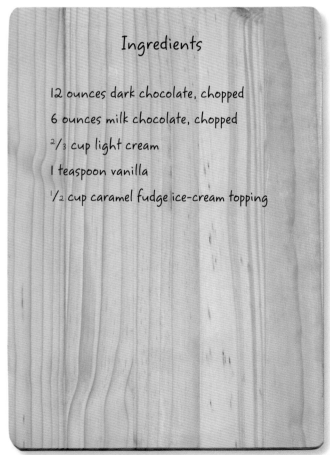

### Ingredients

12 ounces dark chocolate, chopped

6 ounces milk chocolate, chopped

$2/3$ cup light cream

1 teaspoon vanilla

$1/2$ cup caramel fudge ice-cream topping

*Chocolate Caramel Fondue*

- In 2-quart slow cooker, combine chocolates with cream. Cover and cook on low for 2–3 hours, stirring twice during cooking time.

- Stir; if chocolate is melted, proceed with recipe. If chocolate is not melted, cook for another 30–40 minutes on low.

- Add vanilla and fudge topping; stir well. Cover and cook on low for 20–30 minutes longer.

- Serve right from the slow cooker insert with cookies, angel food cake squares, pound cake squares, and fruit for dipping.

**White Chocolate Fondue**
Make recipe as directed, but use 18 ounces of white chocolate bar, chopped. Mix in 2-quart bowl; place in 4-quart slow cooker. Omit light cream and caramel fudge ice-cream topping; add a 12-ounce can of evaporated milk. Cook on low 1–2 hours until melted; stir in 2 tablespoons amaretto, if desired.

**Black and White Fondue**
Make 1 batch Chocolate Caramel Fondue, except omit the caramel fudge topping. An hour later, make the White Chocolate Fondue. Pour both at the same time into a 4-quart slow cooker; stir to marble and serve immediately.

*Chop Chocolate*

*Stir Chocolate*

- To chop chocolate, place it on a work surface and chop using a chef's knife.

- Just cut across the chocolate with a knife, occasionally bringing the pile together, until the pieces are about ½ inch.

- The cream not only adds richness and smoothness to the fondue, it helps shield the chocolate from the heat.

- For an even richer fondue, use heavy cream instead of light cream. You can also vary the chocolate proportions; use more or less milk chocolate.

- Stir the chocolate using a heatproof silicone spatula or wooden spoon. Be sure to scrape the sides and bottom of the slow cooker.

- If you have a newer slow cooker and are afraid of burning, cook the fondue mixture in a bowl inside the slow cooker.

- The vanilla is added at the end of cooking because it has volatile oils that release with heat.

- You want to keep those oils within the fondue mixture, so it won't heat it for long after adding the vanilla.

CHOCOLATE DESSERTS

# CHOCOLATE CHEESECAKE

## Cheesecake cooks to perfection in the moist slow cooker environment

Cheesecake can be quite temperamental. Often, cheesecake baked in the oven has a crack running right down the center.

There are two culprits in this disaster. First, a cheesecake isn't meant to be airy. Don't beat the mixture very long; just enough to incorporate the sugar, eggs, and chocolate. If the cheesecake rises as it bakes, it may crack upon cooking.

Second, the oven's dry heat cooking method can cause

cracking, which is why cheesecakes are often baked in a water bath. The moist environment of the slow cooker helps prevent cracking.

The cheesecake has to be chilled before serving. Remove from the slow cooker and place in the refrigerator for 4–5 hours, then enjoy.

**Yield: Serves 8–10**

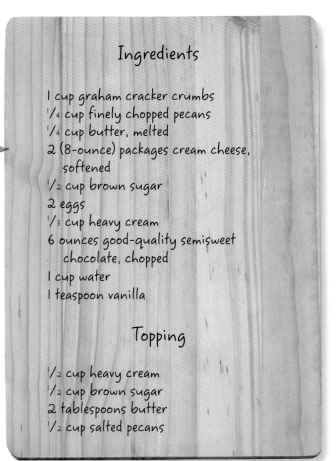

### Ingredients

1 cup graham cracker crumbs
¼ cup finely chopped pecans
¼ cup butter, melted
2 (8-ounce) packages cream cheese, softened
½ cup brown sugar
2 eggs
⅓ cup heavy cream
6 ounces good-quality semisweet chocolate, chopped
1 cup water
1 teaspoon vanilla

### Topping

½ cup heavy cream
½ cup brown sugar
2 tablespoons butter
½ cup salted pecans

*Chocolate Praline Cheesecake*

- Mix graham cracker crumbs, pecans, and ¼ cup butter. Press into greased 7-inch springform pan.

- Beat cream cheese until smooth. Add ½ cup brown sugar, then eggs.

- Melt ⅓ cup cream with chocolate; stir into cheese.

Pour into pan. Cover with foil; place in 6-quart slow cooker. Pour 1 cup water around the pan.

- Cook on high 3–4 hours until edges are set. Cook cream, brown sugar, and butter until smooth. Pour over cheesecake. Top with salted pecans; chill.

220

**Salted Pecans**

Sweet and salty is the latest craze in desserts. To salt nuts, melt 2 tablespoons butter in medium pan. Add 1 cup whole pecans or almonds; cook and stir until nuts are fragrant. Remove to paper towel; spread nuts out. Sprinkle with ½ teaspoon kosher salt; let cool.

**Chocolate Chocolate Cheesecake**

Make recipe as directed, except use chocolate cookie crumbs in place of the graham cracker crumbs. Stir 1 cup dark chocolate chips into cheesecake batter. Omit brown sugar topping; melt 1 cup chocolate chips with 3 tablespoons cream; pour over top and chill.

*Beat Chocolate into Cheesecake*

- Beat the cream cheese with an electric mixer just until smooth, then beat in the sugar and eggs until smooth.

- Make sure that the chocolate is completely melted, but not very hot when added to the batter.

- You can melt the chocolate ahead of time, then let cool until lukewarm. Then stir into the batter.

*Cover Pan Tightly*

- Wrap the springform pan completely, from top to bottom, in 1 large sheet of heavy duty foil so no water leaks into the cheesecake as it cooks.

- Pour the water carefully around the foil-covered pan. Don't let any get on the cheesecake

- Don't start cooking the topping until the cheesecake is done; it will harden quickly.

- Stir the topping while it cooks. It will seem like it is not coming together, then all of a sudden the sauce will blend.

CHOCOLATE DESSERTS

# CHOCOLATE BREAD PUDDING
## Chocolate is a wonderful addition to bread pudding

Chocolate is the perfect addition to turn bread pudding into an elegant dessert. You can use white chocolate, milk chocolate, dark chocolate, or even the newest kinds of chocolate chips: chocolate swirled with caramel or peanut butter.

Bread pudding was originally a very humble dessert, created to use up leftover stale bread. It has evolved into quite a treat, served at the best restaurants in the world.

Chocolate is very important in this recipe, so buy the best you can find. Makers like Godiva, Lindt, and Callebaut make the best chocolate, with a high percentage of cocoa butter. That is what makes chocolate smooth and creamy.

Serve this rich pudding with some plain heavy cream.

**Yield: Serves 8–10**

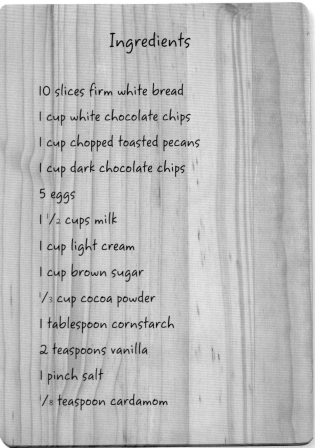

### Ingredients

10 slices firm white bread

1 cup white chocolate chips

1 cup chopped toasted pecans

1 cup dark chocolate chips

5 eggs

1 1/2 cups milk

1 cup light cream

1 cup brown sugar

1/3 cup cocoa powder

1 tablespoon cornstarch

2 teaspoons vanilla

1 pinch salt

1/8 teaspoon cardamom

*White and Black Bread Pudding*

- Cube bread and layer in slow cooker with white chocolate chips, nuts, and dark chocolate chips.

- In medium bowl, combine remaining ingredients and beat until smooth. Pour into slow cooker.

- Cover and cook on high for 4 hours, or until pudding is puffed and set.

- Serve with vanilla ice cream, chocolate sauce, or hard sauce.

**Chocolate Sauce**
Combine 3 tablespoons butter, 2 tablespoons brewed coffee, ¼ cup dark corn syrup, ½ cup brown sugar, and ⅓ cup cocoa powder in saucepan. Cook and stir until thick. Stir in 1 pinch salt and 1 teaspoon vanilla; remove from heat. Store in refrigerator; reheat in saucepan to use.

**Dark Chocolate Bread Pudding**
Make recipe as directed, except add 1 cup semisweet chocolate chips to the bread mixture. Omit the white chocolate chips. Omit the cardamom; increase vanilla to 1 ½ teaspoons. Cook as directed; serve with vanilla ice cream.

*Cube Bread*

*Layer Ingredients*

- The bread should be cubed evenly and into fairly small pieces, about ½ to ¾ inch square. Layer evenly with the chocolate chips.

- It's important to toast the pecans before adding to the pudding mixture so they retain some crunch

in the middle of the soft pudding.

- To toast, place pecans in a dry saucepan. Cook over low heat, shaking the pan occasionally, until fragrant.

- Let the nuts cool completely before adding to the bread mixture.

- Place a layer of bread in the slow cooker before you add the chocolate chips. The chips should be suspended in the bread.

- You can use any combination of chocolate chips and nuts that you'd like.

- Chopped cashews, natural (not dyed) pistachios, walnuts, pecans, and even mixed nuts are excellent.

- This dessert is meant to be decadent; don't use low-fat ingredients. Just eat small portions and enjoy.

# CHOCOLATE CUSTARD
## Add chocolate to custard for a decadent twist

Chocolate custard is like a pudding, but thicker. It will hold its shape when cut or lifted with a spoon.

Recipes in the custard family include crème caramel and flan. Custards are creamy, rich, and smooth when properly made. It's important to follow the directions carefully and take your time when assembling the ingredients.

Like all egg desserts, custard can be temperamental. There's a fine line between smooth custard and scrambled eggs. It's best baked at low heat for a long period of time; that's where the slow cooker comes in. Blend all the ingredients well, and make sure to strain the mixture before cooking.

Serve this custard warm or cool, with a drizzle of chocolate sauce or some whipped cream.

**Yield: Serves 6–8**

## Ingredients

1 cup milk

1 cup heavy cream

2 tablespoons cocoa powder

½ cup brown sugar

6 ounces semisweet chocolate, chopped

3 eggs

1 egg yolk

1 pinch salt

1 teaspoon vanilla

1 cup hot water

*Chocolate Custard*

- Grease 1-quart baking dish with unsalted butter. In saucepan, combine milk, cream, cocoa, brown sugar, and chocolate.

- Cook and stir over low heat until chocolate melts and mixture is smooth. Remove from heat.

- Add eggs and egg yolk, salt, and vanilla and mix well. Strain into baking dish and cover with foil.

- Place on rack in 5-quart slow cooker. Pour hot water around dish. Cover and cook on high 2–3 hours until custard is set. Cool 1 hour; chill.

### Pots de Crème
Make recipe as directed, except strain the chocolate mixture into a bowl. Grease 6 (6-ounce) ramekins or small baking cups with unsalted butter. Divide chocolate mixture among cups. Place on rack in slow cooker; add water. Cook on high for 1 ½ –2 ½ hours until just barely set; cool.

### Chocolate Ginger Custard
Make recipe as directed, except reduce semisweet chocolate to 4 ounces. Add ½ teaspoon ground ginger to mixture; strain. Then stir in 2 tablespoons very finely minced candied ginger. Pour into baking dish and cook as directed.

## Strain Chocolate Mixture

- Beat the mixture until smooth and combined. Like cheesecake, you don't want to add too much air to a custard.

- Egg custard should be perfectly smooth. To accomplish this it has to be strained.

- Straining removes any lumps from chocolate or sugar, and removes the chalazae, the part of the egg that attaches the yolk to the white.

- Use a fine-mesh strainer, not a colander, to strain the custard mixture.

## Cook Custard

- Make sure that the pan fits in the slow cooker with at least an inch to spare around all sides.

- The rack ensures that heat circulates evenly around the custard as it cooks.

- The custard is covered with foil; still, when you pour the

water into the slow cooker, pour it around the pan, not on top of it.

- Custard is best served chilled; chill for 3–5 hours in the refrigerator before serving.

# CHOCOLATE CANDIES
## Melt the candy in the slow cooker for some delicious and easy treats

Homemade chocolate candies are quite the delicacy, and will impress everyone. Yet they're easy to make, especially in the slow cooker.

This isn't a recipe that you can walk away from. Don't make the recipe, turn on the slow cooker, and leave the house. Because of chocolate's low burning point, it has to be stirred often, even when melted in the slow cooker.

There are several types of chocolate, defined by the amount of cacao they contain. Baking chocolate and cocoa powder have the highest content, 100 percent. Dark or bittersweet chocolate ranges from 30 to 90 percent cacao, and milk chocolate has 10 to 20 percent.

Pick your favorite and make some fabulous candies.

**Yield: 24 candies**

### Ingredients

2 cups dark chocolate chips

2 cups semisweet chocolate chips

2 tablespoons heavy cream

1 (1-ounce) square baking chocolate, chopped

1/2 cup creamy peanut butter

3 cups dry roasted peanuts

*Chocolate Peanut Candies*

- In 3-½ quart slow cooker, combine chocolate chips, cream, and baking chocolate.

- Cover and cook on high for 1 hour and stir. Reduce heat to low. Cover and cook for 1–2 hours longer until mixture is smooth, stirring once.

- Stir well, then add peanut butter. Stir until peanut butter melts and mixture is smooth.

- Add peanuts and stir to coat. Turn off slow cooker; drop candy by tablespoons onto waxed paper; let stand until set.

226

Chocolate, in moderation, is good for you. It contains antioxidants, compounds that help protect you from free radicals. Dark chocolate is one of the best sources of flavanol antioxidants because it has a high percentage of cacao, the nib or center of the cocoa bean.

## · · · · · RECIPE VARIATION· · · ·

**Chocolate Truffles**
Melt 2 cups dark chocolate chips, 2 cups milk chocolate chips, and 1⅛ cups heavy cream in slow cooker. Stir together, then add vanilla. Pour into bowl and refrigerate until firm. Beat with electric mixer until fluffy; form into balls; roll in cocoa powder.

## *Prepare Ingredients*

- You can use chocolate bars instead of the chocolate chips if you'd like. The chips make a slightly sweeter candy.

- If using chocolate bars, chop by cutting with a chef's knife. Cut into pieces about ½ to 1 inch in diameter.

- You can use any combination of dark, milk, or semisweet chocolate in this recipe.

- Just keep the proportion of chocolate to cream and peanut butter the same so the candies will set.

## *Form Candies*

- Waxed paper or a Silpat liner works well for holding the candies as they cool.

- To speed up setting, you can refrigerate the candies until firm to the touch.

- Don't store the candies in the refrigerator. If chocolate is exposed to temperature

contrasts, it will "bloom," or form a grayish coating.

- Make several different kinds of candy with different chocolates and nuts and make your own chocolate box for Valentine's Day.

# WEB SITES, TV SHOWS, AND VIDEOS
## Information for slow cookers

In these times, there are many places you can turn to for help with your slow cooker. Online, there are lots of videos, recipes, tips, and hints to make your slow cooking experience perfect.

Product manufacturers, books, magazines, and catalogs can also help. You'll be able to find information about products, many recipes, slow cooker tips, and where to find special ingredients, tools, and replacement lids and inserts for your slow cooker.

Online message boards and forums are wonderful resources as well. On popular boards, you will get answers to your questions very quickly. Don't be afraid to ask for help!

## Slow cooker Web sites

### Crockpot@CDKitchen
http://crockpot.cdkitchen.com

- This Web site features recipes submitted by bloggers. More than 4,200 old-fashioned and updated recipes are reliable and delicious.

### Crock-pot.com
www.crock-pot.com/recipescat.aspx?catid=6

- This site, run by Rival, has lots of recipes specially developed for the slow cooker.

### AllRecipes
http://allrecipes.com/Recipes/Main-Dish/Slow-Cooker/Main.aspx

- AllRecipes, which features reader-submitted recipes that are rated by members, is a reliable source of slow cooker recipes.

### Southern Food at About.com
http://southernfood.about.com/library/crock/blcpidx.htm

- This venerable site has more than 1,400 slow cooker recipes for everything from desserts to pot roast.

### BH&G
www.bhg.com/recipes/slow-cooker/

- *Better Homes and Gardens* offers hundreds of simple and interesting slow cooker recipes, all tested in their test kitchens.

### RecipeZaar
www.recipezaar.com/recipes/crockpot

- Thousands of slow cooker recipes are submitted by readers and rated by viewers.

# Slow cooker videos

## YouTube
www.youtube.com/watch?v=87sAHQ5x5gk

- Thousands of videos will teach you how to make lots of slow cooker recipes.

## Expert Village
www.expertvillage.com/video-series/1758_crock-pot.htm

- You'll learn how to make everything from apple pie to Chicken Artichoke Soup at this site.

## Busy Cooks at About.com
http://video.about.com/busycooks/How-to-Cook-With-a-Crock-pot.htm

- Video shows you exactly how to safely and efficiently use a slow cooker.

## AllRecipes Videos
http://allrecipes.com/HowTo/Secrets-of-Success-for-Slow-Cooker-Chicken-Video/Detail.aspx

- AllRecipes.com has a lot of excellent videos made in their test kitchen.

## About.com Food Videos
http://video.about.com/food.htm

- Dozens of sites offer hundreds of videos teaching you how to use the slow cooker in every ethic cuisine imaginable.

# Slow cooker TV cooking shows

## America's Test Kitchen

- Cook's Illustrated is responsible for this show on PBS that teaches you how to cook. Lots of great slow cooker recipes.

## Robin Miller on the Food Network

- Robin Miller, in her show Quick Fix Meals, uses the slow cooker a lot to efficiently prepare meals for the week.

## Semi-Homemade Cooking with Sandra Lee on the Food Network

- Sandra Lee developed the concept of "30 percent fresh food, 70 percent prepared food." She often has slow cooker episodes.

229

RESOURCE DIRECTORY

# BOOKS AND MAGAZINES
## Hundreds of slow cooker books and magazines are here to help

## Slow cooker books

Alley, Lynn. *The Gourmet Slow Cooker*. Ten Speed Press, 2004
- Surprising and unusual recipes include White Truffle Risotto, Chicken Mole, and Anise Biscotti.

Better Homes & Gardens. *Biggest Book of Slow Cooker Recipes*. BH&G, 2002
- Kitchen-tested recipes for your slow cooker; lots of kid-friendly recipes.

Betty Crocker. *Betty Crocker's Slow Cooker Cookbook*. Betty Crocker, 1999
- Excellent collection of triple-tested slow cooker recipes from the giant of cooking.

Editors of Cooking Light Magazine. *Cooking Light Slow Cooker*. Oxmoor House, 2006
- Slow cooker recipes from Cooking Light Magazine's "Essential Recipe Collection."

Finlayson, Judith. *The Healthy Slow Cooker*. Richard Rose, 2005
- Healthy recipes use natural ingredients and whole foods. Recipes include Winter Vegetable Casserole and Ribs 'n Greens with Wheatberries.

Good, Phyllis Pellman. *Fix-It and Forget-It Big Cookbook*. Good Books, 2008
- From one of the first "modern" slow cooker authors, this book is part of a popular series.

Gurley, Chris, and Tom Hamilton. *Crock-Pot Incredibly Easy Recipes*. Publications International, 2007
- Book of recipes assembled by Rival, a leading slow cooker manufacturer.

Hensperger, Beth, and Julie Kaufmann. *Not Your Mother's Slow Cooker Cookbook*. Harvard Common Press, 2005
- This book offers updated slow cooker recipes that don't use cream of mushroom soup, but explore ethnic cuisines.

Rachor, JoAnn. *Fast Cooking in a Slow Cooker*. Family Health Publications, 2005
- Recipes designed for quick preparation and slow cooking. Color photographs, lots of tips and information.

Robertson, Robin. *Fresh from the Vegetarian Slow Cooker*. Harvard Common Press, 2004
- Book offers information on cooking vegetarian meals in the slow cooker along with many recipes.

Rodgers, Rick. *Slow Cooker Ready and Waiting.* William Morrow, 1998
- Delicious, gourmet recipes from your slow cooker, like Coq au Vin and Sweet and Sour Brisket.

Schloss, Andrew, and Yvonne Duivenvoorden. *Art of the Slow Cooker.* Chronicle Books, 2008
- Book offers eighty recipes, with advice about entertaining and cooking charts for perfect timing.

Spitler, Sue, and Linda R. Yoakam. *1001 Best Slow Cooker Recipes.* Agate Surrey, 2008
- Great time-saving strategies and family-friendly recipes that cook in your slow cooker.

## Slow cooker magazines

*Better Homes & Gardens Special Interest*
- Magazines devoted entirely to slow cookers are offered several times a year.

*Family Circle*
- This magazine offers lots of slow cooker recipes and menus, seasonal recipes, and tips.

*Slow Cooker*
- By the editors of *Slow Cooker Magazine,* this little volume offers lots of recipes and tips.

*Taste of Home Slow Cooker*
- This venerable magazine focuses on reader-submitted recipes, tested in their test kitchens.

*Woman's Day*
- Magazine has many slow cooker recipes in each issue, along with cooking lessons and tips.

# EQUIPMENT RESOURCES
Find equipment through these resources to stock your kitchen

## Catalogs for slow cookers

### Brylane Home
- Catalog has lots of kitchen equipment, including specialty tools, utensils, and dishware.

### Chef's Catalog
- A good selection of utensils and kitchen equipment.

### Hammacher Schlemmer
- Catalog offers high end appliances, including stainless steel slow cookers and other kitchen equipment.

### Solutions
- Lots of new equipment and tools to make cooking quick and easy.

### Sur la Table
- Catalog offers lots of kitchen equipment along with dishes, serving utensils, and flatware.

### Williams-Sonoma
- Top of the line equipment, along with cookbooks and many appliances, tools, and accessories.

## Web sites for slow cooker equipment

### Amazon.com
- Many appliances are for sale on this large site, including slow cookers of every size and shape.

### Chefsresource.com
- Cutlery, flatware, gadgets, tools, knives, and brands like Cuisinart are featured.

### ConsumerSearch.com
- Web site rates slow cookers and gives you links to purchase them online.

### Cooking.com
- Kitchen fixtures, large appliances, cutlery, cookbooks, and tools can be found at this site.

### Cookingequipment.about.com
- Site reviews cooking equipment and gives tips about buying the appliances and utensils you'll use the most.

### Crock-pot.com
- The Web site for Rival slow cookers, this site offers customer service, replacement parts, and recipes.

### eHow.com
www.ehow.com/how_2135456_buy-slow-cooker.html

- "How to Buy a Slow Cooker." Article relates tips on choosing the best appliance for you.

### The Gourmet Depot
www.thegourmetdepotco.com/store/

- Replacement parts for many kitchen appliances, listed by manufacturer.

### Kitchen.ManualsOnline.com
- Web site offers contact information for dozens of slow cooker manufacturers.

### Sears.com
- Site offers dozens of slow cookers from many manufacturers.

# METRIC CONVERSION TABLES

## Approximate U.S. Metric Equivalents

### Liquid Ingredients

| U.S. MEASURES | METRIC | U.S. MEASURES | METRIC |
|---|---|---|---|
| ¼ TSP. | 1.23 ML | 2 TBSP. | 29.57 ML |
| ½ TSP. | 2.36 ML | 3 TBSP. | 44.36 ML |
| ¾ TSP. | 3.70 ML | ¼ CUP | 59.15 ML |
| 1 TSP. | 4.93 ML | ½ CUP | 118.30 ML |
| 1¼ TSP. | 6.16 ML | 1 CUP | 236.59 ML |
| 1½ TSP. | 7.39 ML | 2 CUPS OR 1 PT. | 473.18 ML |
| 1¾ TSP. | 8.63 ML | 3 CUPS | 709.77 ML |
| 2 TSP. | 9.86 ML | 4 CUPS OR 1 QT. | 946.36 ML |
| 1 TBSP. | 14.79 ML | 4 QTS. OR 1 GAL. | 3.79 L |

### Dry Ingredients

| U.S. MEASURES | | METRIC | U.S. MEASURES | METRIC |
|---|---|---|---|---|
| 17⅗ OZ. | 1 LIVRE | 500 G | 2 OZ. | 60 (56.6) G |
| 16 OZ. | 1 LB. | 454 G | 1¾ OZ. | 50 G |
| 8⅞ OZ. | | 250 G | 1 OZ. | 30 (28.3) G |
| 5¼ OZ. | | 150 G | ⅞ OZ. | 25 G |
| 4½ OZ. | | 125 G | ¾ OZ. | 21 (21.3) G |
| 4 OZ. | | 115 (113.2) G | ½ OZ. | 15 (14.2) G |
| 3½ OZ. | | 100 G | ¼ OZ. | 7 (7.1) G |
| 3 OZ. | | 85 (84.9) G | ⅛ OZ. | 3½ (3.5) G |
| 2⅘ OZ. | | 80 G | 1/16 OZ. | 2 (1.8) G |

# GLOSSARY
Learn the language first

**Al dente:** Italian phrase meaning "to the tooth"; describes doneness of pasta.

**Baking Powder:** A leavening agent used in baking and candy making.

**Beat:** To manipulate food with a spoon, mixer, or whisk to combine.

**Braise:** Cooking method where meats or vegetables are browned, then simmered slowly in liquid until tender.

**Broil:** To cook food close to the heat source, quickly. Used in slow cooking to add color and flavor.

**Brown:** Cooking step that caramelizes food and adds color and flavor before cooking in the slow cooker.

**Caramelize:** To cook until the sugars and proteins in a food combine to form complex compounds. Refers to browning of food and flavor.

**Chop:** To cut food into small pieces, using a chef's knife or a food processor.

**Coat:** To cover food in another ingredient, as to coat chicken breasts with breadcrumbs.

**Curry Powder:** A blend of warm spices used in Indian cooking to flavor meat, vegetable, and fruit dishes.

**Deglaze:** To add a liquid to a pan used to sauté meats; this removes drippings and brown bits to create a sauce.

**Dice:** To cut food into small, even portions, usually about 1/4 inch square.

**Dry Rub:** Spices and herbs rubbed into meats or vegetables to marinate and add flavor.

**Flake:** To break into small pieces; canned meats are usually flaked.

**Fold:** To combine two soft or liquid mixtures together, using an over-and-under method of mixing.

**Grate:** To use a grater or microplane to remove small pieces or shreds of food.

**Grill:** To cook over coals or charcoal, or over high heat.

**Marinate:** To let meats or vegetables stand in a mixture of an acid and oil, to add flavor and tenderize.

**Melt:** To turn a solid into a liquid by the addition of heat.

**Mince:** To cut into very small, even pieces with a knife or food processor.

**Pan-Fry:** To cook quickly in a shallow pan, in a small amount of fat over relatively high heat.

**Pare:** To remove the skin of fruits or vegetables, usually using a swivel-bladed peeler.

**Roux:** A mixture of butter and flour, used to thicken a white sauce.

**Shred:** To use a grater, mandoline, or food processor to create small strips of food.

**Simmer:** A state of liquid cooking, where the liquid is just below boil.

**Slow Cooker:** An appliance that cooks food by surrounding it with low, steady heat.

**Steam:** To cook food by immersing it in steam. Food is set over boiling liquid.

**Stir:** To mix with a spoon or whisk until foods are combined.

**Toss:** To combine food using two spoons or a spoon and a fork until mixed.

**Whisk:** Both a tool, which is made of loops of steel, and a method, which combines food until smooth.

**White Sauce:** A sauce made by cooking flour in fat, then adding liquid and cooking until smooth. Used to stabilize sauces in the slow cooker.

**Zest:** The colored part of the skin of citrus fruit, used to add flavor to food.

# FIND INGREDIENTS

There are many resources for ingredients other than the grocery store

KNACK SLOW COOKING

## Catalogs and online resources

### Amazon Grocery
www.agrocerydelivery.com/

- Amazon.com has a grocery delivery service. Offers general foods and hard to find items.

### The Baker's Catalog
- From King Arthur's Flour, this catalog offers cooking equipment and baking ingredients, including specialty flours and flavorings.

### Cub Foods
http://cubfoods.com

- National grocery chain offers delivery in some areas; large selection of foods.

### EFood Depot
www.efooddepot.com

- Service specializes in ethnic foods from Europe, India, Japan, and China.

### Local Harvest
www.localharvest.org

- Use this site to find the freshest organic foods in your area. Lists of farmer's markets and local businesses.

### NetGrocer.com
www.netgrocer.com

- For a small fee, groceries are delivered to your door. Personal shopping services.

### Nuts Online
www.nutsonline.com

- Store offers nuts, snack mixes, spices, seeds, chocolates, and dried fruit, shipped quickly.

### Peapod
www.peapod.com

- Online grocery store serving some areas of the United States

### Safeway.com
- Grocery chain offers delivery of food items, as well as recipes and tips for healthy living.

### Schwans
- Home delivery service for groceries, serving parts of the United States.

### Sunrise Foods
www.sunrisefoods.com

- You can order prepared foods and ingredients from this all-inclusive online store.

# Farmers' markets

## Farmers' Markets
www.farmersmarketla.com

- Los Angeles Farmers' Market Web site; the original farmers' market.

## Farmer's Market Search
http://apps.ams.usda.gov/FarmersMarkets/

- USDA site lets you search for a farmers' market by state, city, county, and zip code, as well as methods of payment.

## National Directory of Farmer's Markets
http://farmersmarket.com/

- Site has index of U.S. farmers' markets listed by state.

# HOTLINES AND MANUFACTURERS

Find help with cooking problems and equipment manufacturers

## Hotlines

### Butterball Turkey Holiday Line
1-800-323-4848

- Hotline available year round; answers questions about turkey cooking and preparation.

### Empire Kosher Poultry Hotline
1-800-367-4734

- Year-round hotline answers questions about poultry.

### Perdue
1-800-473-7383

- Year-round hotline helps with cooking questions, especially poultry products.

### Reynolds Turkey Tips
1-800-745-4000

- Year-round hotline answers consumer questions about turkey preparation; free recipes.

### USDA Meat and Poultry Hotline
1-800-535-4555

- Year-round line offers information about food safety; answers consumer questions about meat preparation.

## Manufacturers

### All-Clad
www.all-clad.com/

- One of the first manufacturers to make metal inserts for the slow cooker.

### Cuisinart
www.cuisinart.com/

- Company can completely outfit your kitchen, from ranges to slow cookers.

## GE Appliances

www.geappliances.com/

- Outfit your entire kitchen with GE appliances. Online service and customer support.

## Kitchenaid

www.kitchenaid.com/home.jsp

- Lots of high-quality appliances offered, from refrigerators and stoves to slow cookers.

## Rival

www.rivalproducts.com

- Manufacturer of the original Crock-Pot, with product information, recipes, and an online store.

## West Bend

www.focuselectrics.com/catalog.cfm?dest=dir&linkon=section&linkid=54

- Slow cooker manufacturer, with service, support, and how to use appliances.

# INDEX